Technology as symptom and dream

Technology as symptom and dream

Robert D. Romanyshyn

ROUTLEDGE
London and New York

First published in 1989 by Routledge
11 New Fetter Lane, London EC4P 4EE
29 West 35th Street, New York NY 10001

© 1989 Robert D. Romanyshyn

Typeset by Pat and Anne Murphy, Highcliffe-on-Sea, Dorset
Printed and bound in Great Britain by
Biddles Ltd, Guildford and King's Lynn

British Library Cataloguing in Publication Data

Romanyshyn, Robert D.
   Technology as symptom and dream
   1. Phenomenological psychology
   I. Title
   150.19′2

Library of Congress Cataloging in Publication Data

Romanyshyn, Robert D. (Robert Donald), 1942–
   Technology as symptom and dream
   Robert D. Romanyshyn.
   p.   cm.
   Bibliography: p.
   Includes index.
   1. Technology — Philosophy. 2. Technology — Psychological aspects.
   I. Title.
   T.14.R58   1990   89-3527 CIP
   601 — dc19

ISBN 0-415-00786-0 (hbk)
      0-415-00787-9 (pbk)

Contents

Contents

Figures

Acknowledgements

A book is born in strange circumstances. This one began in a museum on a rainy Sunday afternoon when my younger son said that the bodies in a Giotto painting looked like the artist did not know how to draw. He was young then, but old enough to have been educated into the cultural medium of central perspective vision. That innocent comment started me wondering about the ways in which we see and take for granted our visions. It started a journey which has taken six years to complete. Along the way I have gathered many debts and I have made many new friends. I want to express my gratitude to all of them.

Particular thanks are owed to Doug Gerwin, Mary Vernon, David Levin, Don Johnson, and Andrew Samuels. Each of them read all or significant portions of the manuscript along the way, and I benefitted greatly from their advice and criticisms. They were supportive of, and enthusiastic about, the effort. Andrew Samuels in particular deserves my thanks for the significant role he played in bringing this work to the attention of the publisher.

I must also acknowledge the very generous and critically detailed reading which Ivan Illich, Barbara Duden, Wolfgang Sachs and Dirk von Boetticher gave to the entire text. Their patient efforts have greatly improved the manuscript and the shortcomings which it still possesses are the consequence of my own limitations. My debt to Ivan and Barbara, moreover, extends to their generosity in inviting me to be a part of their annual seminars on the cultural history of the body. Significant portions of the work were developed in the give and take of those meetings. Ivan's invitation to Göttingen, Germany, in the summer of 1985 to meet Rudolf Zur Lippe has proved to be a lasting benefit. Zur Lippe's work on the geometrization of humanity has been most helpful in guiding my own thinking about the historical and cultural consequences of linear perspective vision.

Apart from the circumstances of its beginning and the nurturing support of the colleagues and friends mentioned above, a work needs a place. There have been several over the years which I must acknowledge.

Certainly The Dallas Institute for Humanities and Culture deserves my thanks for providing an arena for reflection and thought. The invitation of Bob Sardello, a friend and colleague of many years, to participate in a special seminar with Ivan Illich in February 1985 gave me the first public opportunity to try out some initial ideas of this work. I am also grateful to Dean Robert Corrigan of the Arts and Humanities School of the University of Texas at Dallas for inviting me to teach in his program. In a series of graduate courses, many of the ideas now presented in the text were shaped and refined. My thanks to those students whose creative response in examinations and projects helped to further the work. The Centre for Traditional Acupuncture in Columbia, Maryland, has also been instrumental in providing a place of support. Through the generous efforts of Bob Duggan and Dianne Connelly I have been able to share my views with a host of scholars concerned with body history. I trust that they realize how very much I have gained from those seminars. Finally I should thank my colleagues at the University of Dallas whose support of my work was instrumental in obtaining the sabbatical which allowed me to complete the journey. Special thanks is owed to Liota Odom not only for typing the manuscript but also for her endurance and patience.

Circumstances which surround its beginning, the helpful and sustained support of colleagues and friends, and the many places offered to present the work in progress nearly complete the acknowledgement of the debts that I owe. There remain only a few final words to speak: To professor J. H. van den Berg, I owe again my thanks for having been and continuing to be my teacher. This book, like my earlier one, owes much to his vision; to my oldest son, Jeff, who has listened to many of these ideas, initially with bemused patience and more recently with conviction and understanding; to my younger son, Andrew, who seeded the beginnings of the work with his innocent words; and to my spouse, Janet, who shared the place on Ocracoke, Island, where the writing was done. For the many walks and the ferry rides across the waters.

For permission to use quoted material in the text, grateful acknowledgement is hereby made: extract from 'Little Gidding' in *Four Quartets*, © 1943 by T. S. Eliot, renewed 1971 by Esine Valerie Eliot, reprinted by permission of Harcourt Brace Jovanovich, Inc.; the excerpts are reprinted outside the United States, its dependencies, and the Phillipine Republic by permission of Faber and Faber Ltd; extract from 'Forever in Blue Jeans', © 1978 Stonebridge Music, all rights reserved, by Neil Diamond and Richard Bennett; extract from 'The Ninth Elegy' in *Duino Elegies*, © 1939 by W. W. Norton & Co., Inc., copyright renewed 1967.

Prologue
Address to the reader

I Beginning: a first fantasy

On an island off the coast of North Carolina, a place called Ocracoke, a man or a woman can isolate himself or herself from the events of the world. It is very secluded, a thin strip of sand and grassy marshes, part of the Outer Banks, which form a barrier between the ocean and the mainland. There are of course many such places in the world, and it is not this specific island which matters to this story. Rather what matters here is the fact that this place, like, I suppose, almost any other island of seclusion, can so easily be tied back into the network of the world. Through those thin wires which stretch from pole to pole outside my house, wires whose fragility is marked by their movements in the wind, the world outside my island can enter my front door. Those wires generate an invisible electric web which knits together our entire globe, creating in McLuhan's phrase, a 'global village',[1] so that here on this island at night, when there is only the sound of the wind across the marsh and the starlight of the black sky, one can soften the isolation and believe that one is not alone.

Those images of light which dance on the screen before me always seem miraculous, however much I may understand the explanations for how television works. They are, if truth be told, more like ghosts come to visit and perhaps, depending on one's turn of mind, to haunt us in our isolation. Our explanations in fact can desensitize us to the magic of technology. They can fill us with a false sense of understanding which robs us of the *awe-ful* experience which technology provides, for in fact the experience of living in a technological world fills us with awe in spite of our explanations. To realize for even one brief moment that with the touch of an index finger on a channel selector one can command into presence the image of events and persons far removed in space and even time is humbling and exhilarating. No magus of the ancient world ever possessed such power, not even Merlin, who is said to have been the greatest and wisest of all wizards who has ever lived. And no medieval monk or saint, however holy, had the power to draw into presence or banish into absence angels or demons. They came

1

unbidden, like the demons who haunt and tempt St Anthony in the fifteenth century landscapes of Hieronymous Bosch.[2] But technology seems to invest us with such power, although we seem to employ it without either wisdom or holiness. Without much effort we can summon into presence any number of figures and just as easily with the press of a button can we condemn them to the fading light of absence. We can light up the night and banish the darkness. We can withdraw from the minerals of the earth billions of years of stored energy of the sun. We can even re-create that energy here upon the earth by releasing from within matter itself the radiating energies of a star. And perhaps most awe-ful and miraculous of all, today we stand poised and ready to reach beyond island earth for the stars themselves.

Technology is the magic of the modern world and every man and woman and child, however humble their circumstance, can be a practitioner of its art. Here in my island house, in the stillness of a dark night, I can sense Merlin's envy. My finger is a wand and I am invested with his cloak and cap of ancient times. *Technology is awe-ful.* And what is awe-ful, what fills us with awe, invites us to wonder and dream.

II Beginnings two: a second fantasy

I sat there early in the morning, just before the sun began to rise. It was cool and silent and in the hide you are more or less invisible, like an unseen witness to a drama, the coming of the animals to the water hole. In groups they came, in collections of their respective kind, appearing out of the mist of the bush almost miraculously. Where a moment ago there had been nothing but the dry African plain, animals now appeared as if born by the bush itself, as if formed out of the morning mist itself. The bush was a womb of time pouring out life onto what had been an empty, silent landscape. It was as if one was witnessing the birth of creation, watching life congeal itself out of formless vapor into visibility. The animals just appeared — suddenly. Their appearance was effortless, slow, graceful, silent. The breath of God stirring over the formless waters of creation? It was dawn and it could have been the very first day.

It is the *silence*, really, which is overwhelming: not the absence of sound — one hears the animals, the birds, and the other sounds of the bush — rather it is a silence which has no sound of the human, a landscape whose silence bears witness to our exclusion, a silence which speaks *our* absence. A sleepy kind of dumbness lies over this landscape of mist and bush and animal and sun and cool morning breeze and water. Earth is in repose, folded in on itself, asleep. Earth seems unconscious of itself.

The land was empty again. As silently as they had appeared out of the early morning, the animals disappeared back into the bush. They were taken back into invisibility, dissolved again into formless mist.

One could stay there forever, for all eternity, and again and again one would see the same procession of creation, of appearance and disappearance, repeat itself. One could stay there forever in that silence, in that sleepy dumbness of the earth's quiet sleep. And if one waited long enough, could one also dissolve into that landscape, become part of it, be received by the mist in the endless cycle of appearance–disappearance, of form and dissolution?

The silence of the landscape said 'No!' I (we) had already been placed at a distance. (Or is it that we had placed ourselves at a distance?) The silence of the bush seemed already to have spoken: the earth had been waking itself *through* us, had been doing so already for countless ages. Earth itself had broken the cycle of repetition and *through us* (were we chosen?) had been coming to its own realization. Rilke, the poet, had known this secret of the earth. 'Earth! Isn't this what you want: an invisible re-arising within us?'[3] Into that silence there had come *word*. Into that silence had come language. Through the word we had become (were chosen to be?) *agents* of the earth.

Agents of the earth! Poets sow strange seeds, but perhaps they reap the most bountiful and truthful harvest. Perhaps technology has been part of the earth's long history of coming to know itself, and perhaps in that effort we have been its servant. The silence of that African plain, however, suggests how dispensable we really are. That silence echoes an absence and perhaps even our eventual disappearance. In the shadow of the bomb our technological mastery of the earth seems a bad dream, and in the shadows of Chernobyl and the space shuttle disaster our service to the earth seems to have gone terribly awry. On a dry African plain, in the silence of the early morning, one can still imagine technology as *vocation*, as the earth's call to become its agent and instrument of awakening. But in the shadows, the imagination falters and technology seems less the earth's way of coming to know itself and more the earth's way of coming to cleanse itself of us.

On some future morning the sun will rise and there may be no human eyes to bear witness to it. Rising there on the horizon as it has always done, but now lighting a barren and burnt landscape of broken, twisted forms, the sun on that day will have changed. Rising on a void, it will have lost its splendor and in time it will die. And this death will slowly spread over the face of everything on earth, including earth itself. Perhaps this death will even reach into the heavens. The silence then will be most complete and perhaps forever, and when night comes the stars themselves may cease to shine when there are no longer any inquisitive eyes to look at them and to praise their glory.

III Beginnings three: the imagination of events

The two illustrations in Figures I and II belong respectively to the world of science and to the world of art, and presented together they suggest the strong affinity which exists between science and art. C. H. Waddington[4]

3

Figure I Space shuttle at lift-off

Source: NASA

has made this same point and he has beautifully illustrated the affinity in our age between painting and physics. Indeed, the overlaps which he demonstrates between the physicist's and the painter's visions are astonishing. The painter's brush and the physicist's instruments take the same measure of a new reality in the late nineteenth and early twentieth centuries. The atom fragments at roughly the same time that non-representational

Figure II Paul van Hoeydonck, *Little Cosmonaut*

Reproduced by permission of Koninklijke Smeets Offset, Weert, The Netherlands

painting fragments the forms of things. It might even be said that matter conceived as fixed points in space is transformed into temporal relations at the same time that time enters the canvas of the painter. Picasso and Einstein see the same thing simultaneously. Applying a recent argument made by the poet and literary critic Frederick Turner, it might be said that 'Picasso' is a higher but less fundamental 'Einstein'. In the pyramidal image of knowledge which Turner advocates, 'the arts and humanities are a more advanced, but less basic, area of study than physics.' Indeed, stated in the most radical way, 'the arts and humanities *are* higher physics.'[5] The physicist and painter envision a common reality but in different ways, and at different levels of complexity. The images of art and the events of science converge.

Technology is, I believe, a strong force in this convergence, and indeed in technology the separation of image and event is all but erased. The cosmonaut depicted in Figure II is the body fashioned and invented for the shuttle depicted in Figure I. That astronautic body belongs to the spacecraft as much as it belongs to the canvas. It is as much a work of art as it is of science.

Whatever else technology does, therefore, it does indicate that events are also images and that images are events in the world. The little cosmonaut in Figure II belongs to the shuttle as much he or she reveals the *imaginal* lining of this technical event. That fantastical figure is the *depth* of that event, the deepening of what would otherwise remain a mere surface reality. On the other hand, that event of lift-off depicted in Figure I is the means by which that imaginal lining is enacted in the world. It is a surface through which that depth appears, the surface without which the figure of the little cosmonaut would remain a mere fantasm, an illusion. We should say, then, that technology marries surface and depth. We should say that it reveals and uncovers the imagination of events. We should say that it is that power to realize (to make real) the imaginative depths of the world.

We should say all this, but then we would go too far, because technology is only the possibility of that power, and because in large measure technology has eclipsed the life of imagination more than it has been its realization. Figure III illustrates this point.

The event portrayed in Figure III is a familiar one. It is a specter which haunts our time, the mushroom cloud of an atomic explosion. Atoms have been split here, and from this destruction of real atoms the energy of the stars has been released from matter. I look at this event and I cannot help but marvel at how different these atoms are from those described by Democritus. Once, a long time ago, this Greek philosopher imagined matter to be made up of tiny, hard, indivisible units of being, and through these atoms the bewildering array of the world's surface changes was ordered. These atoms were, if you will, images of reality, that is, ways of experiencing the events of the world. They were invisible beings, not in the sense, however, of something that could be made visible, but invisible in the sense of the depth of the visible, the power and means by which the visible world could be what it is. With our technology, however, we have transformed the invisible depth of the world. We have made the invisible visible, *and literally so*. We have transformed the atoms from a way of experiencing the events of the world into an event itself capable of being experienced. We have, in short, exploded the depths.

In speaking of the invisible I do not mean to be intentionally vague or vaguely poetic. On the contrary, I mean only to point to that dimension of reality where myth and dream, hope and promise, belief and image, animate our lives. And I mean to point us in this direction only because technology, even while it is the power to open this dimension, to realize the life of imagination, very much seems to take us in an opposite direction.

Figure IV can illustrate this point. It is a detail of a painting entitled *Kissing* by Alex Grey. One aspect of this painting to be noticed is how the

Figure III Nuclear fireball: H-bomb explosion at Bikini Atoll

Source: US Department of Defense

experience of kissing has been made visible as an event, specifically a neuro-chemical event. Something of the 'inside' of the kiss is rendered visible here, and indeed it is this aspect of the painting which is emphasized in a section of *Esquire* magazine, where it was featured. In that presentation, the artist is quoted as saying, 'The inside tells me about the outside,' while the interviewer, Paul Bob, goes on to say that 'Alex Grey paints our insides.' Bob continues: 'To him, everything starts there: our power, ideas, and desires. The kiss comes from within, and our outsides are just along for the ride.'[6]

Grey, of course, is right, at least with respect to the notion that the kiss does come from *within*. But in transforming that 'within' into a visible interior, an interior, moreover, which has been opened up as the unquestionable reality of the anatomical body, at least we need to wonder if there is some confusion between the artist's words and the image. Is it from *that*

Figure IV   Alex Grey, *Kissing*, 1983

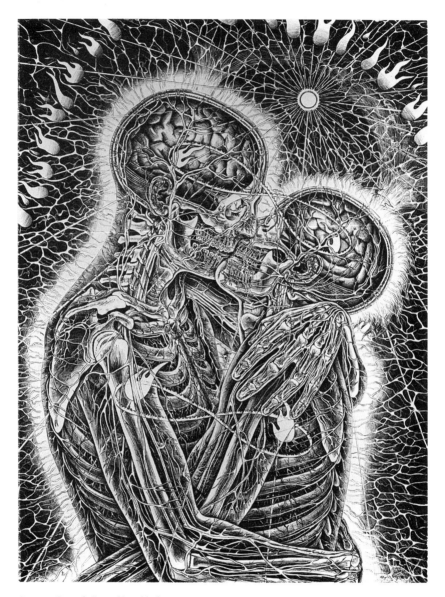

Source: Stux Gallery, New York

interior that the kiss begins, from that inside space of the anatomical body of neurochemical functioning? Is the 'within' about which the artist speaks that real, material, inside space, formerly an invisible, now made visible? I do not believe that this is what the artist means, and for this reason I do believe that this painting can and does illustrate the way in which technology, often quite subtly, poses a crisis to the life of imagination.

In an interview about his work Grey has said that '. . . a materialist attitude leaves no space for the human spirit.' Moreover, in this same interview — after quoting Andy Warhol's wish 'I want to be a machine' — Grey says 'I don't think his attitude is basically survival-oriented for the human race . . .'[7] Such statements clearly indicate that for the artist Grey human life is more than a material matter, and they accord well, therefore, with the notion that the 'within' is not just a previously invisible made visible. On the contrary, they indicate that the 'within', from which the human kiss begins, is the human imagination, that invisible power to deepen the event of a kiss into a promise, a hope, a fantasy, or a dream. The image in the painting, however, can eclipse all this, and it could have us believe that what we are seeing here is only another illustration of the power of technology to make visible something that was previously merely hidden. Then the kiss is in danger of becoming a rush of neurochemical processes initiated by pressure contact between two pairs of mucous membranes of two people. There is no doubt, of course, that in one sense the kiss is such an event. But there is also no doubt that *that* kiss lies at an immeasurable distance from the experience and imagination of a kiss in human life. Moreover, should it ever come to pass that the kiss, as an imagined invisible promise, hope, or dream, does become for us really and only a neurochemical event, the pressure contact of two pairs of mucous membranes which fires off these events in a real, material, interior space, the character of human life will have been as thoroughly destroyed as life itself would be by the fires depicted earlier in Figure III. And lest we miss the point about how Grey's painting, in presenting the challenge which technology poses to the life of imagination, invites us to consider both the dangers and opportunities of technology, we should note these words. Speaking about his work within the context of the ever-present threat of nuclear war, he says that 'It becomes crucial that we see we are in an ethical dilemma — about the way we treat the earth, the way we treat each other.' The painting says as much in awakening us to the possibilities of, and perhaps, therefore, even warning us about, the dangers of treating the kiss as only a material event. 'We have to forge,' he says, 'a new attitude, create a sacred response.'[8] To do so will require of us the wisdom and intelligence to use the power of technology to open the surfaces of events into their invisible depths, and to avoid the use of that power to raise (reduce) all depths to a visible surface.

Later I will have much more to say about the four illustrations presented in this third beginning. For the moment, however, I want to underline the central point about technology which these four illustrations have given. We may, perhaps, state the point this way: technology is a *crisis* of the imagination. As such, technology is both a danger and an opportunity with respect to the imagination. It is a danger in so far as it can be the death of imagination through its literalization. It is an opportunity in so far as it can be an awakening to how the events of the world have an imaginal depth, and how the life of imagination inscribes itself within the events of the world.

IV Technology as shadow, symptom, and dream: some remarks about approach

Three beginnings, and all of them perhaps a strange way to consider technology. Why begin a work about technology with fantasy and image, with questions about technology and art, image and event, with reference to the shadow of the bomb and the breakdowns of technology? The three beginnings themselves, I believe, answer the question. Technology is not just a series of events which occurs over there on the side of the world. It is, on the contrary, the enactment of the human imagination in the world. In building a technological world we create ourselves, and through the events which comprise this world we enact and live out our experiences of awe and wonder, our fantasies of service and of control, our images of exploration and destruction, our dreams of hope and nightmares of despair. I begin this way, therefore, because I mean to approach technology from the side of its depths, from the images of the events and happenings which comprise the technological world. It is not a philosophy of technology which I offer here, nor a history. Rather I offer a study of technology as a psychological reality, a study of technology as the creation, the making, the working out, of a shared cultural dream.

As a working out of a shared cultural dream, the technological world, like all psychological realities, is a labor of creation which, while it takes place in the light of day, nevertheless draws upon and is nourished by the darkness of the night. The technological world is a work of reason but of a reason which reaches deeply into dream. Conscious intentions shade into unconscious motivations, some and perhaps even most of which are not just unknown but also repressed. Creation is conflict and the struggle which becomes the technological world leaves traces of itself in the work. The space shuttles we build as much as the bombs we make are products of reason lined with desire. Freud and the art of psychoanalysis have taught us as much and we risk a potentially fatal ignorance if we forget or deny the basic insights which psychoanalysis has gathered about the human soul. At the very least, no account of human achievements is possible today without some consideration being given to the interplay of unconscious and conscious motivations, to dreams as a legitimate source of knowledge, and perhaps, most fundamental of all, to the erotic character of the human body and the dynamic role which it plays in shaping the human world. Indeed, as we shall discover, the technological world is in a very radical way a cultural dream of reincarnation. The body is central in technology and the shared cultural dream which guides our creation of a technological world is in many respects a record of our continuing debate with the fact of our incarnation and the limits it imposes, not the least of which, of course, is the fact of death.

One does not need to be, however, a Freudian psychoanalyst to acknowledge the pivotal role of the human body in shaping human culture. It is a shared insight of our age. The painter and the poet, the philosopher and the physician, the sociologist and the anthropologist all bear witness to it. And even closer to home, in the midst of our daily living, we find evidence of the omnipresence of the body in technological culture. From sports to spas, from advertising to medicine, our age seems obsessed with the flesh. It might even be said that the technological world is the discovery of the body, and perhaps, even more significantly, a playing with the possibilities of its transformations. Moreover, that such play is not without anxiety is attested to by recent films like *The Thing*, *Alien*, and *The Fly*. Films are cultural daydreams and in each of these films our culture is inventing and dreaming new ways of remaking the body and expressing its underlying concerns about this power of creation.

The approach which I am taking in this work is, moreover, not without precedent. A concern with what we might call the underside of culture, with the unconscious of history, is not even new. In the postscript to his classic work, *Europe's Inner Demons*, the historian Norman Cohn writes that what he has been investigating in his study of witches in European history is '. . . above all a fantasy at work in history . . .'. 'It is fantasy, and nothing else,' he says, 'that provides the continuity in this story.'[9] The fantasy which has shaped the event; the story which has guided the history; the cultural dream which has lined the exterior actions of men and women has been his domain. And while it is history which he practices, with all the respect for evidence and data appropriate to the historian's craft, Cohn acknowledges at the very end of this same postscript the need for something more. Beneath the terrain he has charted, he has felt, he says, 'depths which were not to be explored by the techniques at my disposal.' Others are needed 'to venture further downwards, into the abyss of the unconscious.'[10] Events, like ideas, have a history but, as this historian knows, they also have a shadow.

In addition to the historian Cohn, the Dutch psychiatrist J. H. van den Berg[11] has written extensively and brilliantly on the question of how the cultural world incarnates humanity's psychological life, and indeed the spirit of this work owes much to his thought and influence. The way in which an age paints its paintings and builds its buildings, for example, embodies the spirit, the style, the character, and the dreams of that age. A fourteenth-century Gothic cathedral, for example, announces a sense of spirituality which is radically different from the sense of spirituality made visible in a seventeenth-century Baroque church. A visitor need not be either a believer or an architect to feel this difference. The two buildings shape the dreams of faith in radically different ways. Something of the spiritual dreams of the Gothic and the Baroque worlds, and the differences between them, are chiseled in stone. The majesty and power of a divine presence, which still broods over the space of a Gothic church, have retreated in the space of the Baroque. In this latter space it is less the power of God and more the glory of man which is celebrated. Moreover, when Descartes (most probably for reasons of expediency) places God at the beginning of his philosophy as a watchmaker who, having set the mechanism of the universe in motion, is no longer needed, except perhaps for an occasional repair, otherwise called a miracle, which soon will have no place, he unknowingly complements this space of the Baroque church. They go together, this Cartesian God and this Baroque space. They cohere as one cultural world. In both spaces, philosophical and architectural, the presence of the divine has been removed to a new, discrete distance.

With Cohn and with van den Berg, then, we are able to appreciate that history is a psychological matter and that humanity's psychological life, its hopes and its dreams, its fantasies and fears, its images and inspirations, are shaped as a cultural world. For much the same reasons the work of Marshall McLuhan[12] must also be cited here, specifically his insights regarding the shaping influence of technological means of communication on the social and psychological character of an age. In his work as well as in the work of Harold Innis, Walter Ong, and most recently Donald Lowe,[13] one discovers how the shift from oral to written means of communication, especially the shift to typography in the sixteenth century, has shaped the character of our modern world. To mention only one item, which in this context is the most obvious, the shift from ear to eye (from oral to written culture) is most visibly apparent in the fifteenth-century invention and widespread dissemination of the printed book. As we shall see later on, some very ordinary themes of modern life, like uniformity, homogeneity, standardization, repeatability, are already inscribed in the creation of a book, as are certain values like privacy, interiority, and individualism in the creation of the silent reader of the book. The very thing which you, the reader, are doing right now at this moment, reading these words, most probably silently to yourself, demonstrates a self formed by a technology (in this case printing) which defines in large part the character of our age.

Books surround us, and yet they are but one small item of the body of technological inventions which flesh out our time. Radio and television, newspapers and films, automobiles and airplanes, computers and spacecraft, nuclear power plants and nuclear bombs are also part of our world.

They are the social and psychological body of our age as much as Gothic cathedrals formed in part the body of the late medieval world. These things and events incarnate the dreams of the world we have built and in so doing they tell the story of who we are and who we imagine ourselves to be.

To approach the technological world as a cultural dream is an invitation to the reader to adopt a style of thinking receptive to the undertones of life. In dreams we are addressed by the underside of events and things, by the unspoken in what has been said, by connections and allusions which may otherwise be unnoticed. Dreams shadow waking life and what we, individually and culturally, cannot bear in conscious life we dream. To attend to the cultural dream of technology, then, is to attend to the shadows and silences of technology. It is, moreover, also something more, for in presenting the shadows and the silences every dream, whether individual or cultural, preserves them. In this respect every dream is also a call to remember what would otherwise be forgotten on the surface of events and things.

These rhythms of presentation and remembrance and remembrance and forgetting characterize, however, not only the dream but also the symptom. Hence, in attending to technology as a cultural dream, the reader is also being invited to attend to it as a cultural symptom. This second invitation, moreover, does not merely repeat the first one. It also adds something.

To be sure, a symptom as a way of ignoring or forgetting something is also a way of preserving or remembering it. But beyond this rhythm a symptom is also a way of saying not only that something is wrong, but also how that something can be made right. In every symptom there is, so to speak, the whisper of a direction, the hint of a path about how one can find one's way back to health or balance or, perhaps most descriptively, home. Symptoms are a memory of this path, this way home, this way back to what has been forgotten, lost, ignored, or otherwise left behind. Almost one hundred years of psychoanalytic work should be sufficient to persuade us of this redemptive quality of the symptom, but lest we remain unconvinced there is a recent and most readable work by Dianne Connelly entitled *All Sickness is Homesickness*.[14] It is an elegant work in which the reader is continually reminded that the symptom as a sign of illness is also a guide home. In attending technology as a cultural symptom, then, the reader is being invited to recover in the happenings and events of technology, especially in its extreme moments, in its moments of crises and breakdown, a call of return.

This prologue, then, extends this work to the reader with a double invitation. In the invitation of the dream, the reader may find in those images of space travel and the cosmonaut the tale of technology as an epic journey. The reader may also discover how these and other events and happenings of technology preserve and remember dreams of distancing ourselves from the body and of departing earth, dreams of a distancing which dream on about images of reincarnation and fantasies of disincarnation, and dreams of a departure which becomes escape. And through the call of the dream as symptom, the reader may learn how in living these dreams forgetfully, in tending only to the surface of technology as event while forgetting its imaginal lining, these dreams can become a nightmare of destruction. Attending to the symptomatic character of technology, the reader may, however, also recover how technology as an epic journey of departure is also a journey of return, how technology at its deepest cultural–psychological levels is a dream about home.

The hope and desire which animate this work are that if we can attend to the dreams and symptoms of technology, we may be able to imagine the shadows and silences of technology in ways that are not literally destructive.

V Ending: by way of apology

Dreams speak the language of images not the language of reason, and while there is always a story told by a dream there is no *storyline*. Lines belong to books and books belong more to the path of logic than to the way of dreams. The lines of a book inscribe a logic of linear connections where sequence means consequence, where effect follows cause, and where dispassionate argument is valued over the passion of emotions. Dreams, however, are not at all like that. They have no linear logical lines. On the contrary, they are patterns, webs of interconnections which more often than not follow aesthetic values rather than logical rules, and in listening to a dream, in attending to the story it unfolds, one is, more often than not, taken up by the dream, moved by it. This dream frightens and that one feels like a warning, while another strikes the dreamer, as most dreams often do, as peculiar, odd, and strange. Dreams solicit us. They beckon and call, establish a mood, invite us to move, and move us. At times they might even shake us up. So it is also with symptoms. The difficulty, then, is obvious: in the form of a book I want to offer technology as symptom and dream. Hence the ending of this prologue is by way of apology, both in its first sense of a defense of what follows, and in its second sense of begging the reader's pardon.

By way of defense I want to anticipate for the reader how very much the matter of technology requires that our thinking move with it in non-linear ways if we are to catch hold of its shadows. As we shall discover, technology is deeply rooted in a special kind of historical vision, a linear vision which gives a special place to a notion like perspective or point of view, with its implications of fixity or stability and its preference for processes like inspection and detached, objective analyses and observation. Such a fixed perspective tends to eclipse movement. If we apply this perspective to technology, then the ways in which technology as a cultural–historical dream and symptom moves and as an emotional reality moves us are cast into shadow. In place of the awe and terror of technology we establish the illusion of a well ordered, highly rational world, the illusion of technique, in Barrett's phrase.[15] Or in place of the often dizzying pace of technology's breakthroughs (and breakdowns), we plot its line of progress which extends into infinity. To attend the shadow side, then, requires a change in our thinking. A cool, rational, dispassionate analysis will not suffice, for it will only apply technical thinking to technology. We might then succeed in taking the measure of technology by keeping our distance, by staying on the surface, when in fact we need to fall into its depths. The reader, therefore, has to enter that space where, beckoned by the shadows and called by the symptoms of technology, he or she feels drawn into its dreams, moved by its symptoms, affected by its mood. An incarnate response is in order, not one so high up in the head that one misses the awe and terror of this world we have created. If we are to be moved by the soul of technology, then we need to suspend the sure, stable, and fixed ground of a thinking which, in adopting a perspective or viewpoint, would line things up for dispassionate inspection.

How disproportionate, however, is this work to that plea. We are so much the unconscious product of that linear vision which has seeded our technological world, so much the consequence of a book culture, that this effort seems doomed to fail. But better to acknowledge the limits in the beginning, and, by way of asking pardon, petition the reader to make the effort to fall as deeply as he or she can into the story and the images which follow and which reveal the symptoms and the dreams, the moods and the emotional impacts of technology. In doing so, we may realize *something* of the psychological depths of technology. In doing so, we may be stirred by something in the depths and heights of its soul.[16]

Chapter one

Lift-off: we are all astronauts

I Abandoning the body

Naked exposure, stripped of clothes and skin, two electric bodies exchange a kiss. Sparks do fly, as we have always known, but here it is no mere metaphor. The kiss inflames and stirs electric circuitry into life. Touching, holding, pressing, kissing radiates, leaps beyond its boundaries, jumps the gap between two beings and fuses them as one. Meltdown at the core!

Here, at the moment of lift-off, the reader is invited to look again at Figure IV. A sun is in the background. It radiates its energy and between it and the kiss a web is generated. These electric bodies, these bodies of fusion and radiation, belong to the stars. They are bodies of atomic children, cosmic creatures.

When we previously considered this painting by Alex Grey, I indicated that its appearance in *Esquire* magazine was accompanied by a quote from the artist. 'The inside,' he said, 'tells me about the outside.' Now in reply to these words I want to say No and Yes. No, because the image itself goes further. It says more. It says the inside is the outside. All is energy and energy is all. Body melts into cosmos. And Yes, because the last four hundred years of the history of the body have been a history of this telling, of an opening of the inside to tell us about the outside. We can appreciate the significance of the latter reply when we know that the appearance of this painting in *Esquire* magazine was accompanied not only by the artist's words, but also by a photo. In that photo there is the artist and behind him the figure of a skeleton. That skeleton behind the artist who speaks these words about the inside and the outside is a witness to these last four hundred years of history. The two who kiss are not alone. They are observed.

Vesalius, whom we shall meet again later, is a witness. In 1543 he created modern anatomy. Before Vesalius the non-living body was a dead body. Dead bodies are buried with rituals of remembrance. After Vesalius the dead body became a corpse. Corpses are designed to be opened for inspection. They are invented so that the inside can be instructive about the outside. The English physician William Harvey, whom we shall also meet again, is there too. The corpse lies still on the dissecting table. It does not move. Harvey resurrects this corpse. In 1628 he reanimates it by making the heart into a pump. A crude machine in comparison with those electric bodies, but their ancestor nonetheless. The skeleton in the background is a reminder of this lineage. Something of the corpse haunts these cosmic creatures, these electric bodies which belong to the stars.

A   The corpse and the cosmonaut

The corpse is present in the figure of the Little Cosmonaut (Figure II). But it is hidden, or better, it has been transformed, re-dressed in the guise of its technical functions. The pumping heart is there and so much more. The eye of optics, the lungs of respiration define this body, a chiasm of physics and physiology. It is the medical body as an artist's dream:

> All the natural activities — of hearing, breathing, speaking, and making gestures — are . . . replaced by technical functions. The body has no contact with the surrounding atmosphere; it is protected by impenetrable suits. Van Hoeydonck gave us twentieth-century man as this man created himself: an almost inhuman abstraction, further removed from nature than at any other moment in history.[1]

Activity has become function: inspiration and expiration as respiration; communion as ingestion, digestion, elimination. The body is a technical matter, a problem to be solved. I know this body. We all know it. But it is known at a *distance* from life, from the body in its living situations. Vision may be a matter of what meets the eyeball, but seeing never is. The awesome power of the rising space shuttle is a sight which can take one's breath away. But that is a different matter from respiration.

An invented body! A created body! A manufactured body! And perhaps above all else a body without context, isolated from its surrounding atmosphere, a visible body, a spectacle. The inside has truly become the outside when all bodily activities have been rendered visible as technical functions. Like Le Centre Pompidou in Paris, that building with exposed interior, with its pipes and ducts, beams and girders on the outside, this body is exposed for inspection. A spectacle for observation, a specimen: nothing secret, nothing hidden, nothing shamed. Can the Little Cosmonaut blush? Can the astronautic body escape the gaze of an observing eye? The corpse, lying on the dissecting table, is pure spectacle. It is the body exposed in its isolation to the full light of objective consciousness: a blinding, antiseptic whiteness; a body of purity. So too is the body etherized on the surgeon's table, the medical body, the body as object of the medical gaze. Are we all astronauts? We are in so far as we all share this reality of the objective body, the body as technical function. Baby Fae was given a baboon's heart and it hardly made a difference. A pump was exchanged and her mother said, 'There are a lot of sentimental ways of talking about the heart. The soul of the human is in the brain.'[2]

The location, of course, is not the issue. The eclipse of the *difference* between the heart as a pump and the human heart, between technical function and human activity, is the issue. Do you think that if for one of those two electric bodies the kiss is a bitter disappointment his/her *broken heart* can be fixed? It is easier to repair a broken pump than it is to heal a broken metaphor, especially when we have forgotten the difference. Without the difference, a heart cannot be broken out of love, or if it can it really does not matter. Without the difference, the broken human heart has become only a metaphor, while the pump that can be broken can be exchanged.

B   *Homo sapiens astronauticus*

The body of the Little Cosmonaut is a spectacular body. It is a spectacle, a body of pure visibility, and a spectacular wonder in the sense that it is the same for all. It is an anonymous body, a democratic body, an empty shell. It is the body from which a self has taken flight and in this respect all of us truly are astronauts, perpetually 'in orbit' as Walker Percy says and perhaps also as he says 'lost in the cosmos'.[3]

A shell! Enshelled according to the artist! And it is true. One can see it. The Little Cosmonaut is enshelled in his/her space suit. Has a metamorphosis occurred? Has the invention, creation, and manufacture of the spectacular specimen body become a reincarnation? Is this body even to be viewed perhaps as a new stage in evolution, 'homo sapiens astronauticus', space man, cosmic woman, a universal creature?

If so, it is a very curious stage in evolution, because the body of the Little Cosmonaut amusingly resembles a kind of hard-shelled bug. The inside which has become an outside is like an exoskeleton. Is the cosmonautic body then a creature which reverses the actual movement of evolution, from the shell on the outside protecting the soft interior of the creature as is the case, for example, with crustaceans like crabs and lobsters, to the skeleton as support on the inside?

A reversal, perhaps, but no mere repetition of an earlier stage. On the contrary, the astronautic body is more a new twist in the spiral of evolution. It is the body turned inside out, re-dressed in terms of technical functions *on the way to being discarded*. It is a first step, perhaps, on a path toward 'exosomatic evolution',[4] a temporary bridge which initially joins us and machine, and wires us to (as) a computer. As a first step the shell is an external womb and the astronaut in suit and ship a foetus. The closing scenes of *2001: A Space Odyssey* vividly portray this image, as the astronaut David Bowman, floating in an amniotic bubble, is reincarnated as a foetus against the background of earth. A rebirth of humanity is being imagined here, a rebirth in space, but whether it is apart from earth or still in its shadows remains a mystery. In either case, however, from cybernetics to cyborgs, a new bionic woman and a six million dollar man loom on the horizon — and a new offspring, the boy Daryl in the film of the same name: *D.A.R.Y.L.: Data Analyzing Robot Youth Lifeform!*

Either as shell or embryo, the astronautic body becomes a temporary body on a path which ultimately leads to the abandonment of the body. In the generative fantasies of Timothy Leary, 'We are all neurogenetic robots'[5] programmed to leave the earth and destined by our genes to shed this skeletal husk of the human body. From the vantage point of the Little Cosmonaut the human body of flesh and bone, blood and muscle has been a necessary but only temporary expediency. Man, says the Nobel geneticist Herman J. Muller, is 'a giant robot created by DNA to make more DNA'.[6] In this vision, the body which belongs to the earth, which is tied to the earth by the natal bond of gravity, the body which each one of us is, is secondary. It is the genetic code which is primary and which is primarily human. We need to pause for a moment to imagine our reaction to this news. Is it a sudden, sharp sense of alienation from one's own body? Does this news make one feel like an agent of some alien force? Or is the other side a more appealing possibility? Is there some comfort in feeling guided by some higher wisdom, by a kind of universal intelligence coded as DNA?

Whatever one's reaction, no less an authority than Francis Crick, who with James Watson decoded the structure of DNA, gives the fantasy of DNA-programmed departure another twist. He speculates in his recent book *Life Itself*[7] that the stuff of DNA could have originally come only from the stars. If that be so, then the message coded in our genes is to journey in search of home. The astronautic body, then, is destined to depart. It is a body made by DNA to engineer its departure, the invention of DNA which will allow it to return to its home in the sky. Evolution with a cosmic purpose, blueprinted as the genetic code, and all of us under the same injunction: Little Cosmonaut as E.T. — 'Phone home!'

C The shadow of the alien

Crick's speculation, however, has a shadow side. If the astronautic body is DNA's way of redesigning the body to depart earth in search of its original home in the stars, then the earth is not our home. We are, then, in a very fundamental sense, aliens with respect to earth.

Film portrays the mythology of an age. It is a shared myth, a cultural daydream, and as such it is in film that we obtain perhaps the best images of our alien status. In films like *E.T.*, *Alien*, *Aliens*, *Close Encounters*, *The Thing*, *2001*, *Invasion of the Body Snatchers*, and the *Star Wars* series we encounter through the alien figure reflections of who we imagine we once were or will be. The alien is us, and in the context of Crick's proposition regarding the extra-terrestrial *origins* of life on earth, the alien creature is psychologically an image of an ancestor. In the guise of the alien creature we encounter our imagined heritage. For astronautic man/woman on the journey home, the alien figure wears the face of mother and father, the symptomatic face of our dreams of disincarnation.

But even without Crick's hypothesis, the alien still mirrors our own imagined face. Even if the earth is originally our home and the astronaut in departing is obeying another destiny coded in the genes, as Leary, for example, suggests, the alien is an encounter with an imagined future, with what we imagine we will be. As heritage and destiny, then, 'homo astronauticus' encounters himself/herself in the guise of the alien, and what is most significant in this encounter is the ambivalent character of our technological dreams of departure from earth and abandonment of the body.

The aliens of *Close Encounters*, for example, are decidedly different from those we meet in films like *Invasion of the Body Snatchers* or *The Thing*. In the former the alien is a figure of salvation; in the latter a figure of destruction. Such films, as expressions of our cultural daydreams, enact for us our optimistic hopes for, and pessimistic fears of, technology. Perhaps nowhere else is the ambivalent character of our daydreams more visible than in Japanese science fiction films. The only people on the face of the earth to have suffered the unforgettable fire of atomic war, the Japanese often instill in one and the same alien figure the dread and the hope of technology. A creature like Godzilla, for example, which is spawned by nuclear technology, is destructive and protective at the same time. In so many of these films, humanity looks to this creature for deliverance from some threatening evil, even while this creature itself is something which is feared. Moreover, the attribution of quasi-human qualities and emotions to Godzilla, while amusing and even silly, nevertheless strikes a deep chord in the human soul. It is an effort, I believe, to humanize and hence to tame the dread of technology's monstrous face. It is an effort to scale down the monstrous proportions of technology to human terms.

From the inside which tells about the outside (the corpse), through an inside which has become the outside (the two kissing figures), to a body either discarded as shell or temporarily used as embyro (Little Cosmonaut), the telos of technology's dream to refashion the body is toward abandonment of the body, toward disincarnation. This dream is, however, inseparable from the dream of departing earth. Disincarnation is a moment of departure. We can deepen our appreciation of the dream of technology, therefore, by attending to this moment.

II Departing earth

The images in Figure I and III mirror two prominent possibilities of our time. Indeed, they are the primary images of our age. The space shuttle at lift-off rises against the pull of earth's gravity, and in that powered ascent the earth grows smaller and farther away. In this image and event we have unmistakeable testimony that our technological power over nature is, and always has been, a matter of obtaining distance from it. The departure of the shuttle from earth is only the latest, and perhaps most dramatic, enactment of that distance, for distance belongs to technological knowledge as much as nearness belongs to intimate knowledge, to what might be called a knowledge of the heart. To know one's own body as a technical function, to know that the heart is, for example, a pump, requires a measure of distance neither obtainable nor suitable in the context of daily life. Although one may know one's body and heart in this fashion, they are known in this way only on the condition that one withdraws from them, that one places between oneself and the passion of one's heart, which in thirsting for knowledge of the other whom one loves necessarily draws near to that other, a distance which is not a matter of measure but of attitude.

Joseph Weizenbaum, one of the early pioneers of computer technology, portrays this dream of technology as distance in his work. Describing the role played by a group of American scientists in advising the Defense Department during the Vietnam war, Weizenbaum writes:

These men were able to give the counsel they gave because they were operating at an enormous psychological distance from the people who would be maimed and killed by the weapons systems that would result from the ideas they communicated to their sponsors. The lesson, therefore, is that the scientist and technologist must, by acts of will and of the imagination, actively strive to reduce such psychological distances, to counter the forces that tend to remove him from the consequences of his actions.[8]

Weizenbaum's work, moreover, insists that unless such acts of will and imagination occur, unless the distance between us and nature, between us and our own bodies, between us, is recognized, acknowledged, and understood, the final consequence of this power to distance ourselves from our bodies and from earth will quite probably be disaster. His words on this matter are quite direct:

Even physicians, formerly a culture's very symbol of power, are powerless as they increasingly become mere conduits between their patients and the major drug manufacturers. Patients, in turn, are more and more merely passive objects on whom cures are wrought and to whom things are done. Their own inner healing resources, their capacities for self-reintegration, whether psychic or physical, are more and more regarded as irrelevant in a medicine that can hardly distinguish a human patient from a manufactured object. The now ascendant biofeedback movement may be the penultimate act in the drama separating man from nature; man no longer even senses himself, his body directly, but only through buzzing sounds produced by instruments attached to him as speedometers are attached to automobiles. The ultimate act of the drama is, of course, the final holocaust that wipes life out altogether.[9]

That ultimate act of the drama, to which Weizenbaum alludes, is, of course, the image in Figure III, the fiery mushroom cloud of a nuclear explosion. That act is and would be the ultimate distance. Weizenbaum's words, however, make it quite clear that this ultimate separation is part of a larger web of occurrences which reaches into the fabric of our daily lives. In a sense, he is saying that the bomb is already present in the distance we put between ourselves and our bodies, in the ways in which the body has become, for example, an object of medicine. The bomb is *not* an exterior thing lying outside the circumstances of our living. If it is the final act it is *not* the period of the last sentence in the story of technology. Rather, it is already written into the letters and words, the sentences and the paragraphs which make up the tale. In these everyday acts of distancing, the bomb has already been armed. Indeed, in a sense it has already exploded.

We live in the year 44 PH, the forty fourth year after the atomic bombing of Hiroshima and Nagasaki. The nuclear bomb is a central image of contemporary life. We live forevermore in a nuclear-armed world. Even with total disarmament, the bomb, as Jonathan Schell[10] points out, can never be dis-invented, because we shall forevermore have the knowledge to build it. This one unalterable fact links together the images of Figures I and III. In their connection a deeper sense of technology as departure becomes visible.

A Flight as escape

In Walter Miller's classic science fiction novel, *A Canticle for Leibowitz*, first written in 1959, the two images of space flight and nuclear annihilation are wedded. The world, already once devastated by a nuclear holocaust, has resurrected itself out of the ashes, and after long centuries of struggle it has once again risen to the level of technological civilization. At the close of the novel, however, the world teeters again on the brink of catastrophe, and as the novel ends the sky erupts in fiery explosions as a group of monks, who for centuries had preserved remnants of the ancient knowledge, prepare to depart.

They sang as they lifted the children into the ship. They sang old space chanteys and helped the children up the ladder one at a time and into the hands of the sisters. They sang heartily to dispel the fright of the little ones. When the horizon erupted, the singing stopped. They passed the last child up into the ship.

The horizon came alive with flashes as the monks mounted the ladder. The horizon became a red glow. A distant cloudbank was born where no cloud had been. The monks on the ladder looked away from the flashes. When the flashes were gone, they looked back.

The visage of Lucifer mushroomed into hideousness above the cloudbank, rising slowly like some titan climbing to its feet after ages of imprisonment in the Earth.

Someone barked an order. The monks began climbing again. Soon they were all inside the ship.

The last monk, upon entering, paused in the lock. He stood up in the open hatchway and took off his sandals. *'Sic transit Mundus,'* he murmured, looking back at the glow. He slapped the soles of his sandals together, beating the dust out of them. The glow was engulfing a third of the heavens. He scratched his beard, took one last look at the ocean, then stepped back and closed the hatch.

There came a blur, a glare of light, a high thin whirring sound, and the starship thrust itself heavenward.[11]

Miller's tale indicates that the fires of lift-off are akin to the fires of destruction. The rocket is, psychologically speaking, powered by the fires of nuclear annihilation. Indeed, the fires of nuclear catastrophe are the symptomatic side of the fires of departure. Wedded in this fashion, departure takes on the character of psychological necessity. On an earth wired for destruction, space flight becomes a means of escape.

As disturbing as it may be to recognize that our departure is motivated as escape, it may be even more disturbing to realize that this connection between departure and destruction also works the other way. An earth from which we *can* depart, an earth from which we *can* escape, is one whose destruction would be less of a catastrophe. To be sure, this is a difficult notion to accept, but consider that something of this motive is already apparent in Francis Crick's perception of the earth as originally not our home. Earth so regarded is already psychologically abandoned. The ground, literally and figuratively speaking, is already prepared for lessening the impact of destruction. I am not saying here that such destruction is intentionally pursued. Rather, I am saying that the possibility of departure from earth is a way of lessening the emotional effects of the fear of its destruction. I am saying that the two images work upon each other, feed upon each other, as it were, creating an emotionally laden vicious circle. Threatened with destruction, as imaged in the nuclear cloud, there is the need to escape, imaged as space flight. And feeling the need to escape, as promised in the possibility of space flight, it becomes necessary to devalue the earth we would leave behind, to lessen the impact of the loss.

The image of home is perhaps the oldest, deepest, and most powerful image of the human soul. In stripping the earth of this image, we sever its hold upon us and thereby deaden for ourselves the impact of its loss. Initially devalued, the emotional disaster of its loss is somewhat tamed.

This effort is, of course, an illusion, but illusions become necessary when reality is too hard to bear. The destruction of the earth is, for the incarnated human soul, whose entire history is inseparable from and has been shaped by its place on the earth, an unbearable reality. At the most primitive and emotionally powerful levels, the very rhythms of the earth — the tides of the sea, the cycles of the seasons, the rising and the setting of the sun — have been a kind of guarantee of our own continuity. In knowing them, something of us, not individually but collectively, is also known, recognized and acknowledged. In the most extreme circumstances, we have been able to believe that there will always be another tomorrow.

But what if tomorrow when the sun rises there is no living human being to see it? Then the earth which has linked together the generations of humanity falls into a kind of sleep, and we are forevermore forgotten.

The breakers beat monotonously at the shores, casting up driftwood. An abandoned seaplane floated beyond the breakers. After a while the breakers caught the seaplane and threw it on the shore with the driftwood. It tilted and fractured a wing. There were shrimp carousing in the breakers, and the whiting that fed on the shrimp, and the shark that munched on the whiting and found them admirable, in the sportive brutality of the sea.

A wind came across the ocean, sweeping with it a pall of fine white ash. The ash fell into the sea and into the breakers. The breakers washed dead shrimp ashore with the driftwood, then they washed up the whiting. The shark swam out to his deepest waters, and brooded in the old clean currents. He was very hungry that season.[12]

That is the end of Walter Miller's tale. After the bomb and even after departure, for those few who have *perhaps* managed it, there is one final movement in the drama, never to be witnessed, only to be imagined. Oblivion! Consider the tides continuing their relentless pursuit upon the shores! Or consider the sun still rising and setting in its perpetual round! Or the wind without sound blowing its way across barren fields! And consider all this now occurring apart from our presence and even indifferent to our absence! Even the dinosaurs never passed into such complete and total darkness. These things, these simple rhythms of nature, which once were a guarantee, become in the light of the bomb a testament to our oblivion.

There is sufficient anxiety in these considerations to fire wishes, however illusory, to lessen the impact of earth's destruction, to devalue it and thereby diminish its loss, and to prepare for and to pursue our departure.

That we do numb ourselves to this loss has been indicated in another way by Paul Boyer in his recent book, *By the Bomb's Early Light*. Speaking about television, a very concrete and universal expression of our technological world, and speaking specifically about how difficult it has been for this medium to awaken us to the horrors of nuclear catastrophe, he notes that, '*The Day After* had less impact than predicted.' We lessened its emotional effects, devaluing it much as we have devalued the earth to lessen its loss. 'Perhaps,' he then writes, 'the only adequate television treatment of nuclear war would be two hours of a totally blank screen in prime time.' Would we be able to pull off the same psychological trick of devaluation here, with this habit of television viewing so close to home, as we perhaps can do with the earth? Or would we perhaps be forced to admit that our world does matter, even in something as simple as our television habits and preferences? If we could do the latter, then perhaps the possibility of departure, from the earth and from the world we have built upon it, would no longer require that initial devaluation which makes their destruction less of a catastrophe. If the earth and the things of our world could again begin to matter, if we could allow ourselves to feel again the pain of their loss, then the insidious connection between the images of space flight and nuclear annihilation might be broken. Then, threatened with destruction, imaged as nuclear annihilation, the need to escape, imaged as space flight, might *not* lead to that act of devaluation yielding the illusion of a lessened catastrophe. Then, threatened with destruction, we might in the face of the bomb reaffirm our connection to the things of the world and to the earth. Out of distance we might draw closer, to be touched again by these things and by the earth. And in this context, we might recover other motives for space flight, for our journey to the stars. As Boyer, however, asks of his television suggestion, 'But who would sponsor it?'[13] And that is, as we shall see, a key issue of technology. Having dominated the earth out of our increasing distance from it, we have come to believe that we are masters, and even creators. And in so doing, we have lost the sense that we are *sponsored*, which means supported, upheld, and already sent on the way. In this respect, we have lost something of the *religious* sense of human life, in the root meaning of that term, the sense that we are already bound, and connected to, and limited by something beyond ourselves. In breaking the bond of gravity we have broken more than a physical restraint. We have broken the spiritual condition of humanity.

The artist Alex Grey again offers us a visual presentation of our theme. Entitled *Nuclear Crucifixion* (Figure 1.1), it disturbingly juxtaposes not only two dominant symbols, but also two different world views. The figure of Christ crucified makes sense within a world where issues of sin,

Figure 1.1 Alex Grey, *Nuclear Crucifixion*, 1980

Source: Stux Gallery, New York

redemption, and salvation belong. The figure of the mushroom cloud of nuclear annihilation belongs to a world which almost completely cancels that symbol and has fallen asleep to those issues. Cloud eclipses cross, crucifying it, as it were, on a fiery cross of hubris, fashioned out of the arrogant and unchecked use of our power. In the clash of these two symbols, however, we may be shocked enough to ask the question of who, then, can *sponsor* a reawakening? Or what? And shocked enough to wonder if such a reawakening, a new genesis of humanity's spiritual condition, is possible in a technological age? From within technology and not outside it, we need to consider whether the dream of technology itself can spur such an awakening.

III Escaping death

In the epilogue to his book *Time of Need*, a reflection on the life of the imagination in our technological century, William Barrett writes that 'That mere leap into space by itself does not signify.' Rather, 'it is as a symbol that it captures the imagination, a symbol of the departure from the earth in which we are all swept along.'[14] In the long journey down the corridor of evolution, along with all the other species of life which have inhabited this planet, we have been nurtured and nourished, sponsored by the earth. Now, having refashioned ourselves in our own image, we stand alone poised to depart, to break free of that natal bond which gave shape to who and what we are. There on the launchpad we can awaken to a new beginning or our final end. Departure can be another step in the history of human evolution or the harbinger of its end. The *event* of departure as *symbol* has multiple possibilities.

Timothy Leary, in a brilliant and hilarious commentary on the sixties, *Neuropolitics*, celebrates the symbol of departure as a new and necessary beginning. 'Space migration,' he writes, 'is the inevitable next step in evolution,'[15] and he has even coined a memorable slogan for our departure. It is S.M.I.²L.E.: Space Migration, Intelligence Increase, Life Extension. Indeed, something of the character of the manifesto marks his words:

> We live at the bottom of a 40-mile gravity well. It has taken all of four and a half billion years of terrestrial evolution to produce nervous systems capable of devising a technology with which to climb out of that well and launch migratory-colonization cylinders into space. There is no reason for us to ever climb back down into such a planetary hole again. Our evolutionary mission is to fly free through timespace. The original sin of 'Genesis' is gravity: the fall.[16]

Others share this optimism, viewing the continuing tie to the earth as a kind of retardation of the species, as illustrated for example in Isaac

Asimov's now famous phrase, 'planetary chauvinism',[17] which is vividly descriptive and diagnostic of how he perceives those who would temper such optimism. But even without the optimism, there are those for whom the event of departure symbolizes a step which must be taken. In the vision of one like Gerard O'Neill,[18] for example, colonizing the higher frontier of space is the only solution to the four major problems which are a consequence of the limited size of earth. Without departure and colonization, the swelling population of earth will fast deplete our supplies of energy, food, and living space. For O'Neill departure is necessary in order to survive.

O'Neill, Asimov, and Leary characterize earth departure in different ways, but in each characterization there is, I believe, a shadow which is ignored. To discover its presence we need to turn to Barrett once again.

Noting the conjunction in our age of our knowledge of the stars and of the primitive peoples of the earth, Barrett writes: 'The appearance of space man seems secretly timed with the disappearance of archaic man. Primitive peoples are in fact dying off or being drawn into the orbit of civilization so rapidly that in a few years there will be no more left.'[19] What does this disappearance of archaic man indicate about the character of our departure?

The body of the space man, as illustrated in the figure of the Little Cosmonaut, is a body of technical functions, a body created or born in and made for distance from the earth. As a body of departure it is a body apart from the earth. In contrast, the body of archaic man is a body of ritual, a body in intimate connection with the earth, a body which is a part of the earth. And just as we are all swept along in the symbol of departure, just as we are all astronauts, so too do we all remain, at least for the moment, a primitive body rooted to the earth, a body which, if not of ritual and remembrance, still remains at least a body of human activity within the layers of technical functions by which it is enshelled. In this context, then, the disappearance of archaic man indicates a war we are waging against the body of life. This disappearance is perhaps nothing less than a displaced expression of the increasing objectification and medicalization of our own bodies, processes which replace flesh with function.

To displace the body which is a *part* of the earth by a body which is *apart* from it, to displace flesh by function, to wage a war with the body of life, is, however, to symbolize in our departure from earth a dream of escaping death. The archaic body about which Barrett speaks, this primitive body which in ritual performances like burial practices remembers its ties to earth, is a living body. In contrast with a technical body, which can cease functioning, a living body is one which dies. The conjunction of space man's appearance and archaic man's disappearance is, therefore, nothing other than a harbinger of our wish to take leave of a flesh so fragile and so frail, flesh which is always finally heir to death.

Departure as a flight from death is a dream of technological humanity. 'Homo Faber' or 'Technological Man,' as Jeremy Rifkin puts it, 'wants to overcome death.'[20] But that is an impossible dream, in part because in order to escape death our departure from earth would have to be total and complete. As Barrett, however, again notes, although 'one part of our knowledge provides us with the instruments to get free of earth, another part tells us how much, deep down, we are formed of the muck and slime of that same earth from which we can never be quit.'[21] We carry death with ourselves, therefore, as deeply as we carry earth with ourselves as embodied creatures. We carry death as carnal knowledge. To escape death, then, we would have to do more than simply depart earth, more than simply break that natal bond of gravity between body and earth, that bond inscribed in our flesh by which the earth holds fast its claim upon the body and finally reclaims it. In our departure, we would even have to do more than destroy the earth, because we would still carry within ourselves, within every bone and muscle, within every gesture, a living reminder of our tie to earth. To cheat life of the death we owe it we would have to cleanse ourselves completely and totally of all that, of every touch, taste, and smell of matter, of its stench of corruption. To defeat death we would have to rid ourselves of the scourge of aging and its signs of decay. To conquer death we would have to purify ourselves of all traces of how we matter. Our ascent would have to be an act of purification. Our departure, perhaps reminiscent of the fall but reversed by the will of technological humanity, would have to be as angels.

What we would deny returns, however, as symptom, and in this light the threatened archaic body of humanity, coincident in its increasing disappearance with the appearance of the astronautic body of humanity, struggles to hold a place for death in the midst of human life. It is a symptom of our flight from death, a reminder, therefore, that as carnal creatures we do owe life a death. This body, however, maintains a precarious existence, present as it is on the margins of technological culture and, as Barrett notes, increasingly threatened by extinction. Moreover, this body, a body of human activity in contrast with technical function, is becoming increasingly marginal even within technological culture, as we remake the body in terms of the image and definition of the Little Cosmonaut.

Symptoms ignored, however, do not disappear, and thus the death we would deny only appears elsewhere, perhaps in more virulent forms. For example, are our diseases, especially those of epidemic proportions, symptoms of cultural denials? In a recent book edited by David Levin,[22] several investigators from diverse fields propose and examine such a notion, and it is within this context that we may wonder if we have already gone so far along the road of fashioning the body apart from earth, an astronautic body whose shadow side is that of the alien, that the living body increasingly distant from the earth has itself become so alien that it no longer has its natural defenses? In short, is AIDS a cultural symptom of the alienation of ourselves from our bodies, a disease of the 'alien'? As questionable as this might appear, already we tend to perceive AIDS in this fashion, in so far as we struggle to keep it associated with those whom we would regard as alien to the mainstream of society, to gays and drug users. In this regard, then, do we unknowingly and unwittingly arrange for our diseases to carry the shadow of our culture, and, more to the point here, do we 'choose' and designate victims to suffer our cultural symptoms?

We need not, however, limit ourselves to this suggestion, because the death we would deny is more immediately apparent in another virulent return. In our dream of escaping death by departing earth we have surrounded ourselves with it. We court death even as we would flee it. The earth we would depart is also the earth we have wired for destruction. Thus the death we would escape comes back to haunt us in the shape of the nuclear cloud of annihilation. In this form, the death we would shun embraces us. In this respect, the death from which we would depart becomes the bomb as cultural symptom.

IV Turning the dream

On the launchpad we stand alone and it is there, more than in any place in our present world, that the distance which has marked our technological mastery of the earth is most visible. There on the launchpad we get some rough measure of how far we have come along the long road of evolution toward separating ourselves from the earth and the rest of creation. Truly as astronautic man and woman we stand isolated and apart, the new masters of creation, and it is an *awe-ful* vision. That it promises a new beginning there is little doubt. But that it is equally harbinger of a final end must also be considered, for we have arrived at this point by becoming, in the fine phrase of Loren Eiseley, 'world eaters',[23] energy consumers on a planetary scale.

In attending to the dream of technology we have assumed that technology is humanity's dream. That is quite natural. But what if, as James Hillman notes about dreams,[24] we are in the dream and the dream is not in us? Then, perhaps, something which Loren Eiseley has wondered about in one of his more melancholic visions becomes plausible. Suppose technology is the earth's dream? Suppose it is the earth's way of cleansing itself of the 'planet virus' called humanity, of ridding itself of those wishes and dreams which would court its own destruction. 'The fruition time of the planet virus is at hand' Eiseley says,[25] by which he means our rocket century. It is, I agree, a fanciful notion. But what if from earth's point of view technology is a dream, an experiment in self-knowledge, which has failed? On the launchpad, alone, at least we have to wonder about technology from nature's point of view. And perhaps *in* that wondering there is the beginning of an awakening, a way in which we can hear the earth's dream and become agents more of construction than destruction. Maybe we need to learn only how to listen. 'Earth, isn't this what you want: an invisible re-arising in us?'[26]

V On the launchpad

In this moment of lift-off we have attended to technology as symptom and dream by attending to some of its images. Later, in the final chapter, at the moment of re-entry, we will return to technology as symptom and dream and attend again to its images. In between these two moments, however, we will inquire into how we have arrived at this place of departure, bearing these dreams of distance and disincarnation and their shadow sides of annihilation and a flight from death. To do so, we need to listen to the dreamer, since every dream is dreamed by a dreamer. History will be this dreamer for us, and we will journey through history and attend to the story which has fabricated these dreams, to those historical events and happenings from which the images of these dreams have been woven. Lest there be cause for misunderstanding, however, we shall listen to the dreamer's tale, to these events and happenings of history, with our ear already attuned to the shadows. In other words, we will take this journey already carrying the images of technology as symptom and dream. These images will be the background, the depth, from which we will listen to this tale.

The journey begins in the next chapter with a tale of beginnings, with a consideration of how the dream of mastery through distance originates in the imaginal eye of the artist some five hundred years ago. It is a tale about windows and cameras, a story about vision and the hegemony of the eye. It is a tale, finally, of how the artistic technique of perspective vision, in becoming a cultural habit of mind, transforms the landscape of the world, the geography of the soul.

In subsequent chapters, we will discover how within this landscape of linear perspective vision the self becomes a spectator ensconced behind his or her window on the world, how the body, now divorced from this self, becomes a specimen, and how the world, as a matter for this detached and observing eye, becomes a spectacle. Then, in a final chapter, at the apogee of our journey after lift-off, we will attend to how technology itself, as a story of departure, may also be the possibility of return, remembrance, renewal, a return which is not just a going back home but a coming home, perhaps, with a nod to the poet Eliot, to know the place for the first time.[27]

Chapter two

The window and the camera

I A window on the world

J. H. van den Berg[1] has written extensively on how the cultural world mirrors or reflects the changing nature of humanity. We who live in the twentieth century differ as much from men and women of the Middle Ages as their world differs from ours. Van den Berg has specifically considered the history of western Church architecture in this way, demonstrating how humanity's changing conceptions of spirituality and the space of the world are reflected in these transformations. Architecture is a visible expression of how a specific historical–cultural era shapes its space and draws its boundaries between the inside and the outside. Church architecture in particular reveals how an age carves in stone its boundaries of the sacred and profane.

Painting also provides this kind of mirror through which we can read the image which an age has of itself and the world. As a celebration of the visible world painting reflects, among other things, not only the ideas which a particular age has about the space of the world and its place within that space, but also the space itself of that world. The canvas records not only the style of the painter but also the style of the world in which he or she lives and paints. A Cezanne canvas radically differs from one by da Vinci, and that difference attests to the different worlds in which each has lived *and* to the different eyes with which each has perceived his world. Between a da Vinci and a Cezanne the human world and the human eye have changed. Painting indicates not only that styles of human perception change but also that the world itself changes.

The invention of linear perspective painting in fifteenth-century Italy is one such moment of change, and the tale to be told in this chapter concerns how the invention and development of this artistic technique became the cultural vision which has shaped our contemporary technological world. Linear perspective vision, in the words of art historian Samuel Y. Edgerton, is 'the "innate" geometry in our eyes,'[2] and although this way of perceiving space is no more natural to humanity than, say, a Picasso canvas in which multiple perspectives appear simultaneously, the latter remains for us abstract and unreal while the former defines for us what is real and what is natural. Before we know that we know it, we have learned to see the world as a three-dimensional plane where depth is a matter of spatial distance from the viewer and where all objects decrease in size as they recede from the viewer toward a vanishing point. In short, before we know that we know it, we have learned to see the world as if we were focusing through the lens of a camera, or as if we were standing on a railroad track looking at the parallel rails converging in the distance.

What linear perspective vision achieves is a kind of geometrization of the space of the world, and within that space we become observers of a world which has become an object of observation. Linear perspective is a celebration of the eye of distance, a created convention which not only extends and elaborates the natural power of vision to survey things from afar, but also elevates that power into a method, a way of knowing, which has defined for us the world with which we are so readily familiar. It is the transformation of the eye into a technology and a redefinition of the world to suit the eye, a world of maps and charts, blueprints and diagrams, the world in which we are, among other things, silent readers of the printed word and users of the camera, the world, finally, in which we have all become astronauts.

To assign so much importance to an artistic technique invented over 500 years ago may seem, however, to be too bold a claim, the consequence perhaps of too liberal an imagination. And yet that this technique, a way of representing three-dimensional space on the two-dimensional plane of a canvas, has become a cultural vision is beyond doubt. The art historian Helen Gardner notes, for example, that linear perspective 'made possible scale drawings, maps, charts, graphs, and diagrams — those means of exact representation without which modern science and technology would be impossible.'[3] And William Ivins, noted cultural historian, supports this view. 'Many reasons are assigned for the mechanization of life and industry during the nineteenth century,' he says, 'but the mathematical development of perspective was absolutely prerequisite to it.'[4] Finally, as if to secure this point beyond any shadow of doubt, Samuel Edgerton notes that 'space capsules built for zero gravity, astronomical equipment for demarcating so-called black holes, atom smashers which prove the existence of anti-matter — these are the end products of the discovered vanishing point.'[5] Linear perspective, artistic technique become cultural vision, is central, therefore, to the story of technology being told in this work, and in its invention we shall find something of the origins of those dreams of distance, departure, and disincarnation which have already been mentioned. In continuing our story in this fashion we shall hear how linear perspective vision, in making the eye the world's measure, has transformed the self into a spectator, the world into a spectacle, and the body into a specimen. We shall hear how this vision has become our window on the world. Before we continue the tale,

Figure 2.1 Vanishing point as launchpad to the stars

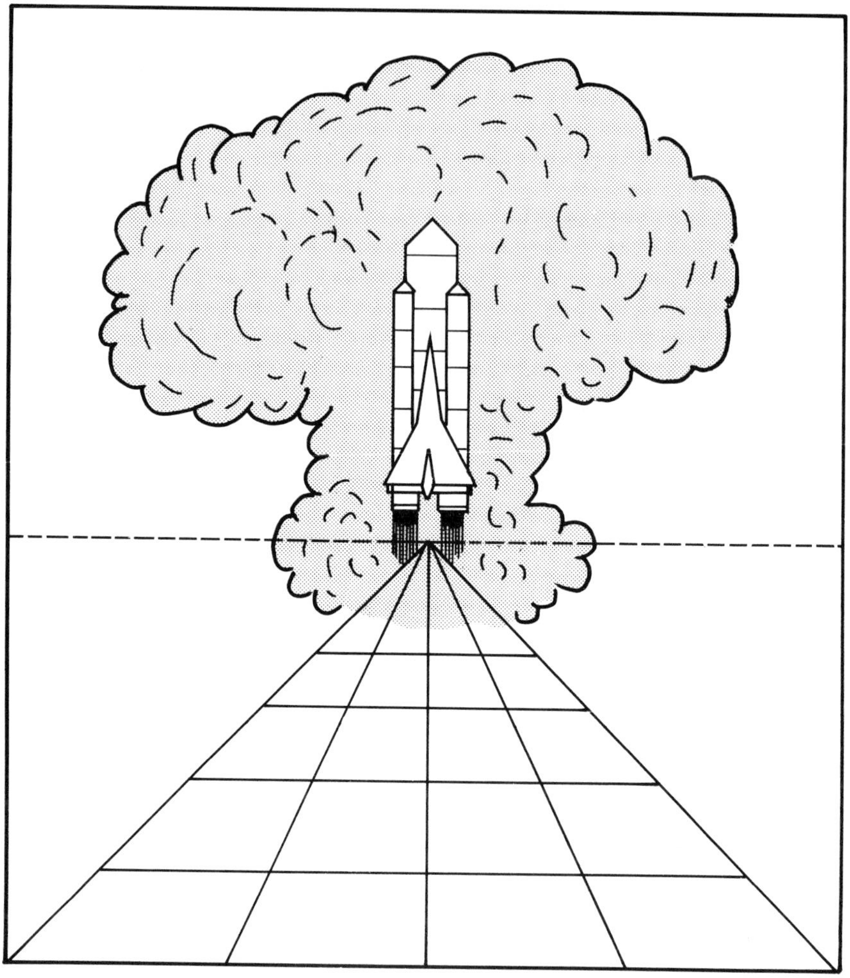

Drawing by Liota Odom

however, it will serve us well to gather in the image presented in Figure 2.1 the things which have already been spoken. The vanishing point is the launchpad of the modern world. It is there, in that distance and at that point where the figure of the astronaut, already reincarnated for departure, takes leave of the world.

II Linear perspective: some necessary technical considerations

A An opening image

To begin our discussion of some of the necessary technical matters involved in linear perspective technique, let us first familiarize ourselves with our own linear perspective style of vision, that innate geometry of our eyes. To do so, consider the two illustrations of the city of Florence presented in Figures 2.2 and 2.3. The first one dates from approximately 1350 while the second one, known today as *Map with a Chain*, dates from about 1480. They lie on either side of the invention in 1425 of the technique of linear perspective by Filippo Brunelleschi and later codified in Leon Battista Alberti's treatise on painting, *De Pictura*, which was published in 1435–6. Between these two paintings there is a world of difference; between them a new world has emerged.

Perhaps what is most striking about the earlier portrayal is its sense of clutter and confusion. The buildings of the city crowd in upon each other, presenting a multiplicity of perspectives simultaneously. Our eyes cannot find any one point from which to view the city, and in this respect the painting may remind us of a young child's drawing of his or her house, in which front, side, and back views are given all at once. Indeed, from the point of view of the later painting we might be tempted to dismiss this earlier one as naive, crediting to the later view a more realistic presentation.

The later view is not, however, more real, and such a judgement would express only our preference for what has become most familiar. The difference between the two views is not a matter of the real and the unreal. It is rather a difference between one world and another. 'The painter of the earlier picture,' Edgerton says, 'did not conceive of his subject in terms of *spatial homogeneity*.' On the contrary, his painting reflects a belief that 'he could render what he saw before his eyes convincingly by representing what it felt like to *walk about*, experiencing structures, almost *tactilely*, from many different sides, rather than from a *single, overall vantage*.'[6] In short, what we have with this earlier painting is a rather vivid impression of what it must have been like to live in another, earlier, medieval world. The painting tells us that it was a world marked by time and by the presence of the body in the midst of things. If we find it confusing, then it is because there is time and body in this earlier painting. If we find it confusing, it is because with the advent of linear perspective vision we have managed to spatialize time, to distance ourselves from the body, and to remove ourselves from the midst of things. It is confusing because it is a city which has not yet become for us a spatial landscape mapped by a bird's eye view.

The Florence of 1480 which is depicted in Figure 2.3 is, however, such a city. It offers that bird's eye view above the city, a 'fixed viewpoint' in Edgerton's terms, which is 'elevated and distant, completely out of plastic or sensory reach of the depicted city.'[7] It is the perspective of the figure in

Figure 2.2 Panorama of Florence, fresco, Loggia Del Bigallo

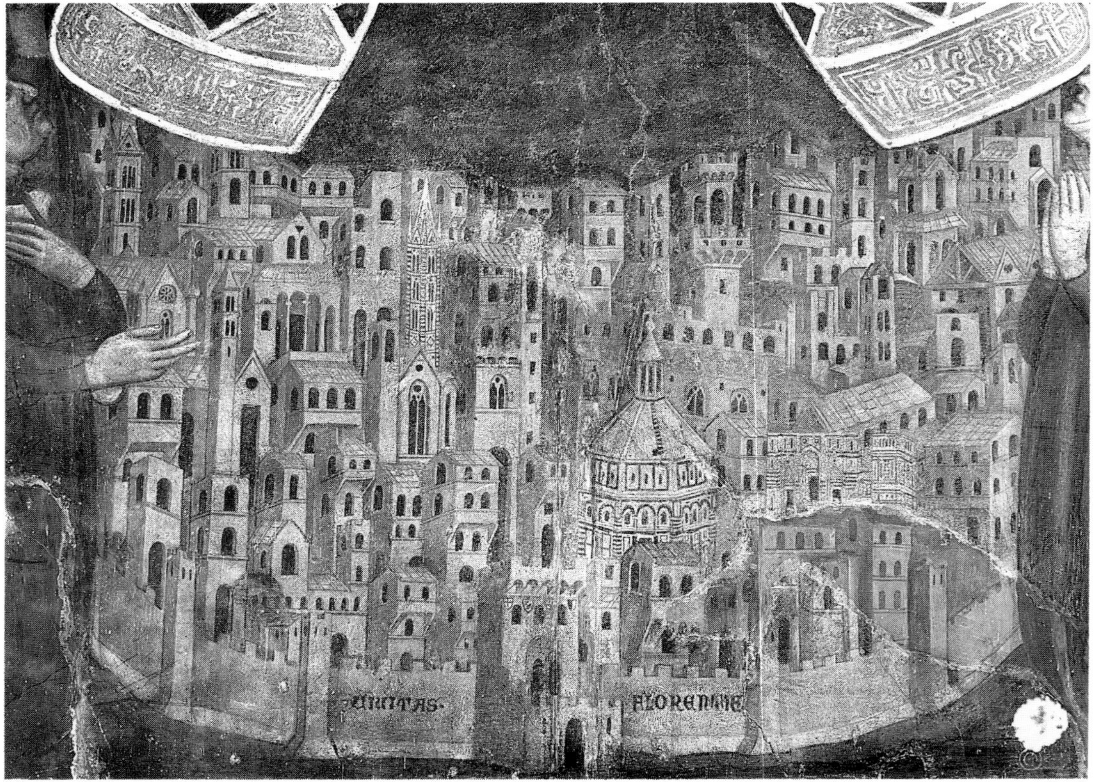

Reproduced by courtesy of Alinari/Art Resource, New York

Figure 2.3 Map of Florence: copy of the Carta Della Catena, Museo de Firenze Com'era, Florence

FIORENZA

the lower right hand corner of the painting, the man on the hill above the city with his sketchpad in hand. Is he, perhaps, sketching a map of the city? Of course, we cannot know. But we can know that from his high-altitude vantage point he is a man of distant vision, perhaps the first expression of the self we have become, perhaps even, we might say, the father of the astronaut. Seated there as he is above the city, he incarnates at its birth a new ideal of knowledge according to which the further we remove ourselves from the world the better we can know it. It is an ideal, however, which by definition means a knowledge of the world which is increasingly disincarnate. On the hill above the city only his eyes remain 'in touch' with the world observed below. But at that distance such eyes, unrelated, for example, to ears and hands, can no longer know the words of anger or of love uttered by those *living* in the city.

One looks at this anonymous work painted so long ago and one recognizes a kinship with the perspective it portrays. It is a view with which we are familiar, a perspective which finds a favorable reception in the geometry of our eyes, in the way in which we perceive the world. Closer in chronological time to the earlier view of Florence than it is to our time, it is nevertheless culturally and psychologically closer to us, and anyone who has ever approached a city in an airplane can affirm this affinity. And yet while this later view of Florence manifests that style of vision which defines for us what is real and which we unquestioningly regard as natural, we still retain in our muscles and bones, so to speak, the vision of the world depicted in the earlier view. That earlier view, as Edgerton notes, is, for example, the truth for the tourist arriving for the first time in a strange city with heavy baggage and an unfamiliar hotel address in hand. It is the truth of the city inscribed in one's tired legs, aching feet, and sore shoulders. It is the city measured not by the gaze of the distant eye but by the history of the body. Regardless, therefore, of the distance which we practice and achieve, we remain in our everyday living situations bodily creatures with a carnal knowledge of the world. It persists, this life of the body, in the shadows of our technological vision, forming the underside of our technological world. In treating next a few key points of Alberti's linear perspective technique, we shall hear how the body fares at the origins of this tale of technology.

B Alberti's linear perspective technique

Alberti's procedure for making a linear perspective drawing involves two steps: the construction of a vanishing point and of a distance point. We shall follow his procedure in somewhat simplified form and indicate several conditions and implications of these two steps which have shaped and influenced our sense of body, self, and the things of the world.[8]

1 The vanishing point

The term 'vanishing point' is not Alberti's. It is of more recent coinage. Alberti's term was the *centre point*, which, interestingly enough, was also called in his time the *punto di fuga*, the point of flight. At the outset of our consideration, therefore, echoes of our earlier discussion about flight and departure are heard, and we recall here Edgerton's comment about how our space flight technology is the product of the discovered vanishing point. Perhaps the way in which the first historical and cultural appearance of a phenomenon is named contains a nascent wisdom and genius (or even wish?) concerning its nature and its destiny. We shall hold on to this earliest designation, even though we shall make use of the term which has become the convention.

The construction of the vanishing point is a relatively simple procedure, and Alberti speaks of it in this fashion:

First of all, on the surface on which I am going to paint, I draw a rectangle of whatever size I want, *which I regard as an open window through which the subject to be painted is seen*; and I decide how large I wish the human figures in the painting to be. I divide the height of this man into three parts, which will be proportional to the measure commonly called a *braccio* [approximately two feet]. With this measure I divide the bottom line of my rectangle into as many parts as it will hold . . . . Then I establish a point in the rectangle wherever I wish; and [as] it occupies the place where the centric ray strikes, I shall call this the centric point. The suitable position for this centric point is no higher from the base line than the height of the man to be represented in the painting, *for in this way both the viewers and the objects in the painting will seem to be on the same plane.* Having placed the centric point, I draw lines from it to each of the divisions on the base line.[9]

A bit later in the text Alberti adds that a horizontal is to be drawn through the centric point. This line, which today is called the horizon, was termed the 'centric line' by Alberti. It is important to note that this line sets the limit for the height of any object to be depicted in the painting and that it is *fixed* at the eye level of an observer imagined to be standing on a *horizontal* plane and *staring straight ahead* at the world. This last point means that the centric line, the horizon, is identical with the viewer's eye level, that the centric or vanishing point and the viewer's eye always lie on the same plane. In this respect each of us, as Edgerton notes, is like a viewer who stands at the water's edge and looks out to the ocean. One's eye level is always synonymous with the horizon which rises and falls in exact concordance with one's position, provided the viewer continues to stare straight ahead. Edgerton notes that this concordance of vanishing point and horizon line, the viewer's eye level, was Brunelleschi's most important discovery.

Alberti's remark concerning the centric or horizon line as a limit for the height of an object to be depicted in the painting establishes what Edgerton calls 'horizon line isocephaly'. It means that 'when the viewer stands on a horizontal plane, looking straight ahead at other persons of the same height and standing on the same plane, all the heads of these other persons, no matter how far distant, will appear to be on the same horizon line'. A decrease in size will occur, therefore, ' "from the feet up" '. Edgerton notes that 'no picture made by any artist in any civilization anywhere in the world before 1425 intentionally shows this phenomenon'.[10] In Alberti's text this phenomenon is described in the following way:

> As it passes through the centric point, this line may be called the centric line. This is why men depicted standing in the parallel furthest away are a great deal smaller than those in the nearer ones, a phenomenon which is clearly demonstrated by nature herself, for in churches we see the heads of men walking about, moving at more or less the same height, while the feet of those further away may correspond to the knee level of those in front.[11]

Figure 2.4 summarizes Alberti's construction of the vanishing point. Note that the centric point (A) is no higher than the heads of the figures represented in the illustration and that their heads remain aligned with Alberti's centric line, the horizon, even as the figures in the distance shrink from the bottom up towards the head. The slanted lines, called today 'orthogonals', are the lines Alberti draws from the centric point to the base of his rectangle. Consider them as the sides or edges of objects receding into the distance toward the vanishing point. An immediate example would be the walls of a tunnel for a viewer staring straight ahead toward its exit.

To appreciate better what has been described so far the reader should imaginatively project this illustration into the world in front of him or her. It will help to get the feel for what we are doing if the reader will lift the illustration to his or her eye level, imaginatively extend its lines into the world, and remember that the figures depicted in the illustration are standing upright and that the heads of these figures are aligned with the horizon or centric line and hence with the reader's own eye level. In doing so, the reader will begin to recover what he or she now automatically lives, that innate geometry of his or her linear perspective eyes.

Perhaps the reader has already begun to recognize how pervasive this way of perceiving the world has become for us. But as natural as it may appear, it is important to say once again that this style of vision is a historical invention. Nothing like it appears earlier in medieval painting, for example, suggesting that men and women of earlier ages simply did not see in this fashion. As incredible as this may sound — for it challenges a most basic and assumed condition of our daily living — it is worth noting with

Figure 2.4 Vanishing point with Horizon Line Alignment

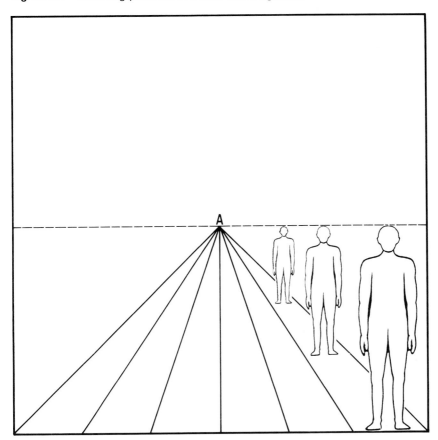

Adapted by Liota Odom from Samuel Y. Edgerton Jr., *The Renaissance Rediscovery of Linear Perspective*

Edgerton that what we regard as a natural fact of vision, that innate geometry which has become ingrained in our eyes (a second nature, as it were), this perspective convergence, was for the medieval science of optics 'a mere *Fata Morgana*', a trick which 'could be disproved by simple geometry'.[12] That linear perspective vision *is* a historical invention recommends, therefore, that we pay close attention to its conditions and implications, for in creating it we have also designed and invented ourselves and our world.

The construction of the vanishing point imposes two conditions. The first one is that the painter (and the viewer) imagines that he or she is looking at the subject to be painted (the world to be viewed) as if through a window. The second condition is that the centric (vanishing) point and the line which passes through this point be placed no higher from the base line than the height of the subject to be depicted in the painting. There are a number of implications of these two conditions, each one of which has had a decisive effect in bringing to birth the technological world. At this point in our story we shall only briefly describe these implications, leaving to a later time (the subsequent four chapters) a more extensive telling of the tale.

The condition of the window implies a *boundary* between the perceiver and the perceived. It establishes as a condition for perception a formal *separation* between a subject who sees the world and the world that is seen, and in so doing it sets the stage, as it were, for that retreat or withdrawal of the self from the world which characterizes the dawn of the modern age. Ensconced behind the window the self becomes an observing *subject*, a *spectator*, as against a world which becomes a *spectacle*, an *object* of vision. Almost two centuries before Descartes will establish the philosophical grounds of a consciousness, a self, separated from the world, the imaginal eye of the artist has already prepared the space for that achievement. With the condition of a window, the 'twofold flight from the earth into the universe and from the world into the self,'[13] which Hannah Arendt says characterizes our modern alienation, has a beginning.

In addition to this separation between perceiver and world, the condition of the window also initiates an *eclipse of the body*. Looked at from behind a window the world is primarily something to be seen. Indeed, a window between me and the world tends not only to emphasize the eye as my means of access to the world but also to de-emphasize the other senses. Like the man on the hill in that later view of the city of Florence, my vision of the world from behind the window tends to lose touch with the sounds, tastes, smells, and feel of the world. And with this eclipse of the body fostered by the window, the world on the other side of the window is already set to become a matter of *information*. As a spectacle, an object of vision, it is already well on the way to becoming a bit of data, observable, measurable, analyzable, and readable as a computer print-out, for example, or as a blip on a radar screen. Moreover, as an object of vision, as something to be seen, the world is also well on its way to becoming a *matter of light*. The camera as an instrument of technology will have its possibility here, and so too will the television. Indeed, the television screen, on which the world actually is reassembled as light, will become our window on the world.

Between Alberti's window and our television screen, there is, however, a series of significant steps. With Alberti the window is still open, but in the later stages of our story we shall have to pay attention to the ways in which it is closed. For the moment, however, it is sufficient to note what we already have said about the window condition of linear perspective vision.

Alberti's second condition about the centric point has a number of inter-related implications. Insofar as the placement of the centric or vanishing point is no higher from the base line than the height of the figure to be depicted in the painting, Alberti notes that 'in this way both the viewer and the objects in the painting will seem to be on the same plane.'[14] In other words, a linear perspective vision is one which places everything on the same level and in this respect the imaginal eye of the artist has already prepared the space for the sixteenth-century emergence of the scientific world of *explanations*. Galileo, for example, will presume such a space for his law of falling bodies, a space where all objects fall equally fast. In such a space all things, regardless of what they are and regardless of the context to which they belong, are equal and the same. They are, in short, ex-plained, that is, reduced to the same plane or level of reality. They are, so to speak, flattened out, within a space that is neutral and homogeneous, a space within which all things become calculable objects in a mathematical equation. That the truth of Galileo's law of falling bodies was demonstrated on the moon during the flight of *Apollo 15* is significant. It indicates that the space opened up by a linear perspective vision is even at its origins an imagined space apart from the earth. There is in this space where all is on the same plane already more than a hint of departure.

The power of such an equalizing vision is, of course, quite obvious, and without a doubt this vision has played a central role in allowing us to take the world's measure. Perhaps it might also be said to have played a part in the social realm as well, preparing the way for that equalizing vision which animates science *and* democracy. Certainly a claim can be made that technology fosters a democratic vision. The view of earth seen from space, for example, lends weight and gives substance to the idea of one single humanity. Of course, the bomb as an instrument of technology shows the other side of this claim. We can all be destroyed equally, a possibility which is quite explicit in the idea of a nuclear winter.[15] In either event, however, it does appear to be the case that what Alberti imagined, technology has to some degree realized: all of us are viewers of the same world. Even if it is only as *consumers* of the same products the world over — a MacDonald's hamburger and a coke — we all stand on the same plane.

A vision which perceives all things as belonging to the same plane is a vision which transforms the depth of the world. Depth as a matter of levels becomes depth as a matter of spatial distance from the viewer. Horizontal depth replaces vertical depth and things, or beings, which either belong to different levels of existence or are marked by different levels of value, like angels and demons, will progressively lose their place in the homogeneous space of the world opened up by linear perspective vision. I mention angels and demons here deliberately because we no longer believe in them, because they have become mere figments of our imagination. Their status, however, is a good measure of the extent to which we have embraced a world of nature in which everything that cannot be explained, that cannot be measured and made equal through the rule of number, disappears. Already by the *late* fifteenth century angels in the space of a linear perspective painting will have to be supported. They will be placed, for example, on clouds, a development which suggests that their appearance in the space of our world is now something of an anomaly.

Angels and demons, however, do not simply disappear, and what I said above about disappearance is too simple. Rather, they go elsewhere, and the two illustrations presented in Figures 2.5 and 2.6 give a very good indication of where they go. The first one is by the fifteenth-century artist Hieronymous Bosch. It is a detail from a painting entitled *The Temptation of St Anthony*. The demons surround him. They are everywhere in the world. The second illustration is from 1794. It is by Goya and is entitled *The Dream of Reason Produces Monsters*. The demons have moved inside. They have become our nightmares and our dreams. I can think of no better contrast to show that when the vertical depth of the world as a matter of levels is replaced by a horizontal depth as a matter of spatial distance, the things which belong to this former depth retreat inside. In the *horizon*-tal space of linear perspective vision the idea of progress *and* the reality of the unconscious are born. The new self, engendered by this vision of a homogeneous world, retreats behind the window, taking with itself its monsters and its dreams. The world of clarity and of light opened up on the other side of the window is complemented by the world of shadows and of night on this side of the window.

Alberti, as we have already said, draws a line through the centric point, and this centric or horizon line produces two more implications. Insofar as the line is fixed at the eye level of an observer imagined as standing on a horizontal plane, staring straight ahead at the world, it establishes the human eye, human vision, as the measure of the world's horizon. In other words, it gives to humanity a central place, an idea which in the fifteenth century is quite new in the scheme of things. In addition, insofar as the line sets the limit for the height of an object to be depicted in the painting, it establishes what Edgerton calls 'horizon line isocephaly', with strong implications for the status of the human body in this space of linear perspective vision.

In speaking of the human eye as the measure of the world's horizon, I am not, of course, speaking of the literal eye. Rather, I am speaking of how the eye becomes a symbol of a new vision of humanity and reality and the relationship between them. A new distance, and even a separation, marks this relationship, and the human eye as the paramount organ of distance comes to represent a humanity which, in increasingly removing itself from the world, becomes less and less touched by it, increasingly less implicated. Moreover, in becoming increasingly detached it becomes increasingly

Figure 2.5 Hieronymous Bosch, *The Temptation of St Anthony*

Reproduced by permission of Alinari/Art Resource, New York

Figure 2.6 Francisco Goya, *The Dream of Reason Produces Monsters*

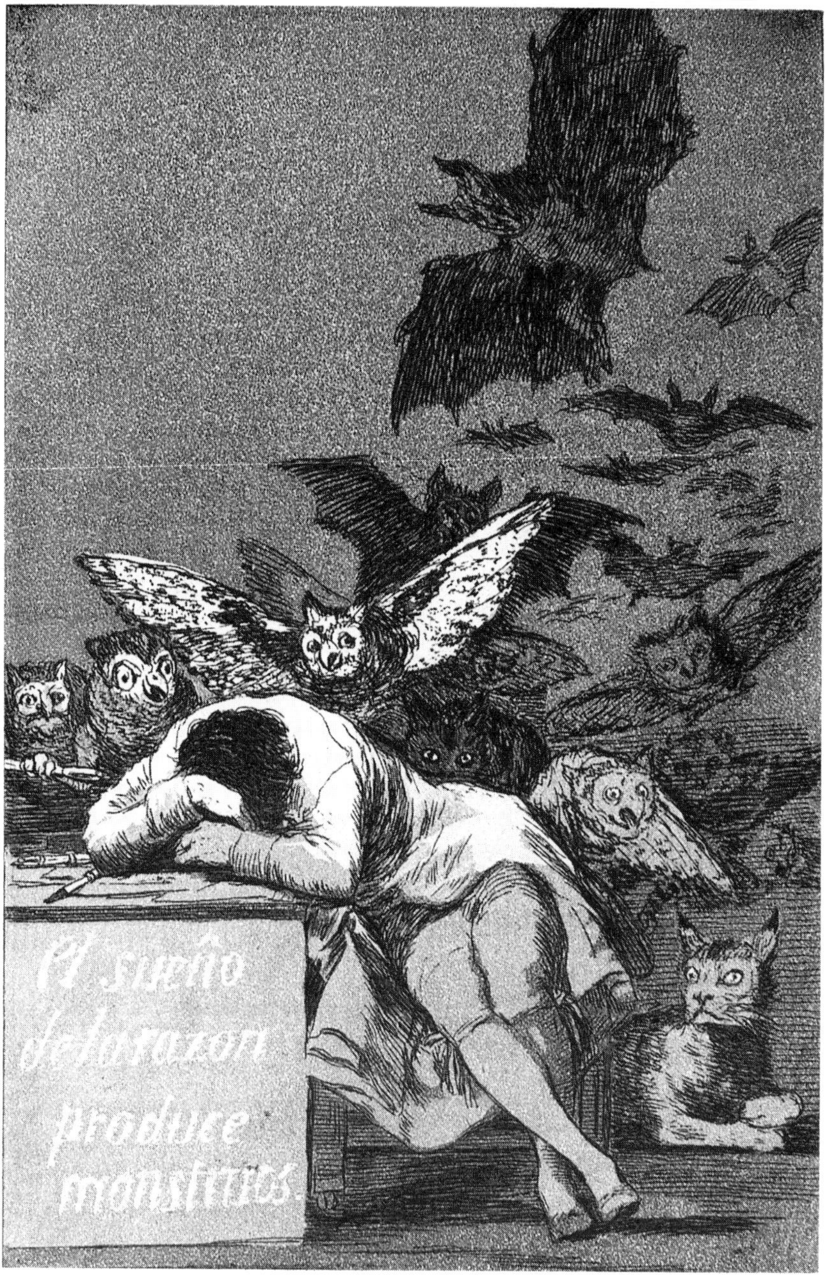
el sueño
de la razon
produce
monstruos

Reproduced by permission of Algur H. Meadows Collection, Meadows Museum, Southern Methodist University, Dallas, Texas possible to imagine that one is in charge and in control of things. With increasing distance it becomes easier to believe that one is really at the center. Like the man on the hill above the city, for example, it becomes possible to believe that with a bird's eye view one now sees all. The higher up one is, as in a business firm for example, the further removed one is from the mix of things, and with this height and distance come power and control. This idea even belongs to the Christian conception of God. His distance from our world belongs with his central position. They are reciprocal items: the further removed the more central one is in the scheme of things. In this respect, moreover, the central position which now settles upon humanity accomplishes a reversal. In the space opened up by linear perspective vision, humanity is on the way to replacing God in the center of things. When human vision starts to become the measure of the world's horizon, the Deity is on the way out. When we ourselves become a god, a deity is no longer needed. God loses his place in the fifteenth century, before he is banished in the seventeenth century by Descartes to the beginning of things as a harmless watchmaker, and declared dead by Nietzsche in the nineteenth. Ironically, however, the same vision which places us at the center of things will also displace us. It already begins near the beginning, with Copernicus, who in 1543 sets the earth in motion by taking up his stance upon the sun. At one and the same time we launch the earth into the heavens *and* we de-center the earth. In Hannah Arendt's terms, we adopt an 'astrophysical view point,'[16] but in doing so we remove the earth from its special place in the center of things. And what begins with Copernicus is furthered by Darwin and Freud. With Copernicus our central place in the cosmos is eclipsed. With Darwin it is our central place in creation. And with Freud it is the central place within ourselves, the ego, which is displaced.

The eye as a measure of the world's horizon is, moreover, a special eye. It is characterized in specific ways by the very conditions which give it its central place. It is an eye *fixed* in its place, a *staring* eye, an eye focused *straight ahead* on the world. Such an eye by definition does not wander over the landscapes of the world, nor does it get distracted to wander over and about things which lie off to the side of its vision. Fixed opposite the horizon, this eye which stares straight ahead has a purposeful intensity, a singular vision. And indeed, as we shall hear at a later point in our tale of technology, it is the singular eye, what the poet Blake will later describe as the single vision of Newton's sleep,[17] which characterizes that human vision which becomes the world's measure. At the moment, however, let it just be noted that it is in the intensity of its singular vision that this eye, which fixes the world's horizon with its stare, gains its power over the world. Fixing its gaze straight ahead it dispenses with the surrounding contexts of things, and so doing it is strengthened, somewhat like a laser beam, to pierce the surface of things, to penetrate inside them. The microscope and the telescope as early instruments of technology will incarnate this fixed, intense, focused stare of the single eye.

The horizon line also introduces the phenomenon of horizon line isocephaly, previously illustrated in Figure 2.4. As the reader probably recalls, it is Edgerton's term to describe the process whereby with increasing distance figures progressively shrink from the bottom up towards the head, which always remains in touch with the horizon line. I doubt that there is a more explicit way to indicate what has already been said in the context of the window: in the space of linear perspective vision the body is progressively abandoned. Indeed, the image here says even more, for it indicates *how* the body is abandoned. As we approach the vanishing point, the body increasingly becomes a matter of the head. In other words, within the space of linear perspective vision and under the fixed gaze which stares at the horizon, the human body is taken up into the heady eye of mind. It becomes an object of thought, and we become, in the memorable phrase of C. S. Lewis, 'Men without Chests.'[18] If on earlier occasions of this tale we heard the whispers of Descartes in this space of linear perspective vision, then here there is no doubt that it is his voice which is prophesied in this space. When he says, 'I think therefore I am,' he simply articulates in philosophical language that distance from the body which the geometry of linear perspective vision has already created. At the vanishing point, at that ideal distance of infinity from the viewer opposite the vanishing point behind the window, the body has been abandoned. In that head space of Cartesian consciousness which is prepared here in this space of linear perspective, in this move toward the infinite, in our vision of infinity, we shall lose our senses. Our senses will make increasingly less sense of the world as the body matters increasingly less than thought. In our later telling of the tale of technology, we shall have to follow the several steps in this process of abandonment. For the moment, however, we shall say that the body abandoned is free initially to become the corpse, the body of anatomical functioning, and we shall end our discussion of the vanishing point, its conditions and implications, by noting that among our inheritances of this invention there lies the corpse. The corpse is the body invented in and for the space of linear perspective vision.

2   The distance point

The second step in Alberti's procedure is the construction of a distance point. It requires a separate drawing which is subsequently mapped onto the drawing made for the vanishing point. Beginning with a straight line which is divided into parts of the same length as the base line of his 'window' in the drawing of the vanishing point, Alberti next places 'a single point above and perpendicular to one end of this line and as high as the centric point is above the base line of the quadrangle (window).' From this point, which is the distance point, or the place (on this side of the window) from which the scene depicted in the painting is to be seen, Alberti draws diagonals to the divisions of his straight line. Then, deciding 'how much distance there is to be between the eye of the spectator [the distance point] and the picture,'[19] Alberti drops a vertical intersection through the diagonals to the base line. Where this vertical line intersects the diagonals, lines can be projected onto the drawing made of the vanishing point, producing in that space transversals. With this procedure the construction of a linear perspective space is complete. The initial *creation* of depth achieved by the vanishing point procedure is herein complemented by the *degree* of depth established by the distance point procedure.

Figure 2.7 illustrates the steps outlined above. In the drawing on the right there is the already familiar vanishing point (A), horizon line (B), and orthogonals (C). The figure on the left contains the distance point (D) and the vertical intersection (E). The dotted lines between the two figures illustrate the projection of the distance point drawing onto the vanishing point drawing, thereby establishing the transversals (F). The transversals are equidistant parallels which, however, appear to be closer together as they approach the vanishing point. Their significance lies in the fact that they illustrate the rate of diminution of objects in linear perspective space. Stated in another way, the placement of the vertical intersection, which allows the projection of the transversals, establishes the *degree of depth* in linear perspective space. The reader can experience this fact for himself or herself. First, repeat the procedures described in conjunction with Figure 2.4 and construct *two* drawings of the vanishing point. Then, following the steps outlined for Figure 2.7, project a distant point drawing onto *each* of the vanishing point constructions. The closer the reader places the vertical line to the distance point the greater the depth of the drawing.

Two conditions characterize Alberti's distance point procedure. First, the distance point, which marks the viewer's position on this side of the window, is *placed at the same level* as the centric or vanishing point. Second, the distance point is *fixed before* the vertical intersection, which establishes the degree of depth, is drawn. A few significant implications follow on these two conditions.

The first condition simply specifies what has already been stated earlier in relation to the centric or horizon line. That line, as we know, is fixed at the eye level of an observer imagined as standing on a horizontal plane, staring straight ahead at the world. The distance point, therefore, simply fixes the place of that imagined observer, and, insofar as it does so, this first condition *reaffirms* the place of the human eye, that symbol of a new idea of humanity and reality and the relationship between them, as the measure of the world's horizon.

In addition, however, the first condition makes it quite clear that the eye which is the world's measure belongs to a fixed, immobile, viewer. Ensconced behind the window, humanity takes its measure of the world by

Figure 2.7 Vanishing point and distance point

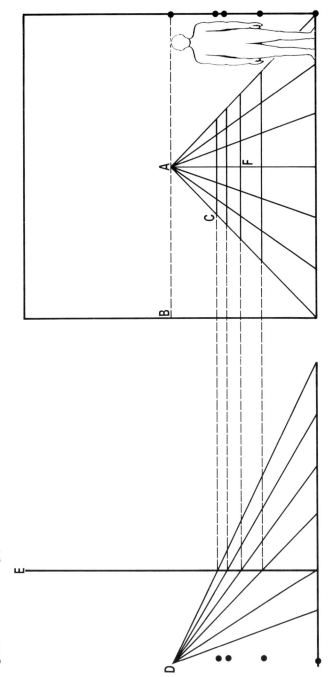

staying in its place. As it has been chiefly *since* the fifteenth century that we have moved over the face of the earth, charting its landscapes and its oceans, this fact of immobility seems in error. It is not, however, a mistake when we realize that the immobility of this eye which takes the world's measure has nothing to do with literal movement or its absence. Rather, this immobility describes a *shift in attitude*, according to which our movement into the world proceeds *on our terms*, which are, moreover, prepared in advance of our encounter with the world. I am describing here nothing other than the rise of the scientific attitude, which, in its *mathematical* character, sketches in advance of our experience of things the conditions according to which things will appear. The philosopher Martin Heidegger[20] spells out this original meaning of the mathematical as a decision to take things in advance of our experience of them, a circumstance which is most explicitly realized in the *experiment*. The immobility of the spectator behind the window describes, therefore, nothing more or less than this way of taking the world's measure by making it an object of experiment. Behind the window the conditions are arranged, so to speak, for how the world can appear. Such a situation is not too unlike that of a person who, in following a map on a journey, may miss the territory. The map projects a bird's eye view of the whole trip in advance of taking it, and while there are numerous advantages to such mapping, not the least of which is a gain in efficiency, a tragic error can occur if and when the map is mistaken for the journey. The map, then, not only precedes the journey, it also replaces it. As we shall see later in this tale of technology, much of this mapping of the world in advance of our experience of it has meant the substitution of quantitative measures for the world's qualities. It has meant the projection of a world without qualities. In a delightful reference to maps, McLuhan points out a specific consequence of this situation: 'The things that hurt one do not show on a map.'[21] And neither do the things that delight.

A further implication of this first condition for the construction of the distance point concerns the *limits* of this eye which is the measure of the world. Insofar as the distance between the distance point and the vanishing point is theoretically unlimited, linear perspective space is theoretically *infinite*. Consequently, the eye which takes the world's measure is, theoretically at least, endowed with infinite vision. At the distance point, behind the window, staring straight ahead at the vanishing point, the fixed, immobile spectator projects a vision which reaches toward infinity. It is a vision which necessarily precedes our actual contemporary flight into the universe. Before we actually become astronauts, we have prepared a vision to carry us into the infinite reaches of space. Before we actually begin the journey, we have prepared a vision of the world with an infinite horizon. A self with infinite vision, however, can also be a self which knows no bounds, an echo of a theme which will sound again in our tale.

The second condition, which fixes the distance point *before* the degree of depth is established, makes the world's depth a matter of human vision, and this much is already implied in what was said above about preparing a vision of a world with an infinite horizon. The infinite universe is a human invention. It is a historical way of envisioning the world. It is, of course, also a discovery of what the world can be so that its invention is not an illusion. Nevertheless, as an invention it serves specific human needs. That we have gone, in the words of Alexander Koyre,[22] from a closed world to an infinite universe does not mean that we have passed from falsehood into truth. The 'closed' space of that earlier view of Florence is as true to human life as is the 'open' space of the latter view of Florence. They belong to different worlds. The invention means, therefore, only that with linear perspective space a new vision of the world *and* a new world is born.

A significant feature of this new infinite world is, as we established earlier in the discussion of the vanishing point, already laid out by the geometry of linear perspective. Depth as a matter of levels is eclipsed by depth as a matter of spatial distance from the viewer, and with this change we exchange depth as an index of the world's mystery for a distance which, in placing the world before us, opens it to our explanations.

The world is, in the concrete tasks of life, 'things'. It is the house in which one lives, the trees of the forest, the things of the world. And in the space of linear perspective vision these are also changed. Look again at the receding transversals in Figure 2.7, or go back to the drawings which you made earlier. Things which occupy transversals closer to the vanishing point appear smaller than those which occupy transversals further away from that point. Now insofar as those transversals are established in relation to the distance point, which describes the viewpoint of the spectator, the size of things becomes a matter of their distance from a viewer. Or to be more precise here, I should say that the size of things becomes a matter *only* of this distance.

It is perhaps this implication of linear perspective vision which demonstrates most emphatically how much this style of engaging the world, this innate geometry of our eyes which we considered earlier, has become for us an unexamined second nature. For what else can the size of things be except what they are in relation to their spatial distance from a viewer? What is more natural than this 'law' of perception, according to which the further something is from you the smaller it appears?

Consider the illustration in Figure 2.8. It is a painting by Jan van Eyck entitled *Virgin and Child in Church*. The body of the Virgin in this painting seems gigantic to our eyes and perhaps even somewhat grotesque because of her size. No one could ever meet such a figure. It is quite unimaginable. But she appears that way to us only because we see her with linear perspective eyes, because even without knowing it we automatically place her in that space where size is a function of distance. She belongs, however, to a different space, to that background space of the painting which is not yet

Figure 2.8 Jan van Eyck, *Virgin and Child in Church*, Rome

Reproduced by permission of Alinari/Art Resource, New York

explicitly executed in linear perspective style. She belongs, in other words, to a different world, where size is an index of significance. Her size registers her importance and while it is true that *this* size is also in relation to a perceiver, it is a relation of value, of meaning, and not of measure.

The size of the things of the world are a register, therefore, of more than a measureable spatial distance. Their size is a register of how they matter in our lives, an index of their meaning. A big car or a big house is always more than an issue of measure, and to one who is poor, for example, the rich man's house is big whether close up or far away, because the space we are speaking of here is not the geometrical, homogeneous space of linear perspective, but the lived, emotional space within which one moves and lives one's life.

We carry such a space within our flesh and bones, so to speak. We make it, actually, in the daily commerce of our lives, in the ways in which we move through the world. In this emotional space of lived life, distance, too, is not yet a metric. It is a meaning, an index of desire, for example, so that the things which one most desires are far away even though spatially near,

Table 2.1 Summary of the relations among Alberti's procedures for the construction of a linear perspective space, the conditions for this construction, and the multiple implications of these conditions

Procedure	Conditions	Implications
I Vanishing point	(1) Window	(a) *Boundary*, even a *separation* between a *subject* as *spectator* and the world which as *spectacle* becomes an *object* of vision.
		(b) *Eclipse of body:* as world becomes increasingly a matter for the eye alone, there is a de-emphasizing of the other senses as legitimate ways of knowing the world. The sound, touch, taste, and smell of the world become secondary qualities as increasing emphasis is placed upon what is visible, observable, measurable, and quantifiable.
		(c) On the other side of the window, as an object of vision, the world is on its way to becoming a *matter of light*, and, as such, a matter of *information*, a bit of *data*.
	(2) Location of vanishing point is no higher from the base line than the height of any figure to be depicted in the painting. In this way the viewer and all objects in the field will seem to be on the same level or plane. In addition, the line through this point, the centric or horizon line, is fixed at the eye level of an observer imagined as standing on a horizontal plane, staring straight ahead at the world.	(a) All viewers and all objects now lie on the same plane of reality. Genesis here of the *equalizing vision* of *modern science* and its world of *explanations* and of *political democracy*.
		(b) An eclipse of the *depths* of the world as a matter of *levels* by depth as a matter of *spatial distance*. An erasure of differences so that things, like angels and demons, which belong to other levels of existence, become a subjective matter. Psychology, as a discipline

Table 2.1 — continued

Procedure	Conditions	Implications
		designed to map the landscape of this subjective, interior domain, is born within this space.[23]
		(c) The human eye, as symbol of a new vision of and relation between humanity and the world, is now given a central place. Humanity's vision now becomes the world's measure. Genesis here of the eclipse of the idea of God, as a theologically ordered universe is replaced by a scientifically explained one.
		(d) The special character of humanity's vision involves: a *focused, singular, intense* vision which, in *staring straight ahead* at the world, penetrates its depths. (The 'single vision' of Newton's sleep).
		(e) *Horizon line isocephaly and the eclipse of the body:* as figures approach the vanishing point they shrink from the bottom up towards the head. Genesis here of *Cartesian consiousness.* The infinite horizon of the world is a correlate of head consciousness.
II Distance point	(1) Distance point is fixed at same level as vanishing point.	(a) See vanishing point discussion, condition (2), implications (c) and (d).
		(b) The *fixed* placement of the distance point, the viewpoint of the perceiver, marks a shift in attitude toward the *mathematical* character of modern science. Humanity's vision fixes the

Table 2.1 — continued

Procedure	Conditions	Implications
		character of the world by *taking* its quantitative measure *in advance of* and even *in spite of* how things appear. The *experiment* becomes the paradigm for how we arrange the space in which nature appears.
		(c) The range of this 'fixed' vision for the viewer placed opposite the vanishing point is ideally *infinite*.
	(2) Distance point is fixed *before* degree of depth is established.	(a) Compare vanishing point discussion, condition (2), implication (b). But also, the world's depth including its ideally infinite character, is a matter of humanity's vision. The *infinite universe is a historical–cultural invention*.
		(b) Size of things as index of *their meaning* and value is eclipsed by size as *measure of spatial distance*. Genesis of things as calculable objects in a neutral, homogeneous space, leading to the modern *economic* calculus of things as supply/demand.

and, even in that far distance, they loom large to tempt one with their appeal. But insofar as we see with linear perspective eyes we come to discount this living relation between our flesh and the flesh of the world, and both size and distance as indices of value are eclipsed by size and distance as measured functions. The former becomes a *subjective* matter while the latter becomes an *objective* account of the way things really are. In this space, then, things are neutralized. Emptied of value, they are arranged in the same homogeneous space of the world, and in that calculable space they are placed well along the path toward becoming calculable objects. Later we shall again consider things and how they have changed in the space of linear perspective vision, but for the moment let us close these remarks by noting that one way in which things do become calculable objects in this space is by becoming items in an economic discourse of prices and costs. Things become a matter of money, of currency, which itself becomes uniform, homogeneous, stable, and relatively fixed. The science of economics in its modern sense, like Galileo's science of nature, is also born in this space of linear perspective vision.

This brief presentation of Alberti's procedure for the construction of a linear perspective space persuasively indicates the importance of this discovery-invention for shaping the modern world. Before we continue our story the reader would do well to pause for a while with this material, which is summarized in Table 2.1.

C Echoes

The invention of linear perspective space inaugurated a revolution in human life. In multiple ways, unforeseen at the time and certainly unintended, these procedures have been taken up, elaborated, and amplified to allow the development of a technological world. The window of Alberti has undergone many changes and we have played out in plural fashion the role of being an onlooker on this side of the window observing a world which in myriad forms has become something to be observed. We have taken the world's measure with a distant vision which truly does seem infinite, and in the process we have, it seems, also fairly well succeeded in remaking the body we first abandoned. As we approach the launchpad of the vanishing point, the body as a carnal knowledge of the world has indeed shrunk into the head. It has become an object of thought refashioned and re-imagined for departure.

Spectator, spectacle, specimen! These are the images we have encountered. They belong together, and each in its own fashion tells that tale of distance, departure, and disincarnation which characterizes the story of technology. In what follows we shall elaborate the tale, following the ways in which the self, as spectator of the world with a body which has become a specimen, already practices that distance which prepares for departure from a world which has become a spectacle. But before the tale continues in this fashion we shall linger for a moment to hear one echo of these beginnings, one way in which spectator, spectacle, and specimen have reverberated through the ages. The camera is in many respects the incarnation of these beginnings, and insofar as it is a most democratic instrument of technology, it further indicates how very much linear perspective vision has become the innate geometry of our eyes.

III The camera eye of distant vision

Linear perspective vision is inherent in photography. The camera is the technological incarnation of the linear perspective eye. Through the lens the world is opened up as a landscape which converges on a vanishing point. In the camera the world truly does become a matter of light, a matter which speaks not to the entire range of embodied sensual life but primarily to the eye and to the eye alone. With the camera we do become a fixed and focused eye, a spectator observing a world which has become a spectacle, an object of vision.

David Hockney, contemporary British artist turned photographer, has taken the camera beyond its limits. In his photography he has deliberately 'broken' the camera eye. By following his photographic studies, we can get a direct appreciation of the origins of linear perspective vision and we can come to appreciate how the camera, as the model of our vision, has been an unacknowledged inheritance of the linear perspective eye.

A   Hockney and the camera

In his book *Cameraworks*, which chronicles the journey of the artist's encounters with the photograph, David Hockney spells out his initial dissatisfaction with photography.

> My main argument was that a photograph could not be looked at for a long time. Have you noticed that? You can't look at most photos for more than, say, thirty seconds. It has nothing to do with the subject matter. I first noticed this with erotic photographs, trying to find them *lively*: you can't. *Life* is precisely what they don't have — or rather, *time*, *lived time*. All you can do with most ordinary photographs is *stare* at them — they stare back, blankly — and presently your concentration begins to fade. They stare you down. I mean, photography is all right if you don't mind looking at the world from the point of view of a *paralyzed cyclops — for a split second*. But that's not what it's like to live in the world, or to convey the experience of living in the world.[24]

The photograph is not lively. It lacks time. It invites the viewer to stare, that is to take up a way of looking which discourages movement. The viewer stares and is invited to stare because the photograph freezes time. The living eyes of perception which roam over the world, which caress the thing they look at, become a camera eye, an eye which belongs to a cyclops who is paralyzed. Camera vision is monocular, fixed, and disembodied. It is the vision of a single, staring eye whose body has been left behind.

The abandonment of the body in camera vision is an issue which Hockney has explicitly challenged. The photographs which Hockney takes are, he says, much like Cubist paintings. They present multiple perspectives simultaneously, and in this respect they introduce time and the body into the photograph and into the viewer's experience of the photograph. With a Picasso painting, for example, one sees things as one sees them while living in the world and moving through it. His paintings, like that earlier view of

Florence, capture time by appealing to the moving body. Cubism restores the body to the viewer. Out of the paralyzed cyclops, it resurrects the living human body engaged with the world over time. In Hockney's words, 'Cubism . . . is about our own bodily presence in the world. It's about the world, yes, but ultimately about where we are in it, how we are in it. It's about the kind of perception a human being can have in the midst of living.'[25] And what Hockney says he also shows in his photocollages. Indeed, as Lawrence Weschler notes with regard to Hockney's work, 'Your eyes go for a walk.'[26]

To the degree that Hockney's photographs, like Cubist paintings, restore the moving body to vision, the inherent distance between and separation of the viewer and the world which characterizes linear perspective and camera vision are also overcome. In a recent *New York Times* interview Hockney has noted both of these features. Photographs, he said, have always given him the 'sensation of being "outside" of the picture', much like his encounters with fifteenth-century crucifixion paintings, executed in linear perspective fashion, made him feel 'left out.'[27] In each instance Hockney noted a sense of distance from what he was seeing, a distance, moreover, which did not seem to fit his experience of seeing the world. The photograph, like the linear perspective canvas, insisted the viewer look at it from afar. It suggested that we become — that we are — spectators, observers, of the world.

What is absent in such a separated and distant vision is the intimacy which exists between our fleshy eyes, so different from cameras, and the textured flesh of the world. Hockney captures this intimacy in one of his comments on Picasso. He says, with respect to the portraits which Picasso did of his lover Maria-Therese Walter, that:

he must have spent hours with her in bed, very close, looking at her face. A face looked at like that *does* look differently from one seen at five or six feet. Strange things begin to happen to the eyes, the cheeks, the nose — wonderful inversions and repetitions. Certain 'distortions' appear, but they can't be distortions because they're reality. Those paintings are about that kind of intimate seeing.[28]

'We live in an age of measurement,' Hockney has said, 'but the great achievement of modern art, of Picasso and others of the Cubists, was to eliminate distance.'[29] That elimination has not been a closing of spatial distance but a shift in *how* we look at the world. No matter how close spatially, the eye of the camera, without a change in attitude, must always look from afar, as a distant observer. Its focus must always be that of a spectator fixed upon a spectacle. And under such conditions, the camera eye of distant vision can only transform intimate vision into pornographic observation. Cubism and Hockney's photographs transform *how* we look because they transform *who* we are as viewers: not spectators whose detached, observing eye fixes the world by staring at it from afar, but involved participants caught up in the circuit of our own vision, seeing and being seen, seeing and seeing how we see.

Hockney's work, however, has not been without its own difficulties, and his struggles are an important witness to how persistent the camera eye of distant vision is in our daily experience. His Polaroid collages, like that of *Celia* (Figure 2.9), for example, are composed of a square matrix-grid pattern which gives the viewer the sense that he or she is looking through a window. At the very same moment, therefore, when Hockney is introducing time and the moving body to the photograph, he is still caught in placing that viewer outside, on the other side of a window.

The window aesthetic, which has so strongly influenced modern life since the fifteenth century, robs the viewer of his/her sensuous body. The window emphasizes vision. It is an instrument of and for the eye. As such, it turns the world primarily into an object to be seen and the viewer into a see-er. Perhaps herein lies the voyeurism of modern consciousness, which in its detached passion for spying on the world wishes to remain invisible, hidden, disembodied. In any case, the viewer is not only a paralyzed cyclops, staring and unmoving, but also *only* an eye. Camera vision not only paralyzes the body it also anaesthetizes it. The smell, taste, touch, and perhaps even the sound of things, are progressively eclipsed. The human body in its erotic and sensuous tie to things is increasingly abandoned.

Much to Hockney's credit, he realized these limitations of his Polaroid grid photographs, and he recognized the necessity to break the window. He noted, for example, how the Oriental influence on the Cubists must have served this task of breaking the window. Oriental art, he says, looks out of doors rather than windows, and the chief difference 'between a window and a door is you can walk through a door toward what you are seeing.'[30] One walks through a door solicited, and perhaps even seduced, by the display which lies beyond it: the *blue* sky, the *cool* breeze, the *sound* of birds, the *smell* of the grass and trees. The real genius of Hockney's camera work is that he has managed to break the window. He has managed, or at least has come as close as possible with a camera, to return the sensuous body to the viewer. His photograph *Merced River* (Figure 2.10), which breaks the square grid pattern, does seem to convey the *sound* of a rushing stream. Here is a photograph which offers a synaesthetic perception. It speaks, as does the world, to a body whose eye is also an ear.

Through Hockney's work one can come to appreciate how linear perspective vision has shaped our modern world and out relation to it. The camera, which incarnates this style of vision, is a familiar object of our daily world, and in breaking the limits of camera vision Hockney's photographs allow us to appreciate what we otherwise would live out forgetfully in our vision. His

Figure 2.9 *Celia*, Los Angeles, April 10, 1982

Composite Polaroid 14 3/8 x 26 3/16", © David Hockney, 1982

Figure 2.10 *The Merced River, Yosemite Valley,* September 1982

Photographic collage 52 x 61", © David Hockney, 1982

work allows us to see how we have been seeing, to see the eye through which we have been viewing the world. In doing so, we can begin to appreciate the *historical* character of this vision, rather than continue to assume that such is a *natural* condition. And, appreciating its historical character, we can perhaps begin to imagine the possibility of seeing in a new way, of envisioning the world not out of separation and distance but in intimacy, through fleshy eyes restored to a sensuous body in time and moving through the world. That such a new way of seeing the world is needed is an insight of Hockney himself. Ensconced behind a window, cut off from the world, separated and distant from it, we are much more likely to forget that the world matters. And forgetting that it matters we are much more likely to destroy it. We have to break the window, return to the world, Hockney says, 'because if we don't, I think we'll blow ourselves up.'[31]

A significant achievement of Hockney's work is that it shows quite clearly that what happened over five centuries ago is not simply past but continues today. In the camera the origins of linear perspective vision have been instrumentalized. The hegemony of the eye, the character of distance, the window aesthetic, the paralysis and anaesthetization of the body, the sterilization of the world of all sensuous qualities save what is visible and observable, are all incarnated in the camera. We enact these attitudes and values, we continue these origins in the use of this simple, popular, and quite harmless instrument. The photograph reduplicates the world and in time even comes to displace it, taking on the character of what is true and what is real. Seeing is believing, we say, a maxim which was unimaginable prior to the invention of linear perspective vision. And with the camera we have further qualified this vision: not any seeing is believing, but only that seeing which duplicates the neutrality and impartiality of the camera eye. If it can be photographed it is real. If it cannot, like the elusive monster of Loch Ness or aliens from outer space, then its veracity remains in doubt.

Much more needs to and can be said of photographs and the camera, because even as Hockney's work indicates, the very same instrument which incarnates the technological eye can also go beyond it. At a later point in our tale, therefore, we shall return to the camera to consider it as an instrument of return from distance. For the moment, however, let us simply acknowledge the wisdom of Hockney's closing remark quoted above. In linking the camera to destruction, Hockney is not, of course, saying that the camera itself will destroy us. Rather he is placing the camera and the vision which it practices within a wider network of values, and in that network the camera eye of distant vision is inseparable, for example, from the figure of the astronaut prepared for departure, who is inseparable from the two kissing figures whose energized bodies have become matters of visible observation, who are inseparable from the fire of energized matter, the fire of destruction. What links these images together are the shared technological dreams of distance, departure, and disincarnation. In these dreams, whose origins we have tried to imagine at this moment in our story, we appear as spectators of a world which has become a spectacle and with bodies which have become specimens. Our tale now continues told along these lines.

Chapter three

Self as spectator

I Introduction

The invention of linear perspective space initiated a revolution in human life. In the space opened up between the distance point and the vanishing point a new self, a new body, and a new world were born. We are the heirs of that revolution and at this point in our story we shall listen to the tale of the self told within the space of this world. It is a tale of how the self as a spectator behind a window has become the world's measure by making the world a matter of its vision, an infinite vision which, in its singular focus and fixed intensity, has clarified the mystery of the world's depth in its explanations.

But before we begin this tale of the self that we are, it is worth remembering that in its origins it was a new, startling, and surprising creation. The self which each one of us is, that sense of self as a solitary, singular atom of individuality, that self which is more or less experienced as an interior reality on this side of our skin somewhere more or less behind the eyes gazing out upon the world — that self is a historical invention. This onlooker self, which we take for granted, was once a novelty and a surprise. This spectating, observing self, which even observes itself observing the world, and which coincides with the detachment of vision from the rest of the senses with the primacy accorded to the eye in the space of linear perspective, was once, in its beginnings, a radically new style of living. And no less a poet than Shakespeare tells us so. In the scene from *King Lear* in which Edgar deceives Gloucester about the place where they stand, we have an early description of what it is like to be a distant self removed to a place high above the world. We have, in other words, an early description of spectator consciousness, of a consciousness which through distance has made the world into a matter of the eye.

> GLOUCESTER: Methinks y'are better spoken.
>
> EDGAR: Come on, sir; here's the place. Stand still. How fearful
> And dizzy 'tis to cast one's eyes so low!
> The crows and choughs that wing the midway air

> Show scarce so gross as beetles. Halfway down
> Hangs one that gathers sampire — dreadful trade!
> Methinks he seems no bigger than his head.
> The fishermen that walk upon the beach
> Appear like mice; and yond tall anchoring bark,
> Diminish'd to her cock; her cock, a buoy
> Almost too small for sight. The murmuring surge
> That on th' unnumb'red idle pebble chafes
> Cannot be heard so high. I'll look no more,
> Lest my brain turn, and the deficient sight
> Topple down headlong.
> GLOUCESTER: Set me where you stand.
> EDGAR: Give me your hand. You are now within a foot
> Of th' extreme verge. For all beneath the moon
> Would I not leap upright.[1]

Edgar, in verbally painting this scene for the blinded Gloucester, commands the Duke to stand still. And from that fixed place, on an imagined cliff high above the scene below, much like the earlier anonymous viewer on the hill overlooking Florence, we learn through Edgar how the eye of distant vision in its early appearance is a strange, unfamiliar, and even fearful vision. Edgar, as a kind of early commentator on this new style of vision, on this new self which has distanced itself from the world, is made dizzy by what he sees and by how he looks. Crows shrink into their heads, and fishermen that walk upon the beach are no bigger than mice. And the 'murmuring surge', the sounds of the world below, disappear. The eye of distant vision eclipses the ear and Edgar, out of touch with the world below save through this eye, will look no more. He turns away from this 'deficient sight', from a sight which has broken its connections with the other bodily senses, and not even for all the world will he leap into and embrace this vision. McLuhan, in commenting on this scene, says that it presents the transition from 'warm, familiar multisensory spaces [to] fragmented visual space.' It presents, he says, the change 'from corporate to private space.'[2]

We live predominantly and much more comfortably than Edgar in this private space, in this singular space which is visual and fragmented, while those corporate, warm spaces which are plural, multisensory, like the space of a kitchen in which bread is baking, a space whose visual dimensions are rounded by the smells, have increasingly become exceptions. The space which Edgar describes has become the familiar space of our world, and we are accustomed to such distant views. We have, as a kind of second nature, an airplane consciousness of the world. We are, each of us, a self which belongs to and is inseparable from a technological world. In telling the tale of the self we have become, we must amplify some of the features of its character, born and nurtured in the space of linear perspective vision.

II The self behind the window

In the space of linear perspective the viewer is imagined to be looking at the world as if through a window. This window has become our habit of mind and through it we have become a self which has learned to keep its eye upon the world. Behind the window we have become distant and detached, a self separated and isolated from the world, a neutral observer and recorder of the world's events.

The figure on the hill above the city of Florence (see Figure 2.3) is perhaps the earliest recorded illustration of this self of distant vision. He is like Shakespeare's Edgar, but predates him by more than one hundred years. There on the hill he sits, sketchpad in hand, above and beyond the city. He commands a bird's eye view, as it were, while the city stretched out before him has been laid bare before his gaze. Perhaps he is sketching the first modern map with which we are today so familiar: the map which we often use to replace the territory, taking it to be the territory itself. Perhaps, however, as we shall see, he is doing other things. In any case, with this figure we have an illustration of that habit of mind which characterizes the modern self as distant and neutral observer, a habit so fundamental to our scientific vision of the world. Helen Gardner in her monumental classic, *Art Through the Ages*, makes this connection between linear perspective art and the scientific vision of the world. Commenting on Alberti's procedure, she writes that 'The position of the observer of a picture, looking "through" it into the painted "world" is precisely that of any scientific observer fixing his gaze upon the carefully placed or located datum of his research.'[3] The gaze of the observer on the hill who has distanced himself from the city leads to the distancing gaze of scientific observation, and the consequence, in both cases, is that the thing seen becomes a spectacle and a specimen. One cannot help but wonder here about the possible connections between Florence, this first city to be viewed from afar, and cities in our own day, like Dresden, Hiroshima, and Nagasaki, which have been objects of distant vision. Certainly, neither Alberti nor his invention are a cause of the latter, and this tale of technology is not concerned with a search for causes. On the contrary, this tale is told in order that we may better understand the fact that we have made use of this invention, that from this gift we have dreamed a world. In telling this tale we are given the opportunity to understand that the events of our age originate as ways of experiencing the world. We are given the opportunity to discover that the bomb, for example, is a way of seeing, that it is not just an event in our world but also, and more fundamentally, the incarnation of an attitude or disposition toward the world, a way in which we have practiced being a self with distant vision behind a window. And indeed, how else could the bomb be imagined except by a self which has already distanced itself from the world? Behind a window it is easier to imagine that one is only an on-looker of the world, a detached and non-involved spectator.

The window which Alberti imagined between the viewer and the world has become for us a style of consciousness marked by our retreat and estrangement from the world. We are familiar with this style which on one hand separates the self as a subjective reality from the world as an objective reality, and which on the other hand locates this self as a private, interior domain on this side of the world. Early on in the tale, in November 1619, Descartes dreamed this self as mind, equating it with our capacity to know the world as a matter of thought, and what mattered most for him in this dream was the essential difference between this self and the body which housed it and the world which it thought. Body and world belonged to matter while self belonged to mind, and in this difference between matter and mind our distance from the world was increased. Here on this side of the world, freed of the body's sensuous entanglements with the allurements of the world, the self could dream a rational world cleansed of qualities, a world reduced to number, a world in which, for example, the colors of things could become measured refractions of light. Ironically, however, the world so dreamed cannot be an inhabited world, a world in which to live, and the self can only become a stranger in this world of its own creation.

Today we know quite well this experience of estrangement, for the distance which separates our knowledge of the world from our experience of it has only increased. Between my body, which I know in living my life with others, and the body of medical knowledge, or between the atomic structure of matter and the things of the world, which I sense with my body, there lies an immeasurable distance, and in most respects each of us remains a stranger to these constructed realities. We *know*, often in fine detail, the world we have imagined and dreamed, the world we have created, but cannot experience it. No matter how hard I may try, for example, to *experience* my sight of a beautiful sunrise as the impact of electromagnetic radiation upon the retinas of my eyeballs where complex electrochemical reactions take place transforming physical stimuli into physiological events, I am doomed to fail. I may succeed, of course, in transforming all of these physical and physiological processes into visual displays which I can see, but the lines and patterns observed on monitor screens are quite clearly *not* the same thing as the sight of a glorious sunrise. And indeed, were I to claim in all honesty and sincerity that I could *experience* that sunrise as a conjunction of physical stimuli and physiological events, I would be judged insane. This is the epitome of estrangement, for the very same world created by a self in distance is judged both to be *real*, the way the world is, a complex of physico-chemical relations transformed into neuro-chemical events, and *illusion*. Small wonder, then, that in this estrangement we should begin to lose our way. The novelist−psychiatrist Walker Percy has recently described this condition in his humorous and quite profound book, *Lost in The Cosmos: The Last Self-Help Book*. He writes that:

Every advance in our objective understanding of the Cosmos and in its technological control further distances the self from the Cosmos precisely in the degree of the advance — so that in the end the self becomes a space-bound ghost which roams the very Cosmos it understands perfectly.[4]

An estranged self, a self in retreat from the world, a self born in distance behind the window as genesis of the astronaut!

But, of course, few, if any of us, are judged insane on these grounds, and probably only a few become aware that they are ghosts lost in the cosmos of their own abstractions. The sun continues to rise in spite of what one knows about the earth's rotation, and each of us continues to see *it* and not the physical stimuli which trigger physiological events. The chasm between the real world which is known and the illusory world of experience is bridged. Or perhaps it is better to say that the dichotomy of reality and illusion is disguised. What is real and known is treated as objective while what is experienced becomes subjective. Nevertheless, the self in its retreat from the world is forced to carry the experienced world inside itself either as illusion or as something merely subjective.

Alberti's window becomes, therefore, a boundary not only between self and world but also a boundary between two worlds. On this side of the window the world of sensuous qualities, of colors and tones, of beauty and charm, becomes a subjective experience of the self, while on the other side of the window another world of measurable quantities and objective events is created. This historical occurrence is a good illustration of what the art historian William Ivins describes as 'the development of perspective from its discovery or invention as a quasi mechanical procedure to a logical scheme or grammar of thought.'[5] Alberti's window, which begins as an artistic device, thus becomes a style of thought, a cultural perception, a way of imagining the world. It is, quite unknowingly, elaborated as a cultural metaphor in which the window begins to resemble a kind of membrane through which the self passes in its retreat from the world, a membrane which filters through all the qualitative dimensions of the world while filtering out the quantities which are left behind. The window as membrane becomes the boundary, the place where the world is divided into exterior and interior domains.

In an earlier work I charted the course of this 'interiorization' of experience, and I noted there how the face of the Mona Lisa may very well be the first explicit face of modern life. Her smile, which van den Berg says 'seals an inner self', is detached from the world, a world 'closed within itself and self-sufficient, an exterior from which the human element has, in principle, been removed . . .'[6] Mona Lisa, whose face appears in 1503, is separate from the world, 'older than the rocks among which she sits,' according to the art historian Walter Pater,[7] and her smile is an index of her separation as well as an expression of a dream which hides within. Her dreams, therefore, like all her experiences, will now have to be guessed, giving rise to a new style of conduct and to new concerns. The smile on the outside will have to be read from the inside, and thus in this space of separation 'the new enterprise of self-expression' will arise and with it a new obsession with the problem of hypocrisy, where as yet ' "There is no art to read the mind's construction in the face." '[8] The discipline of psychology will have its origins in this obsession, called into being by the need for such an art, by the need to explain the outside in terms of the inside, an obsession which will flower into what Christopher Lasch has called 'The banality of pseudo-self awareness.'[9] Moreover, this obsession will even shape our modern sense of the political realm. With deception, including self-deception, now arising as a real human possibility, sanctioned, as it were, by the cultural image of an invisible inside life separated from the external world, Machiavelli, ten years after the appearance of Mona Lisa's enigmatic smile, will describe deception as a principle of political rule. He will tell the Prince who would rule wisely and who would rule well that 'he who deceives will always find one who will let himself to be deceived.'[10]

Mona Lisa is not, however, the only index of this new, separate, interior, self-contained self which appears on this side of the window, distant and detached from the world. The expression of an individual, private self is also registered in the first modern autobiography, that of Benvenuto Cellini, written in 1545, as well as in the rise of portrait painting in the fifteenth century, and in the genesis of self-portraits like those which Alberti and later Rembrandt paint of themselves. Moreover, in a way which highlights the appearance of a new, private self, we find in seventeenth-century Dutch painting, particularly in the work of Vermeer and Jan Steen, that the upper class house is neatly compartmentalized into closed-off private rooms.[11] This compartmentalization of living space dramatically underlines the isolation of self, and we should note that it stands in sharp contrast to the representation of rooms as mere background in the earlier art of Raphael and Titian.

All of these cultural events mirror a radically new style of human life, the private self as self-conscious spectator of the world. Perhaps, however, the clearest expression of this figure is Hamlet, who, says A. C. Harwood, mediates a new type of consciousness, a 'spectator consciousness.' Hamlet, who initially appears in the play, fully engaged in life, a participant, is transformed as the play progresses into a spectator of others and himself, crippled with self-doubts which impede his action. Arranging the play within the play to trap his uncle, Hamlet invites the audience to share the spectator's vision as we watch Hamlet watching the King who is watching the play. This spectator attitude, Harwood claims, alters Hamlet's perception of the world and man. 'The medieval world,' he says, '. . . turns for him into something like the modern world,'[12] a transformation whose effects are expressed in Hamlet's speech to Rosencrantz and Guildenstern.

I have of late — but wherefore I know not — lost all my mirth, foregone all custom of exercises; and indeed it goes so heavily with my disposition that this goodly frame, the earth, seems to me a sterile promontory; this most excellent canopy, the air, look you, this brave o'erhanging firmament, this majestical roof fretted with golden fire, why, it appears no other thing to me than a foul and pestilent congregation of vapours. What a piece of work is a man, how noble in reason, how infinite in faculties; in form and moving how express and admirable, in action how like an angel, in apprehension how like a god, the beauty of the world: the paragon of animals! And yet, to me, what is this quintessence of dust?[13]

Withdrawn from the world and drawn into himself, Hamlet, an early spectator behind the window, now inhabits a different world and dwells upon a different earth. What once was a 'goodly frame' has become a 'sterile promontory,' and we who were once 'in action how like an angel, in apprehension how like a god' have become on this side of the window distant from the world, 'the quintessence of dust.'

But, of course, it is true that Hamlet is a melancholy Dane, and perhaps his judgement about the spectator self, the self behind the window, is, like that of Edgar, too early and too harsh. If we have all become, like the figure on the hill above the city, a self of distant vision, we are not necessarily condemned to be Hamlets or Edgars, Cartesian dreamers or princely deceivers, lost in the cosmos or condemned to a cult of pseudo self-awareness and narcissistic self-expression. We are not condemned, even if behind the window we have taken on these and other guises. What we have made of Alberti's gift has realized one possibility of that invention, and we tell the tale in order to remember that what we have become is precisely a possibility, perhaps now one among many others. We continue the tale, therefore, to further this remembering, turning now to the window itself and its transformations, reading in those changes additional features of the spectator self behind the window.

III Transformations of the window

A The open window

The window from behind which humanity begins to perceive the world is initially, with Alberti, an open window. Windows which are open are, of course, quite different from those which are closed. These open windows are, so to speak, halfway between doorways and windows that are closed. With a doorway one can follow one's eyes into the world. One can walk through a doorway. With a window that is closed one can only look at a world which is for that reason primarily a spectacle, an object of vision, a matter of light. Between these two poles, a doorway which solicits the entire body and a closed window which appeals only to the eyes and to the eyes alone, the open window is something of a compromise. While I cannot walk through the open window, or at least do not do so as an ordinary matter of course, I can nevertheless still hear, smell, and even feel the world on the other side. With a window that is open the world is still more than a matter of light.

The tale we are telling, however, assumes that the window has been closed, for it is only with a closed window that we become the spectator who takes the world's measure by having an eye upon the world. Our assumption, as we shall hear, is well founded. Not only in the ways in which later ages make use of Alberti's invention, but also with Alberti himself and his early successors the window is 'closed'. It is closed in the ways in which the idea or image of the window is transformed.

However, before we follow these transformations it will do us well to remember two things about closed windows. On one hand, a closed window invites the spectator simply to look through it at the world. Alberti's window, however, even when it is open, is never that simple, and even in the beginning we are invited to do more than simply register what we see. Nevertheless, with this simple invitation the possibility is already being created for what will later be realized with the invention of the camera. The camera eye will incarnate a spectator who simply records, reproduces, what is seen.

On the other hand, a closed window has the tendency to reduce the world to a matter of light. If you can imagine a closed window of very thick, clear glass which is moreover at a distance from what is being viewed, then you have an image of the way in which one possibility of Alberti's invention has become a cultural vision of the technological world. At such a distance and through such a thick glass it is the light of the world which matters, and increasingly since the early seventeenth century the world has become a matter of light. Galileo's observations of the moon take place in 1609. They are significant in that they allow Galileo to confirm the Copernican hypothesis of the moving earth, which is a cornerstone of the modern scientific world view. Galileo makes these observations with a telescope, which is an instrument for gathering and focusing light. The telescopic moon which Galileo sees is, therefore, an optical matter — as much a way of looking at the moon as it is a moon to be seen. It is a vision, and it is on *that* moon, a moon which begins its modern period envisioned as a matter of light, a moon that has already become a specimen for a spectator with an eye of distant vision, that we landed in 1969.

Do not misunderstand the meaning of this little aside. There is no criticism being voiced here of what may be the most splendid technological achievement in the history of humanity. There is only the wish to remember the inseparable connections among the moon on which we did land, who we were when we got there and how we got there. We got there in 1969 by

Figure 3.1 The union of the solar and lunar opposites in the alchemical work

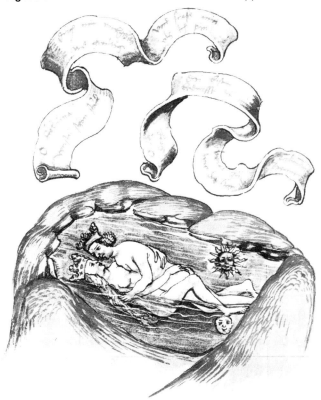

From *Rosarium philosophorum*, by Arnold of Villanova, from *Alchemy* by Stanislas Klossowski de Rola, 1973, reprinted by permission of Thames and Hudson Ltd

traveling the same road that Galileo traveled in 1609. We got there primarily and essentially as spectators, since we landed on a moon that was and had already been for a long time a spectacle, an object of vision. Therefore, as close as we have been to the moon, we remain in one sense quite far away. In the sense that we have been there as a spectator we remain quite distant and detached from the moon. Indeed, I would go so far as to say that Galileo's telescope did not *in effect* bring the moon closer. On the contrary, it moved it further away. Superficially, of course, the telescope did move it closer, but beneath this surface closeness the effect was to distance the moon as an object for the telescopic eye. The telescope, as one of the first technological instruments to transform the world into a matter of light, did not therefore decrease distance, but created it. In effect it opened, enlarged, and expanded the world, making it possible, and perhaps even necessary, to cross that distance. In short we could and perhaps we had to travel to the moon in 1969 because it had gone so far away. Men and women of earlier ages had no need to do so, and had invented no means to do so, because the moon, not yet a distant object of vision, was not so far away. As strange as this may sound to our ears, it is important that we try to hear it. The moon of technological vision is not the same moon which lighted the skies before the invention of linear perspective vision. The moon as a physical object in space is *primarily* and *essentially* a cultural vision, and men and women of earlier ages lived in a different world, and knew and saw a different moon. Figure 3.1 offers an illustration of this different moon and of the different relationship between it and men and women of earlier ages. The reader should note the connection among the moon, the sun and the figures in the drawing. Moon and sun are as close to us here as the carnal knowledge man has of woman and woman of man.

The telescope, of course, is not the only instrument which registers the world as a matter of light. Microscopes and x-rays, laser instruments and television, cameras and radar screens do the same. Perhaps, however, the most important expression of this steady tendency since the seventeenth century to transform the world into a matter of light and thereby make it into an object of distant vision is the mathematical formula which has become the talisman of the age. The physicist's equation $E = mc^2$, is the means by which the world's mass becomes energy mediated by the square of the speed of light. Here light has become the vehicle for a transformation which lies at the foundation of our technological vision of the world. It is the light of nuclear energy, and the light of nuclear holocaust, an ambiguous light with a very ominous shadow. And it is perhaps the supreme realization of the closed window of linear perspective vision.

B The window as veil

The window from behind which the modern self views the world is also a veil of meanings, and Alberti's treatise describes it precisely in this fashion. He writes:

> It is like this: a veil loosely woven of fine thread, dyed whatever color you please, divided up by thicker threads into as many parallel square sections as you like, and stretched on a frame. I set this up between the eye and the object to be represented, so that the visual pyramid passes through the loose weave of the veil.[14]

Figure 3.2 nicely portrays the window as a veil. It is a woodcut dating from 1531 intended to instruct those who would make a linear perspective drawing.

If we allow that linear perspective technique has become the cultural vision of the modern world, then this illustration vividly displays three major ingredients of this vision. There is the window as boundary of separation between viewer and world; there is the self, portrayed in the figure of

Figure 3.2 Johann II of Bavaria and Hieronymous Rodler, woodcut illustration from their *Ein schoen nuetzlich Buechlein und Unterweisung der Kunst des Messens*, Simmern, Germany, 1531

From *The Renaissance Rediscovery of Linear Perspective*, by Samuel Y. Edgerton, Jr., © 1975 by Samuel Y. Edgerton, Jr., reprinted by permission of Basic Books, Inc., Publishers

the artist, on this side of the window looking out at the world; and there is the world, out there, on the other side of the window, which has become primarily an object of vision. But this illustration tells us two other things about the character of our vision. On one hand, it tells us without any sense of hesitation or doubt that the eye through which the spectator behind the window sees the world is a veiled eye. On the other hand, it tells us something about the nature of this veil through which the world is seen. In a few moments we shall take up this latter aspect of the story, but for now we will concentrate on the veiling of vision itself.

The veiling of the eye illustrated in Figure 3.2 is both ordinary and peculiar. It is ordinary insofar as our vision of the world is always veiled. Human vision is always *a* vision. Sight is always insight. Experience is always filtered through a net of culture, and each age envisions the world differently because its eyes are veiled in different ways. In short, every culture *is* the weaving of a veil of meanings through which each age is enabled to perceive what counts for it and what matters to it as real. Culture is, in a sense, a prescription for veiling the eyes, a veiling which brings the world which defines that age into view.

But the veiling depicted in Figure 3.2 is also peculiar because of its explicit, intentional character. The veil here is not one which is given but a self-chosen one, a veiling which the self has itself created. The self here has written its own prescription. It has created its own vision, which is as peculiar as creating one's own language. We are born into and borne by language, as Merleau-Ponty notes,[15] as much as we are born into and borne by perception. The modern self whose situation is portrayed in Figure 3.2 is, however, a radical departure from this position. The intentional, self-chosen character of the veiling proclaims at the threshold of the modern world a new power: the power of the self to be its own creator. In this respect the artist at his table in Figure 3.2 can be regarded as a harbinger of Faust, who is perhaps the most dramatic illustration of the passion and the tragedy of self-creation. And the image of Faust finds a later echo — perhaps more familiar to us today — in that of Dr Victor Frankenstein, whose monstrous and alienated offspring of the same name is the shadow of this passion to usurp the power of divine creation.

The window transformed as veil indicates that the window between self and world is more than a boundary of separation, and that the self behind this window is more than a mere spectator. The window as self-chosen veil is a threshold which changes the world and which reflects a self which is the maker of its own visions. Its vision on the world is also a vision about the world. The world is not just a matter of light for a passive spectator's eye, but also a matter for the eye of mind. Moreover, the departure of the self from the world across the threshold of the window is not simply a retreat and withdrawal from the world. The departure is also a return to the world, a return which re-makes the world in terms of the self's own vision of it. Here, however, we touch upon the nature of the veil which is a further transformation of the window.

C   The veil as mathematical grid

The veil depicted in Figure 3.2, as well as the veil referred to in Alberti's description, writes the prescription for modern vision quite explicitly. We look at the illustration and we recognize beyond any shadow of a doubt the world that has been dreamed (up) by the eye of distant vision, by the self behind the window. The veil is a grid which arranges the world into parallel squares and in this respect the veil through which the modern self as spectator sees the world is a mathematical one.

The veil is mathematical in the *specific* sense that it arranges the world beyond the window into a geometrical spectacle. Edgerton, in commenting on this aspect of Alberti's procedure, makes the same point. The veil, he says, is intended to be 'a means for organizing the visible world itself into a geometric composition, structured on evenly spaced grid coordinates.'[16]

It is important to recognize here that this geometrization of vision presupposes the *fragmentation* of the world. The artist in Figure 3.2 is looking at a world which has been *divided* and *sub-divided* into parts, and Alberti himself notes as much in describing the advantages in viewing the world in this fashion. If, for example, you are viewing a human figure, then your grid allows an easy transfer of the parts apportioned by the grid onto the parallel square sections of your drawing surface. The consequence, however, is that the figure seen has been divided by your way of seeing. Alberti writes, 'for just as you see the forehead in one parallel, the nose in the next, the cheeks in another, the chin in one below, and everything else in its particular place, so you can situate precisely all the features on the panel or wall which you have similarly divided into appropriate parallels.'[17] We have here the genesis of what Rudolf de Lippe, in a brilliant and fascinating work entitled *La Géometrisation de l'Homme*,[18] has indicated has become for us a general condition of our vision: an analytical vision which decomposes the whole into parts, a vision whose power lies in its ability to isolate, decontextualize and anatomize the world. In his work de Lippe shows how this vision projected onto the grid of man produces the measured body and how this measure has transformed our sense of movement. Presenting illustrations from military movements, ballet, and fencing, he indicates how this geometric vision, in fragmenting movements, allows them to be repeated and become subject to a central authority. Later in our tale we shall hear how this anatomizing vision, turned toward the human body, gives rise first to the anatomical body, the body fragmented into parts, the corpse; and second to the body as reflex movement. We shall learn, in other words, how the corpse is the body invented for and within the space of linear perspective vision, this vision which in geometrizing the world cuts the whole into parts. And we shall hear how this fragmentation of movement gets built into our image and conception of the nervous system, of a body regulated by reflex and subject to the central authority of the brain. For the moment, however, it is sufficient to note that insofar as the way one looks reflects who one is, the geometrization of vision means not only the fragmentation of the world into its parts but also the fragmentation of the self. With the window as grid we have also the genesis of the fragmented self, the self of analyzable parts, the self which is capable of dissecting its attitudes, emotions, and beliefs.

Psychoanalysis is born on this side of the window. With the window as grid, the spectator has gone into analysis.

The veil, however, is also mathematical in the *generic* or root sense of this term, and herein lies another important feature of the self whose vision is veiled in this fashion.

In its root sense the mathematical means the projection, in advance of the appearance of things, of precisely how those things are to appear, and the artist at his drawing table in Figure 3.2 clearly illustrates this point. *Before* he looks out the window he has *already* established his grid and hence the way in which the world beyond the window will appear. Martin Heidegger[19] has shown how modern science and technology are essentially defined by this mathematical character, and how this decision to decide things in advance of their appearance according to a pre-established criterion differentiates the modern scientific attitude from any scientific attitude which preceded it. Modern science is not simply mathematical in the sense of the application of numbers to nature — the Greeks, Egyptians, and Babylonians had already done so much earlier; it is also, and more profoundly, mathematical in its decision to regard nature as essentially numerical in character, and to subject the very appearance of things to numerical conditions. Galileo, speaking of the book of nature, says, for example, that '. . . [it] is written in the mathematical language,'[20] and in this respect what counts and matters about things is no longer how we sense them and make sense of them but how they accord with the web of mathematical relations we have already established for them. There is in this attitude a decisive rejection of the sensuous world and its sensible appearances, a turning away from the fleshly world of appearances, and even a distrust of how our bodily sense of the world makes sense of the world, a distrust which is destined to become the methodic doubt of the world which lies at the root of the modern scientific attitude. If a Freudian self is born on this side of the window, so too is a Cartesian self. Indeed, they are twins insofar as each of them shares a radical distrust of how the world appears. Descartes' 'Cogito' and Freud's 'unconscious' begin with a doubt about both our bodily and conscious experience of the world. Both are born on this side of the window.

Doubt occupies in modern thought the same central position which *wonder* in the face of the world occupied in Greek thought. As a doubting self we turn away from the appearance of things and in so doing we take an essential step toward the creation of a mathematical approach to nature which 'ceases to be concerned with appearances at all.' In subjecting geometry to algebraic treatment, a procedure which we all have executed in learning to plot algebraic equations on graph paper, we create a mathematics which liberates us 'from the shackles of earth-bound experience.' Within the coordinates of our graph paper, the grid which has become the window of our minds, we learn to plot as a relation between variables the line, the curve, the power, the shape of things. The shining sun moving across the late afternoon sky yields its place to the mathematical curve which plots its orbit, achieving thereby our 'modern ideal of reducing terrestrial sense data and movements to mathematical symbols.' It is an ideal which allows Newton 'to formulate a law of gravitation where the same equation will cover the movements of heavenly bodies in the sky and the motion of terrestrial bodies on earth.' It is an ideal which erases the difference between such movements, an ideal under which the falling of autumn leaves and the falling of planets in orbital space around the sun are equated in such a way that the difference in these two decidedly different phenomena no longer really matters. It may seem obvious, but it is well worth repeating that such an equation of differences requires an enormous distance — even in principle an infinite distance — from phenomena, from how things appear. The withdrawal of the self behind its window is a first essential step in the constitution of this distance. In projecting onto the world a grid of its own making, the self behind the window imposes upon the world its 'condition of remoteness.'[21]

It is obvious, I think, that the window-veil as mathematical grid amplifies the spectator self in its role as creator. Not only does the self create its own vision, it also creates the world in the image of that vision. Free of our bodily tie to things beyond a window which has already made the world primarily a matter for inspection, we are free to veil the world with our vision of it. The window-veil as mathematical grid has actually become something like a projection device (a movie projector?) and the world a screen. Through the grid of geometrical patterns the world becomes the matrix of numerical relations we have projected, a formal world purified of all but quantity, a world emptied of quality and substance, since the grid, in arranging things essentially as points in space, requires '. . . no principles for its completion beyond those of pure mathematics.' Projecting things as patterns of spatial relations reducible to measure, a projection which is in principle indifferent to the character of things so measured, we 'risk [ourselves] into space . . . certain that [we will] not encounter anything but [ourselves], nothing that could not be reduced to patterns present in [us].'[22] The space into which we launch ourselves as astronauts is, therefore, a world of our own making, a universe which, through the window-veil as grid, is primarily a mathematical space, a space of points and plotted trajectories. Lest our tale be misunderstood here, however, I should add that this way in which we have plotted the space of the world finds a receptive response from the side of the world. In our making we have made one very real possibility of the world come true. In our work of creation we have discovered something of what the world can be. Moreover, it is only into a universe of purely formal mathematical relations that we could launch ourselves as astronauts, because prior to this emptying of the universe of all but mathematical quantities the heavens were either filled with the gods or the home of the one God and his angels. Angels first had to be erased from the heavens by mathematizing the sky before we could launch ourselves into space. It would not do, after all, to bump a spacecraft against an angel!

The grid by which we project the world as a mathematical reality is a habit of mind, a 'new mental instrument . . . more significant than all the scientific tools it helped to devise [which opens] the way for an altogether novel mode of meeting and approaching nature in the experiment.'[23] And indeed it is the experiment — Bacon's wrack upon which the secrets of nature can be tortured from her — that the modern self most fully imposes itself upon nature, and realizes itself as its master and its creator. There is a decisive turn of events here which is quite radical. The modern experiment fosters a shift in the relations between self and world. The phenomena of nature no longer matter as they are given. On the contrary, they now matter only as they are placed under the conditions of mind, that is, under the experimental arrangements established in advance of their appearance. The shift is from *the created order of nature to the creation of meaning established by the self in its withdrawal from the world.* Moreover, insofar as modern science proceeds toward the nuclearization of nature, the experiment establishes conditions which are 'won from a universal, astrophysical viewpoint, a cosmic standpoint outside nature itself'. The mathematical grid which the self projects onto the world increasingly creates a world, therefore, which replaces the 'experience-able' terrestrial world with a world whose processes belong to and occur only in space. Hannah Arendt, in a cogent passage, makes this point in the following way:

> For whatever we do today in physics — whether we release energy processes that ordinarily go on only in the sun, or attempt to initiate in a test tube the processes of cosmic evolution, or penetrate with the help of telescopes the cosmic space to a limit of two and even six billion light years, or build machines for the production and control of energies unknown in the household of earthly nature, or attain speeds in atomic accelerators which approach the speed of light, or produce elements not to be found in nature, or disperse radioactive particles, created by us through the use of cosmic radiation, on the earth — we always handle nature from a point in the universe outside the earth.[24]

When we realize that some of that energy which we produce is released as a nuclear explosion, do not Arendt's words also remind us specifically that the bomb as our creation is inseparable from this historical process of withdrawing from the world to a place behind a window from which we then create and project a new and different reality? Jonathan Schell quotes the words of President Truman in his announcement of the bombing of Hiroshima. With the bomb, Truman said, we had harnessed ' "the basic power of the universe" '. Re-creating here upon the earth ' "the force from which the sun draws its powers,'' '[25] the terrible and awesome power of creation which we have achieved, unmistakably indicates that 'we are actually doing what all ages before ours thought to be the exclusive prerogative of divine action.'[26] Here the self as spectator takes on the image, shape, and appearance of a creator (and destroyer) god.

But if our power to create a world which reproduces here upon the earth the energies which belong to the stars does tempt us with visions of the divine, then because we are not divine we are faced as mortal beings with the problem of boundaries or limits. If the natural world is no longer the measure of our activities — if, on the contrary, we ourselves have become the world's measure — then what contains the power of our creative energies? Do we ourselves now establish the limits beyond which we dare not go? Do we establish the boundaries which in containing our actions give shape and purpose to them?

Joseph Weizenbaum[27] has written with respect to technology that there are things we should not do, even if we possess the power to do them. The history of our century, however, attests to how difficult — indeed, seemingly impossible — this ethical stand can be. Our will toward creation may be more Faustian than otherwise, and given its apparent limitlessness it seems likely that we, like Faust, may court destruction. Indeed, it may very well be impossible for the modern self to exist without some sense of otherness against which to measure itself and to be measured, against which to find itself and to be given its place. Paul Ricoeur, reflecting on the discoveries of Freudian psychoanalysis within the larger context of the modern self's loss of the symbolic in the formalism of its constructed categories, makes this point. He writes: 'After silence and forgetfulness made widespread by the manipulation of empty signs and the construction of formalized languages, the modern concern for symbols expresses a new desire to be addressed.'[28]

Such a desire requires, however, the capacity to listen, and it is precisely this capacity which is so difficult for a self sealed off from the world behind a window, for that man-on-the-hill so distant from the city which he sees. At best we may be able only to feel this desire as an uneasiness, as a vague discomfort. Like Faust we may be able only to say: 'My realm is endless to the eye, behind my back I hear it mocked.'[29] Our unease, our dis-ease, however, may be the very vehicle of return, the means by which we are restored to ourselves, to our bodies, to the world. At the end of our tale we shall consider this issue of return and there I shall say that our salvation, however we may come to understand this term, can arise only from within the technological vision which has spawned our technological world, rather than from outside it, as the fruit of some longing, for example, for the past. But for now let it suffice to note that the mathematization of reality has been the supreme creation of the modern self, for it has been this mathematization of space, time, matter, and the body which has allowed us to take the world's measure and recreate it, not in the likeness of our bodily image but in the image of a self disentangled from the body, in the image of a self which, as distant spectator, has become almost pure mind.

D From window as metaphor to window as map

The illustration presented in Figure 3.2 can be in one respect misleading. In that illustration the window-veil as grid is an actual device. It is present with the portrayed artist in his situation. As a habit of mind, however, the window-veil as grid has actually disappeared, so that what originated with Alberti and his times as a way of seeing has become for us a world that is seen. Or put in other words, what began with Alberti and his times as a metaphor — look at the world through the grid and it looks like a geometrical pattern — has become for us a map. The grid-like structure of the window and even the window itself have become invisible, and all that remains is the reproduction which we now take for the world itself. The window-veil as grid which was originally something to *see through* has become for us a map to *look at*.

That our modern world originates in this mapping is attested to by Gardner. Commenting on linear perspective, she writes that 'it made possible scale drawings, maps, charts, graphs, and diagrams — those means of exact representation without which modern science and technology would be impossible.'[30] Blueprints, scale drawings, computer print-outs, maps, and even labels, as McLuhan points out, are expressions of our technological culture, and in such a culture the advice of the poet James Joyce to 'Love thy label as thyself'[31] makes ironic sense. We have become our labels as much as the world has become our maps. This outcome, however, is not surprising, since the labels and the maps, the blueprints and the drawings, the charts and the diagrams, the print-outs and the graphs, are the self behind the window projected as a world. Our mathematical map of the world is the map of our minds made visible.

To love one's label as oneself, however, is, and requires, a kind of violence, in much the same way as the mapping of the world and our acceptance of the map as the world is, and requires, a kind of violence. It is the violence of a *reductive* vision. The artist in Figure 3.2 is already practicing that vision. His grid *reproduces* the world beyond the window and *reduces* it. The process of reproduction is one of miniaturization. Moreover, as the illustration makes obvious, it is the spatial arrangements, the parallel squares which Alberti describes, which now matter. The geometrical, the quantifiable, the measurable dimensions of the world become primary. In this process of reduction, of miniaturization, qualitative dimensions are destined to become only secondary.

Newton is one of the primary heirs of this vision, as his reduction of the rainbow to the spectrum illustrates. His experimental arrangements betray how the phenomenon of the rainbow, which as '*seen* in the sky . . . is also a *touch* of the air on one's skin, and . . . a change in the rhythm and *sounds* of the day,'[32] must be scaled down to become the spectrum, a matter for the eye alone. Turning his back upon the world of day, he darkens his room to study the light, and then proceeds to cut a small hole in his window shade. Squeezing the light through this narrow opening and bending it through a prism, Newton unweaves the rainbow. Its colors yield to the laws of refraction and, so measured, the rainbow, together with the world in which it appears, is drained of its color. Indeed, near the end of his experiment, Newton makes this claim. Color, he says, no longer belongs to things, but to the light. The green grass and blue sky of experience yield to 'Difform Rays, some of which are more refrangible than others.'[33] When we adopt a look which scales the world to its quantities, the world is leveled of its qualities. In mapping the world, we thereby explain it.

Our mathematical mapping of the world turns out, therefore, to be a reduced vision of the world, and yet this reduction in vision brings about a powerful gaze. As our Newton example illustrates, the reduction of vision is a narrowing of focus which so intensifies the power of our vision that we are enabled to penetrate into the nature of things, to fragment them, to decompose them into their parts. This analytical vision is, however, only one feature of the self behind the window. In continuing our tale we turn to a description of several additional features.

IV The eye of convergent and infinite vision

The construction of a linear perspective space is the construction of the appearance of a depth between a distance point and a vanishing point. In principle the degree of this depth is infinite. At the vanishing point the lines of the world converge toward a single dot, a mathematical point where the world itself as texture, quality, and difference begins to fade. And opposite this point, the viewer at the distance point is in principle infinitely far from the world which converges toward disappearance. We can say, then, that with the invention of linear perspective space the world has been placed at an infinite distance from us. Or we can say that with this invention we have removed ourselves to an infinite distance from the world. Either statement will do, since the convergence of the world toward a vanishing point is the correlate of our withdrawal from it. Linear perspective space opens up a world whose horizons are infinite and generates a self whose convergent vision is infinite in scope.

A Convergent vision

In linear perspective space the eye which sees the world practices a convergent vision which on one hand places the world at an increasing distance from us and which on the other hand mediates our increasing withdrawal from the world. The ideal of this convergent vision is, moreover, an infinite distance, and the greater the distance between us and the world the more sharply focused and precise our convergent vision becomes. To increase the focus and the precision of our vision we have to step back from the world. Figures 3.3 and 3.4 illustrate this point. With increasing distance there is sharpened convergence, and in this respect the convergent vision of linear perspective space gives rise to a new ideal of human knowledge: the further one removes oneself from the world the more precise and pointed one's knowledge of the world becomes.

The habit of mind which underlies our practice of convergent vision has become so routine that now we hardly notice it. We are, for example, readily familiar today with images of earth from space, and while such images can legitimately provide us with a sense of the unitary earth as humanity's home, they also offer images of the earth as a planetary body in space, an object in orbital motion around the sun, an earth, then, which is decidedly not humanity's home but is rather the astronomer's astrophysical idea of the earth. Here, as Hannah Arendt points out, modern humanity's submission to the call of the distant has succeeded in shrinking the earth into a ball.[34] The earth converges to a ball in space, to a mathematical point within a scheme of universal motion, to the degree that we withdraw ourselves from it. Our knowledge of the earth becomes more precise on the condition that we distance ourselves from it. No judgement or evaluation of this distance is being voiced here — on the contrary, I cite this example only to remind us of how easily we assume this habit of distance, thereby forgetting the connection between this habit and the kind of convergent knowledge which brings precision. In a short while we shall consider some costs of this distance, but for the moment it is obvious that this kind of vision and this way of knowing the world has been one of the great achievements of humanity.

Because the distance of convergent vision is so much our habit of mind, we should perhaps get a feel for it. We can do so if we glance for a moment at Figure 3.5. It is a fresco by an unknown artist dating from the early fourteenth century, entitled *Birth of the Virgin*. The space of this painting is one with which we are not familiar, and it seems to us an odd and confused space. This experience of the painting, however, makes sense because it is a presentation of reverse and not linear perspective.

In reverse perspective the sides of objects diverge rather than converge toward a common point, a fact which is clearly visible in the sides and rockers on the Virgin's cradle. If you imaginatively place yourself in the space of this painting, extend the sides and rockers of the cradle, and pay attention to your felt bodily experience, then you may notice how the space of this painting moves you in a different way than the convergent space depicted in Figures 3.3 and 3.4. Whereas the latter space, the space of linear perspective, has the effect of pushing you away from the vanishing point,

Figures 3.3 and 3.4 Relation between distance and convergence

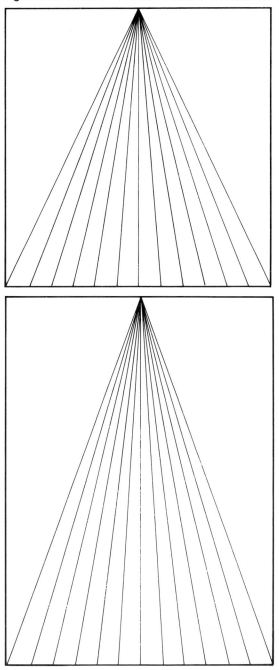

Drawings by Liota Odom

Figure 3.5 Unknown Byzantine artist, detail showing the *Birth of the Virgin* from a fresco in the King's Chapel, Church of Sts Joachim and Ann, Studenica, Yugoslavia, c. 1310–15

From *The Renaissance Rediscovery of Linear Perspective*, Samuel Y. Edgerton, Jr., © 1975 by Samuel Y. Edgerton, Jr., reprinted by permission of Basic Books, Inc., Publishers

Figure 3.6 Bodily felt sense of reverse perspective space

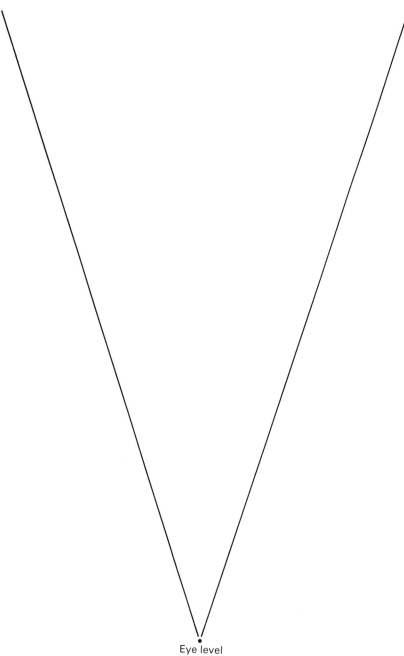

Eye level

Drawing by Liota Odom

Figure 3.7   Bodily felt sense of linear perspective space

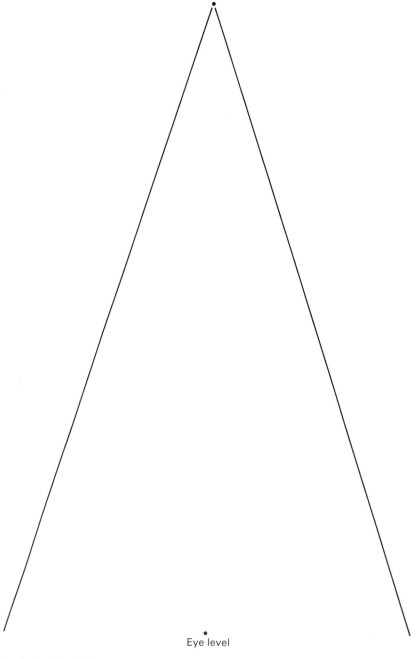

Eye level

Drawing by Liota Odom

the space of this painting seems to invite you into it.

Another way to illustrate this difference is through the two simple examples presented in Figures 3.6 and 3.7. Hold each of the drawings at eye level and note your bodily felt experience of each of these spaces. If you are particularly sensitive to your bodily felt sense of space, you might discover that in addition to drawing you in, the space of reverse perspective resonates lower in your body than the space of linear perspective. In inviting you into its space, reverse perspective is felt near the mid-line of the body, in the gut, whereas in distancing you from its space, linear perspective more often than not is felt higher up near the chest, and perhaps, if the distance seems quite great, still higher, as a sense of dizziness in the eyes and head. In one space, therefore, there is a 'gutty' sense of invitation and in the other a 'heady' sense of distance.

The distance which we experience as a consequence of our convergent vision breeds a kind of passionate concern for dispassionate objectivity. Cool, detached, impartial, and objective, the self of distant vision becomes increasingly indifferent to a world which it views from afar. As things recede toward the vanishing point, as they approach infinity, they become for us, their viewers, less distinct. With each increase in distance they retain less of a tie to us, that tie born in the natal bond between the flesh of our bodies and that of the world. The vanishing point, the point where the world as texture, quality, and difference has shrunk to a geometric dot, has no sound, no taste, no smell, no color, no feel, no quality. It has only measure.

With increasing objectivity and detachment, made possible by increasing distance, we become mere surveyors, whose involvement with the world, while marked by precision, lacks investment. Recall here the figure of the man on the hill looking over the city of Florence. He is perhaps the earliest modern self, the first surveyor of life, the harbinger of what we have become. Seated there on the hill above the city, he has attained, as it were, a bird's eye view of things, and from his position his vision is free to roam over the entire landscape. But while such a distance yields a more comprehensive, broader knowledge of the city than one can obtain by moving through it, that man on the hill — the detached, distant, objective observer of modern life — '. . . will never know from that distance either the words of anger or the sounds of love uttered by those living in the city.'[35] And without that knowledge, a knowledge born within a more intimate space, is not that figure destined to become increasingly indifferent to, and even perhaps incapable of, understanding such knowledge? 'Vision, as our only objective and detached sense, when in high definition, discourages empathy.'[36] Convergent vision, which is the vision practiced by that man on the hill, is vision in its highest definition. It is vision at a distance, which buys scope and precision at the price of intimate understanding.

The fifteenth century is, however, a long time ago and so I want to cite a more recent example of this vision which in gazing from afar becomes alienated from what it sees. It is the vision of Monsieur Roquetin from Jean-Paul Sartre's novel *Nausea*. Roquetin, a modern man tortured by self-doubt and despair, climbs the hills surrounding the city of Beauville, and from that height he experiences with a frightening clarity how distant he has become from life. He says, 'I feel so far away from them, on the top of this hill. It seems as though I belong to another species.'[37]

Roquetin is kin to the fifteenth-century man on the hill. Between the two, however, something has been added. It is Roquetin's words which I consider to be an expression of what was in its origins a possibility. Between the silence of the one and the words of the other lies the path to the modern self, and Roquetin's little speech announces in effect that this is what we have made of this vision. Indifference born of distance has become alienation. The modern self, born in distance from the world, may even be a new species of humanity, 'homo astronauticus', a species whose condition of distance can allow it to contemplate the nuclear destruction of possibly the entire planet and in the face of that possibility still continue to program the planet for destruction.

But if convergent vision is characterized by a dispassionate indifference born of distance, it nevertheless achieves precision, that sharpness of gaze which we have already noted. Convergent vision is focused vision, vision which narrows its gaze to intensify its process of penetration. Our earlier example of Newton's prismatic eye is an apt illustration of this gaze because it analyzes the rainbow, reduces it, penetrates it, discovers a truth about it, by squeezing that phenomenon as it belongs to the world of human history, myth, and experience into the narrow confines of a darkened room.

The poets John Keats and William Blake recognized the awesome power of the sharply focused gaze. In his poem 'London,' for example, Blake wanders the *chartered* streets where the *chartered* Thames does flow, and he notes in the faces of those whom he meets, in these mapped and arranged spaces of the focused eye, 'Marks of weakness, marks of woe.'

London, the city of modern industrialized society, the city blueprinted by a gaze which charters and focuses the world, 'manacles' the human soul. Blake ends his poem with two powerful images of how this sharpness of vision further destroys the human soul:

> But most, thro' midnight streets I hear
> How the youthful Harlot's curse
> Blasts the new-born Infant's tear
> And Blights with plagues the Marriage hearse.[38]

The sharp intensity of this vision blasts and blights, prompting the poet to implore elsewhere, 'May God us keep, From Single Vision and Newton's Sleep.'[39]

John Keats, less pointedly but equally critical of this focused vision, this sharp, intense gaze, asks:

> Do not all charms fly
> At the touch of cold philosophy?
> There was an awful rainbow once in heaven:
> We know her woof, her texture; she is given
> In the dull catalogue of common things.
> Philosophy will clip an Angel's wings,
> Conquer all mysteries by rule and line,
> Empty the haunted air, and gnomed mine —
> Unweave a rainbow. . . .[40]

The 'Single Vision of Newton's Sleep,' the sharp, intense, focused gaze, here unweaves the rainbow to arrange it according to rule and line. This vision, which would even dare clip angelic wings, is a vision which conquers what it sees, empties it of its charms, and tames in the awe-ful power of its gaze what is filled with awe.

This focused vision to which Keats and Blake responded so long ago is perhaps most fully realized today in the figure of the specialist, since specialized knowledge is the outcome of a sharply focused vision. The more narrow, precise, and tight one's gaze becomes the less one has a sense either of the whole, or of the relation of the parts to the whole. But the less one has to bother about the whole the more one can become an expert, a specialist in one's reduced domain. The self which specializes in focused vision, then, comes to possess bits of knowledge, much like a computer is programmed with bits of information. Indeed, we build the computer in our own image, and the understanding we have of it mirrors our own self-understanding. A computer is like a self which is filled with bits of information and which can process that information indifferent to its content. It does not matter what one feeds into a computer. It will process with equal efficiency bits of information concerning airline schedules and bits of information concerning the trajectories of rockets launched for World War III. That is the power of the computer. But if we build the world in the image of ourselves, if the computer is a model of the self we imagine ourselves to be, then this power becomes frightening. Efficiency wedded to indifference is a cold abstraction of a human being.

The specialization of knowledge which follows on sharpened, focused vision virtually surrounds us. There are experts or specialists to handle every aspect of human life. 'With the multiplication of technologies and the ascendance of experts and expertise in all fields,' Walker Percy says, 'the self has consented to the expropriation of every sector of life by its appropriate expert.'[41]

Perhaps, however, the clearest expression of this plethora of experts is provided by the medical profession. As Ivan Illich documents so well in his book *Medical Nemesis*, the 'medicalization of life' could not have proceeded without the 'expropriation of health' by an array of physicians with expertly precise but increasingly narrow vision aided by an equally large support group of medical bureaucrats. The consequence for Illich is a condition of 'social iatrogenesis,' a term which designates 'all impairments to health that are due precisely to those socio-economic transformations which have been made attractive, possible, or necessary by the institutional shape health care has taken.' Under such a condition, he says, 'health care is turned into a standardized item . . . all suffering is "hospitalized" and homes become inhospitable to birth, sickness, and death . . . [and] the language in which people could experience their bodies is turned into bureaucratic gobbledegook.'[42] Precise, narrowly focused, sharpened vision produces a standardized knowledge, a standard held and practiced by those who are specialists of a convergent vision.

Surrounded by specialists and expertise, we hand ourselves over to others, and handing ourselves over in this way we create a distance even within ourselves. The spectator self which begins in distance from the world ends in becoming distant from itself, '. . . a space-bound ghost,' lost in '. . . the very Cosmos it understands perfectly.'[43] Dispersed among the experts, increasingly focused on in increasingly minute terms, the spectator self becomes fragmented and displaced. Like the world which the Irish poet Yeats foresaw, the self too falls apart; its center will not hold. Psychoanalysis, itself destined to become another field of expertise, is born to witness and tragically diagnose this fragmentation of the self. The unconscious, like Blake's chartered London streets, is mapped and tamed by the specialized, standardized language of expert vision. Oedipus becomes a cultural coin and even in its suffering the modern self, born in distance, is handled from afar.

McLuhan and Parker have noted that 'intense stress on visual experience . . . results in fragmentation' and that 'sentimentality, like pornography, is fragmented emotion; a natural consequence of a high visual gradient in any culture.'[44] We might wonder, then, if the pornographic eye is the other side of a convergent, sharply focused vision, that vision of the man on the hill spying on life from above, and if sentimentality is the necessary condition of the self which has withdrawn too far from home in removing itself from the world? Is nostalgic sentimentality the condition of a self which in its distance has grown indifferent to things and is therefore only capable of sustaining the most superficial kind of emotion, only capable of being moved in the instant, only capable of cheap, theatrical sentimentality? In her study of Adolf Eichmann, the technician of death who could see the slaughter of nearly a million Jews only in terms of scheduling problems, Hannah Arendt notes the disproportion between Eichmann's lack of emotion over these monstrous crimes and the easy sentimentality to which he could fall prey over the smallest and most insignificant things.[45] Lost in the world, dispassionately indifferent to it, fragmented within ourselves, we may very well have forgotten how to cry. The eye of distant vision, a convergent vision of specialized, focused knowledge, may very well be, for all its precision, a vision without tears: a vision marked by a dispassionate objectivity leading to an indifferent gaze, and by a sharp intensity of purpose leading, in its turn, to the focused gaze of specialized knowledge, a knowledge which tends to leave the self fragmented within itself — composed of bits of knowledge unrelated to a whole — probably senti- mental in its emotional attachment to the world, and perhaps even essentially pornographic. This vision may very well be a vision incapable of empathic e-motion, a vision incapable of being moved by what it sees.

B Infinite vision/cosmological self

The distance of convergent vision is in principle and in the ideal infinite, and in this respect the self which practices this vision is and must be an unlimited self, a self free to roam the world and indeed the universe, a self for which it would be appropriate to say the sky and only the sky is the limit.

This last phrase about the sky is in fact deliberately chosen because it captures what Hannah Arendt nicely describes as the *astrophysical* world view underlying the modern self. Placed opposite the vanishing point, we are given a central place and in that place we are first re-born as a cosmo- logical species. If technology is the transformation of all of us into astronauts, then the origins of this transformation lie in that moment when the world, receding toward infinity, becomes a mathematical dot, a point set in infinite space, thereby preparing the way for the Copernican earth, the earth as a revolving point in space, 'Spaceship Earth', to emerge. The transformation begins when the horizon of infinity is set opposite to and equal with our vision, making our vision the measure of the infinite and endowing it, and the one who practices it, with infinite status. Alberti's procedure imagines a space reaching toward infinity and in that space we are re-born as cosmic and universe-al. The vanishing point is the place where we launch ourselves from the earth into the universe: linear per- spective grid as a runway for take-off to the stars. Figure 3.8 illustrates this point.

The cosmological self, the self of infinite vision, inhabits a Copernican earth, and indeed it is the Copernican earth which initially best reveals the transformation of the self from a creature bound to a finite earth to one who now belongs to an infinite universe. With Copernicus we begin to dwell in the heavens, and we become, in the words of Arendt, creatures who have now established themselves as ' "universal" beings, as creatures who are terrestrial not by nature and essence but only by the condition of being

Figure 3.8 Linear perspective grid as runway for take-off

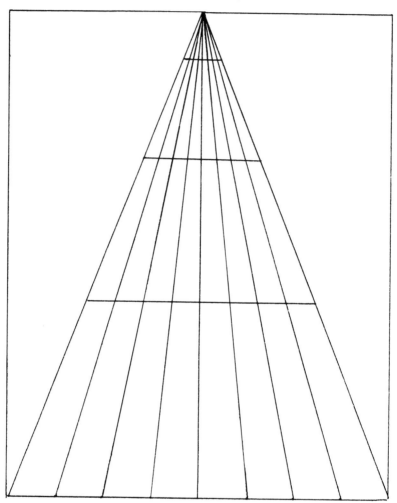

Drawing by Liota Odom

alive, and who therefore by virtue of reasoning can overcome this condition not in mere speculation but in actual fact.' We are terrestrial now only by the condition of being alive, that is only by the condition of our embodiment, and thus the Copernican image of ' "the virile man standing in the sun . . . overlooking the planets" '[46] necessarily intends an abandonment of the body. Infinite vision, which in principle goes further than the embodied eye can ever see, demands the renunciation of the body, the willingness to leave the body behind. It is no surprise, therefore, to discover that the Copernican earth makes its official published appearance in 1543, the same year that the modern anatomical body, the body as corpse, the abandoned body, makes its official published appearance with the work of Vesalius. Elsewhere[47] I have shown that this historical coincidence betrays a cultural necessity, and here I need only repeat that our incarnation is an impediment to the realization of Copernican vision, to the practice of infinite vision. Indeed the daring of Copernicus' imagination, 'which lifted him from the earth and enabled him to look down upon her as though he actually were an inhabitant of the sun',[48] lies in this willingness to dispense with the body in order to achieve a vision of things no longer misled by appearances. It is daring because in principle it acknowledges that the body deceives us, that the appearance of things as carried by the senses is an illusion, and so acknowledging this requires one to renounce the body. And the body *renounced* in this fashion for the practice of Copernican vision, the body *no longer needed* as vehicle for experience, the body now regarded even as *impediment* and *obstacle* to infinite vision, is more easily abandoned to the anatomist's dissecting table. In the same year that the Copernican self officially departs the earth — 1543 — the body of this self is abandoned as a corpse lying on Vesalius' dissecting table.

An artistic anticipation of this confluence of infinite vision and the body as corpse now seen from afar is Mantegna's painting, *Dead Christ*, executed in 1506, and shown in Figure 3.9. Neither the suffering body nor the body which will be resurrected seems present here. On the contrary, it is the corpse which overwhelms us. The dead Christ lies on a plane corresponding to the viewer's perspective, giving the viewer the powerful impression of an ever increasing distance between the feet and the head of the figure. Our vision point is set opposite that receding distance of the figure and the effect is as if we are seeing the figure from above, as if we have become the man on the hill and are now looking down upon the body. The visual genius of this painting is that it makes death so overwhelmingly present *and* so far away, at the same time. Its genius is that it announces most dramatically and persuasively the appearance of the body as corpse and simultaneously establishes our distance from it. It is an eloquent and perhaps even terrifying visual demonstration of the psychological condition of the modern self we have become, a self living in a world where instant death for millions of individuals is so threateningly near and yet so far away.

As selves endowed with infinite vision we have distanced ourselves from our bodies and from the earth. We have become astronauts, beings who by virtue of their powers of vision now belong to the heavens. Earlier we saw how the art historian Samuel Edgerton connected linear perspective space and the infinite cosmic vision which has built our technological world, but it is helpful to repeat his words again. He writes, 'Space capsules built for zero gravity, astronomical equipment for demarcating so-called black holes, atom smashers which prove the existence of anti-matter — these are the end products of the discovered vanishing point.'[49] Psychologically, we have

Figure 3.9 Mantegna, *Dead Christ*

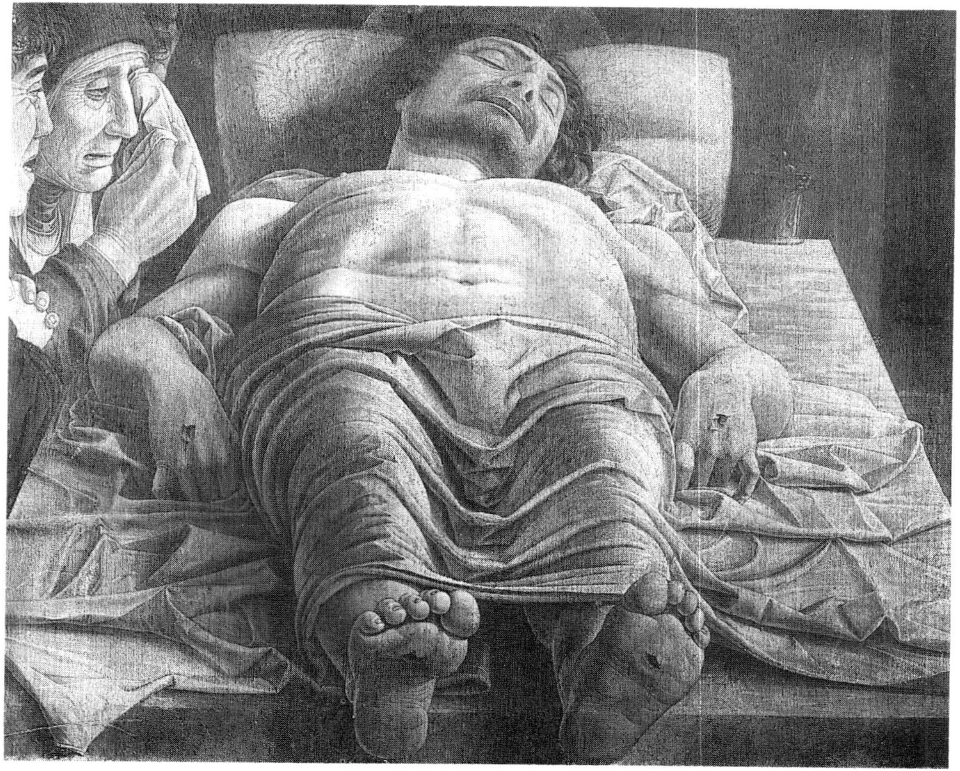

removed ourselves from the earth and in so doing we have constructed a world which incarnates the distance we have created. Technological instruments like the telescope and the microscope, the telephone and the television, the automobile and the airplane, are not merely or even primarily instruments which bridge distance. Rather, they are instruments called into being by the distance we have created, by the distance we have put between ourselves and the world, between our senses and the world of which they make sense. They become possible *and* necessary only when the distance between us and the world has increased. They give flesh to our psychological condition of distance, making visible by their very presence the reality of the self of infinite vision who has become an inhabitant of the stars. They are not merely instruments we use. Rather, they are mirrors which reflect who we are, who and what we have become opposite the vanishing point. They bear witness to the real presence of humanity as cosmological, a humanity which today is even capable of wondering whether the progressively receding universe contains enough matter to allow this process of infinite expansion to slow down and to reverse itself. We cannot help but ask here, however, if this question, like the instruments of technology, also reflects our own psychological condition. In our musings over a progressively receding universe are we discovering in nature only what we are already ourselves? Are we discovering in nature only our own minds? Is the scientific hypothesis of an expanding universe the other side of the psychological condition of the man of infinite vision? Is the universe progressively receding from us, or have we been progressively withdrawing from it? Or are the two questions really the same, so that we read *our retreat from the world*, so that we discover our withdrawal, as *an event of the world*?

However we may answer these questions, what seems undeniable is that the self of infinite vision is today a psychological reality. We are all, psychologically, astronauts. Or in the recent terms of the novelist-psychiatrist Walker Percy, we are all in orbit, our orbiting self lost in the cosmos of its own creation and perpetually faced with the task and the problem of re-entry.[50] What appears undeniable, then, is that distance and re-entry have become matters of the self, psychological matters. In the final chapters of our tale we will take up this issue of re-entry or return as a psychological necessity of modern life.

C An immobile eye on a visible world

Throughout this tale of the self, reference has continually been made to the *eye* of distant and infinite vision, or to the *eye* whose vision of the world is reductive and analytic, or to the *eye* precisely and sharply focused on the world. We have spoken of the spectator self behind the window as if it were one-eyed, Cyclopean in its vision of the world. We have done so, however,

Figure 3.10   Albrecht Dürer, *Artist Drawing a Portrait*, woodcut

Reproduced by permission of Marburg/Art Resource, New York

with good reason, because it turns out that the spectator self of infinite vision truly does keep *an eye* upon the world. It also turns out to be the case that this eye is immobile, that it is fixed in its place. William Ivins, in commenting on the basic idea of linear perspective, puts the matter simply and directly. A person can make a correct image of what he or she sees through a window 'provided that while he does this he uses only one eye and does not move his head.'[51]

The illustration presented in Figure 3.10 demonstrates the fixed singularity of linear perspective vision. It is a woodcut by Albrecht Dürer made in 1525 and intended by him to illustrate the technique of linear perspective drawing.

The fixity of the artist is quite explicit here. The screen or veil is placed between the artist and his model, and the artist has stationed himself quite firmly on one side of this screen. Matching his fixed position we notice the model. We may guess that his apparent rigid posture is the consequence of the artist's command that he not move, echoing perhaps Edgar's opening words to Gloucester, 'Here's the place. Stand still', and thereby suggesting, as McLuhan and Parker note, a link between the artist's understanding of linear perspective technique and the landscape which will appear with Lear, the landscape arrayed before and below one who has become a spectator of the world.[52] We need not, however, confine ourselves to conjecture, since Dürer makes the point about the fixed gaze quite explicit. Notice the artist again! One eye is fixed by a small wooden device which holds his viewpoint and keeps it in place. Here the fixed gaze becomes an actual prescription.

This fixed character of the eye reconfirms an element in our tale of technology which has arisen several times. It reconfirms that linear perspective technique as a cultural vision of the technological world — a way of envisioning the world — dispenses with the body. Fixed in place, the eye no longer needs the body to carry it through the world, and indeed the body, in its movement toward the world, in its sensitive reply to the allure of sensible things, can be only a disturbance. The fixed gaze, like the gaze of infinite vision, is the abandonment of the body, and what begins here as a spectating eye cut off from movement will become the style of a self divorced from the living, moving body. Descartes will lie still in his bed to think. The gaze fixed in its place will become the Cartesian *cogito*, the symbol of thought without movement, the exemplar of a thought which in abandoning the body has itself become disembodied. The irony here is that in time we will 'reincarnate' this fixed gaze which has left the body behind. The computer will give flesh to this eye which in abandoning the body has dreamed of a vision of the world unmoved by the appeal of the world, a vision no longer moved by the allure of things.

The spectator self who trains his or her fixed gaze upon the world also practices a singular vision. It is that single vision of Newton's sleep from which the poet Blake begged deliverance, a literalizing vision which forgets the play of the imagination, which was Blake's point. In taking the world's measure, such an eye knows no play or shadow. It is, we might say, a Luciferian eye, an eye which bears a clear and penetrating light.

The self of singular vision is not, however, merely a silent spectator. The fixed gaze which we train upon the world projects a world. We also speak about what we see, and, as in ordinary life, we speak in terms of how we see. Perception and language are not, as the French philosopher Merleau-Ponty reminds us, separate powers. On the contrary, they interpenetrate each other. 'Perception is a nascent logos,' Merleau-Ponty writes,[53] and language is the amplification and the realization of our perceptions. To be educated within a discipline, for example, is to learn a new language and a new vision. One learns a new way of speaking which issues forth into a new way of seeing, just as the new vision which characterizes the discipline calls forth a new voice.

Insofar as we become accustomed to single vision, to that vision addicted to a fixed perspective or point of view, to a single angle of interpretation, we also become accustomed to a kind of speaking (and thinking) characterized by a passion for certitude, by a passion for fixing the meaning (of words and things) to the letter. I am speaking here about a mind addicted to the literal, about a mind which is as hostile to the play of metaphor in language as singular vision is to the play of shadow in things. And in this respect we should not fail to hear again the connection between linear perspective vision and the rise of modern science, for it is the language of science that we strive most energetically to purify of ambiguity. The exact, precise observations of the scientific eye call for an exact, precise description. We should not be surprised, therefore, to discover early on in the history of modern science, at a time sufficiently removed from the origins of linear perspective vision to have allowed it to become a habit of mind, a rather strong condemnation of the play of language. In 1667 Thomas Sprat, speaking in praise of the scientific members of the Royal Society of London, says:

They have therefore been most rigorous in putting in execution, the only Remedy, that can be found for this extravagance: and that has been, a constant Resolution, to reject all the amplifications, digressions, and swellings of style: to return back to the primitive purity, and shortness, when men delivered so many things, almost in an equal number of words. They have exacted from all their members, a close, naked, natural way of speaking: positive expressions; clear senses; a native easiness: bringing all things as near the Mathematical plainness, as they can.[54]

Metaphor, the play and movement of language, the multiplicity of meaning, is a disturbing extravagance, much as the movement of the eye would be a disturbance to the artist depicted in Dürer's drawing.

Dürer's drawing indicates another feature of linear perspective vision which announced itself earlier in our story. It concerns the connection between the spectator self with its eye upon the world and the world transformed into a spectacle. In calling attention, as it does, to the eye, Dürer's drawing indicates that in linear perspective vision the world is a matter of the eye, of the single eye, and of the eye alone. As such the world matters as a matter of light, and it matters as a visible matter. It matters and counts as real to the degree that it is and can be made into a piece of visibility.

We can illustrate with the example of time how under the gaze of the fixed eye the world has indeed become a matter of increasing visibility. In numerous towns in the late Middle Ages the town clock replaced the cathedral bell as a means of telling time. With this change time was made visible, a matter of measurement, since the clock, registering as it does time on its face, is for the eye. Joseph and Frances Gies, in their study of the Middle Ages, note that with the cathedral bell 'People do not care exactly what time it is; they want to know how much daylight is left.'[55] With the town clock, however, the exact time becomes a visible matter for all to see. The sound of time is inexact to the same degree that the vision of time is exact, a difference which changes the conduct of life in several ways. The inexactness of time heard situates one within the flow and the rhythm of time, whereas the attitude which belongs to time made visible gives one a distance from time, a perspective on it, and allows one to focus more on time as duration. In addition, the cyclic character of time as sounded, for example, by cathedral bells shapes life into a daily round, whereas the linear character of time, which develops with increasing use of the clock, configures our life more as a line, allowing us to dream a new idea like progress, and even perhaps to believe that progress is inevitable and that it moves in a straight line toward infinity.

It is true, of course, that before the invention of the modern clock, on whose face time is made visible, there were water clocks and hourglasses to make visible the passing of time. But these instruments offered a fuzzy visibility, an inexact visibility, in comparison with the modern clock, and, more significantly, they did not lead to another development which marks the hegemony of the eye. I am speaking here of the invention and popularization of the traveling clock, the watch, which allows *each* man and woman to keep a watchful eye on time and in so doing to take time in hand. Such traveling clocks date from approximately 1585, when they were invented by the Englishman Bartholomew Newsam.[56] Taking his or her timepiece from his or her pocket, the modern self looks at time and takes it in hand: time is made visible to the eye and mastered by the eye, which makes everything a matter of visibility. And the end product of this process of visualization is perhaps our digital clock, in which even the face of time disappears into the visibility of a pure number.

V The self without a shadow

In James Barrie's delightful play *Peter Pan*, Peter wants more than anything else to have a shadow. Perhaps as children, probably when we either read the story or saw the movie, we did not appreciate how profound this desire for a shadow really is. But it is a deep desire, because one's shadow is a visible sign of one's substance, because through one's shadow one knows and sees that one is embodied and belongs to this world.

The story of the self behind the window which we have told in this chapter can be summed up by saying that this self is a self without a shadow, a self, then, which is disincarnate. As spectators of the world we have left the body behind. We have abandoned it there on the other side of the window, finding it both unnecessary for a world which has become a matter of light, a matter for the eye alone, and a hindrance for a self with dreams of infinite vision. In the next turning of our tale we shall consider what we have done with and to this body we have abandoned. We shall consider how we have remade it to fit the space of linear perspective vision. For the moment, however, we shall end our tale of the self simply by noting that in our role of spectator we have created a world in which it becomes increasingly possible to believe that we really no longer have to be with our bodies. In projecting our vision of the world on to the world, a mathematical vision which is reductive and analytical, convergent and infinite, fixed and singular, we have made a world where we 'escape' from our bodies, a world, then, in which we cast no shadows. Lest, however, this ending sound too mysterious, allow me to close by saying that many of our technological instruments give flesh to this dream, and as only one example I cite that of the telephone answering machine. The phone rings, a reproduction of your voice answers and invites me, at the sound of a beep, to leave my message. You are there in your words of invitation, and yet you are absent. You are there as a reproduced, disembodied voice, a self without substance, a self which has no shadow.[57]

Chapter four

Body as specimen

I Recollection: of cosmonauts and kisses

At the beginning of our tale we suggested that within the landscape of the modern world each and every one of us has become an astronaut. The actual fact of departure by the few is only an irrelevant detail which does not distinguish those few from the rest of us who in fact, *but only in fact*, remain upon the earth. Overshadowing this minor difference, we all share that same condition of distance from matter whose genesis we have already described. We are all united in that double flight or escape from the world into the universe and from the world into the self. Or perhaps even more dramatically, in the words of the novelist–psychiatrist Walker Percy, we are all 'lost in the cosmos.'

The figure of the Little Cosmonaut whom we met earlier offers an image of the body we have become in the space of linear perspective vision, the landscape of the modern world. It is, in the words of the art critic Charles Wentinck, a body which has become 'an almost inhuman abstraction, further removed from nature than at any other moment in history.' It is a body enshelled, a body where 'All the natural activities — of hearing, breathing, speaking, and making gestures — are . . . replaced by technical functions', a body, finally, which has 'no contact with the surrounding atmosphere', a body closed in upon itself and insulated from the world.[1]

A key issue for our age is to understand the ways in which *we are* this body. It is a key issue because the way in which we understand and treat our bodies is a reflection of the way in which we understand and treat the world. The figure of the Little Cosmonaut displays a cluster of images, from the fires of departure and annihilation, to the anatomical body of neuro-chemical functioning depicted earlier in the two kissing figures.

To understand how the human body has become something quite unknown to us, unfamiliar, an alien abstraction, requires, however, more than an indication of the multiple ways in which the human body has become defined in terms of its technical functions. It will not help very much, for example, only to indicate that this body of the Little Cosmonaut as imagined by the artist is identical to the body of modern medicine, the body which we become when we simply hand ourselves over to the physician. Nor will it increase our understanding very much even to recognize that the cosmonaut is kin — brother or sister — of the Playboy bunny, to the objectified body of pornography. Such connections, while necessary, are not sufficient unless we give some consideration to the genesis of this body, for the simple but most compelling feature of the Little Cosmonaut is that we have invented this body. We have, as the artist says, *created* it. In tracing the genesis of this body, therefore, we are trying to understand as best we can our own (continuing) participation in (and responsibility for) becoming what we are. We need to understand that this body which we have invented is first and foremost a matter of attitude. It is in the *way* we breathe; it is in the *attitude* we adopt toward seeing and hearing; it is the *stance* we take toward eating, walking, sleeping, and all of our other bodily activities; it is in our *disposition* toward illness and health that we exercise our astronautic condition. We are not astronauts, or the artist van Hoeydonck's Little Cosmonaut, because of any superficial, external resemblance to this figure. We are not astronauts only when we assist our breathing, for example, with a technical instrument. Rather we are astronauts when, for example, we regard our breathing as only or merely a technical matter, as a matter of the lungs, and thereby forget that breathing is also, always and primarily, a matter of inspiration. We are astronauts, therefore, because of what we have come to believe about ourselves and our bodies. Before the facts, which are a matter for any eye to observe, there is a belief which is always a matter of the human heart.[2] To trace the genesis of this body, then, is to reclaim the participation and disposition of our human heart in this invention.

Before we take up this theme of how the body *matters* as a *cultural* invention, I want to invite the reader to look again at the two kissing figures we saw earlier. I want to draw attention here to the anatomical depiction of these two figures, which allows the translation of bodily activities into technical functions, which allows the act of kissing to be presented as a neurochemical event. It is a strange perspective, for while it is certainly true that a kiss is such an event, it is also equally certain that I neither know of nor care about such things when I kiss another. No one ever kisses another in this fashion, and to imagine the kiss in this way requires a very special attitude. It requires a withdrawal from the other as he or she presents himself or herself, as well as a withdrawal from my self. It requires a retreat to the body as anatomical object, a retreat into the body. It is a retreat whose code we have already encountered: 'The inside tells me about the outside.' In the course of our tale we shall hear how the invention of the body to suit the space of linear perspective vision is inseparable from a departure from the world and a journey into the interior, anatomical space of the body.

II The body as a cultural invention

I am sitting at my desk writing these words while thinking about the two kissing figures and it occurs to me that my act of writing could be described in the same way as that kiss. The hand which holds the pen is part of my arm which rests upon the desk. But the 'inside which tells me about the outside' tells me that this hand and arm are a composition of nerves, blood vessels, tendons, joints, and muscles within which an array of neuro-chemical events are taking place. Indeed, in principle I can refine this rather gross analysis to a microscopic cellular level and while the categories of my discourse might change, one thing will remain the same. The more that I *distance* myself from the task at hand — the writing of these words and sentences — to retreat *within* the defined spaces of my anatomical arm, the more *my* arm becomes *an* arm, *like any other arm*. In other words, with increasing distance, my arm progressively becomes something objective, a specimen, the knowledge of which serves to detach the human arm from a living situation. Thus, not only is my arm now like any other arm, but also my arm is the same in all situations. The arm which positions itself in relation to this writing pad, the writing arm, is identical (anatomically) to the arm which extends itself in greeting, or to the arm which offers a helping hand to another.

This identical character of the body across all situations is peculiar and it is an essential characteristic of the body we have invented within linear perspective space. We have invented this immutable arm, an arm which belongs to a body which fits all situations and therefore belongs to no situation. The scene depicted in Figure 4.1 suggests the invented character of this arm insofar as it indicates that the body has not always been this way. A brief consideration of it will help us, therefore, to understand the invented character of our present body.

Figure 4.1 is an exterior detail of the bronze doors of St Michael's at Hildesheim, Germany, which dates from approximately 1015. The figure portrayed is that of St Joseph. Notice the arms of the figure. They are extended in a gesture of receiving. The arms are holding a gift, which St Joseph has apparently just accepted from the Magi. The Magi, the three wise men, have traveled a long distance to pay homage to the birth of Jesus, and Joseph, as his earthly father, accepts this honor in Jesus' name. What seems peculiar to us, however, are Joseph's arms receiving the gift of homage. They are too short, and indeed it is easy to imagine that were he to place those arms at his side they would not extend below his waist. What, then, are we to make of this image? It is artist–sculptor merely incompetent? That could hardly be the case, considering the fact that other figures portrayed on this door panel, like the Magi in Figure 4.2, have arms whose length indicates that the sculptor knows the appearance of the body. His figure of St Joseph does not indicate incompetence. Something else is being portrayed here.

Figure 4.1 *Presentation in the Temple*, detail: Joseph with his offering; bronze doors, St Michael's, Hildesheim

Reproduced by permission of Marburg/Art Resource, New York

If we look again at the figure of St Joseph we notice the striking character of his face. The head is slightly bowed, the mouth is pulled slightly downward, and the eyes are closed. St Joseph is receiving a gift of homage in the name of the Son of God from three kings who have journeyed far toward this moment. His head, mouth, and eyes seem to acknowledge this situation.

Figure 4.2 *Adoration of the Magi*, detail: two of the Magi; bronze doors, St Michael's, Hildesheim

Reproduced by permission of Marburg/Art Resource, New York

They *are* humility incarnate. Notice that I do not say here that his head, mouth, and eyes *express* humility. Rather I am saying they are humility made flesh. There is nothing of an inside being pushed outside — expressed — here. On the contrary, there is here 'only' a body 'in' a situation,[3] a body in the midst of a story, a body whose flesh makes visible a moment of that story. Situated within this context, the arms of St Joseph are extremely appropriate, for they fit his face and his situation. Arms of humility do *shrink* in towards the body. That is how we live this type of situation. That is our *felt bodily experience* of such a situation. That shrinking is a bodily lived meaning.

The art historian Helen Gardner lends support to our remarks with her comments on another scene depicted on those bronze doors. Figure 4.3 portrays the tale of Adam and Eve being condemned by God. Again we focus on the arm, this time the left one of God. The arm here is an accusing finger. Gardner writes: 'As he lays upon them the curse of mortality, the primal condemnation, he jabs his finger with the force of his whole body, the force concentrating in the gesture, the psychic focus of the whole composition'.[4] All the drama of that moment is focused on that gesture. If, however, we see this accusing arm of God only through the body as we have invented it, then we are faced with a deity with a withered and shrunken arm, a crippled God. Again, therefore, we need to look in a different way. We need to focus on the body 'in' its situation, and doing so we recognize again that the sculptor—artist has depicted the body incarnating a story. The accusing hand, this gesture of condemnation, gives flesh to that moment of judgement. It emphasizes and even exaggerates what one would perceive in such a moment, the arm as accusing finger. Gardner says of this scene that 'the story is given with all the simplicity and impact of skilled pantomime.'[5] We might suggest, then, that the bodies depicted in these bronze doors are *pantomimic bodies*, bodies whose gestures are inseparable from the emotional situation and the story they enact. As such, the bodies depicted on these doors, these pantomimic bodies, are a far cry from that body whose inside tells us of the outside. The bodies depicted here have no interiors in the sense of an inside which tells one of the outside. They have no inside in the sense of a source which originates the gestures, much less causes them. Rather, the gestures of these pantomimic bodies are directed to a world and, we might say, even originate there. The gestures of these bodies are drawn out toward the world and in this sense we should say that these bodies on the bronze doors are *e-motional* bodies. They are bodies *moved out* of themselves, seduced and solicited by the world. These pantomimic bodies situated within a story are radically unlike the immutable body of technical functioning, of which it can be said that it *has* emotions which are pressed out (ex-pressed) from within.

What the sculptor—artist has depicted in these scenes is something about the living, human body which our invention of the anatomical body has

Figure 4.3 *Adam and Eve Reproached by God*, bronze doors, St Michael's, Hildesheim

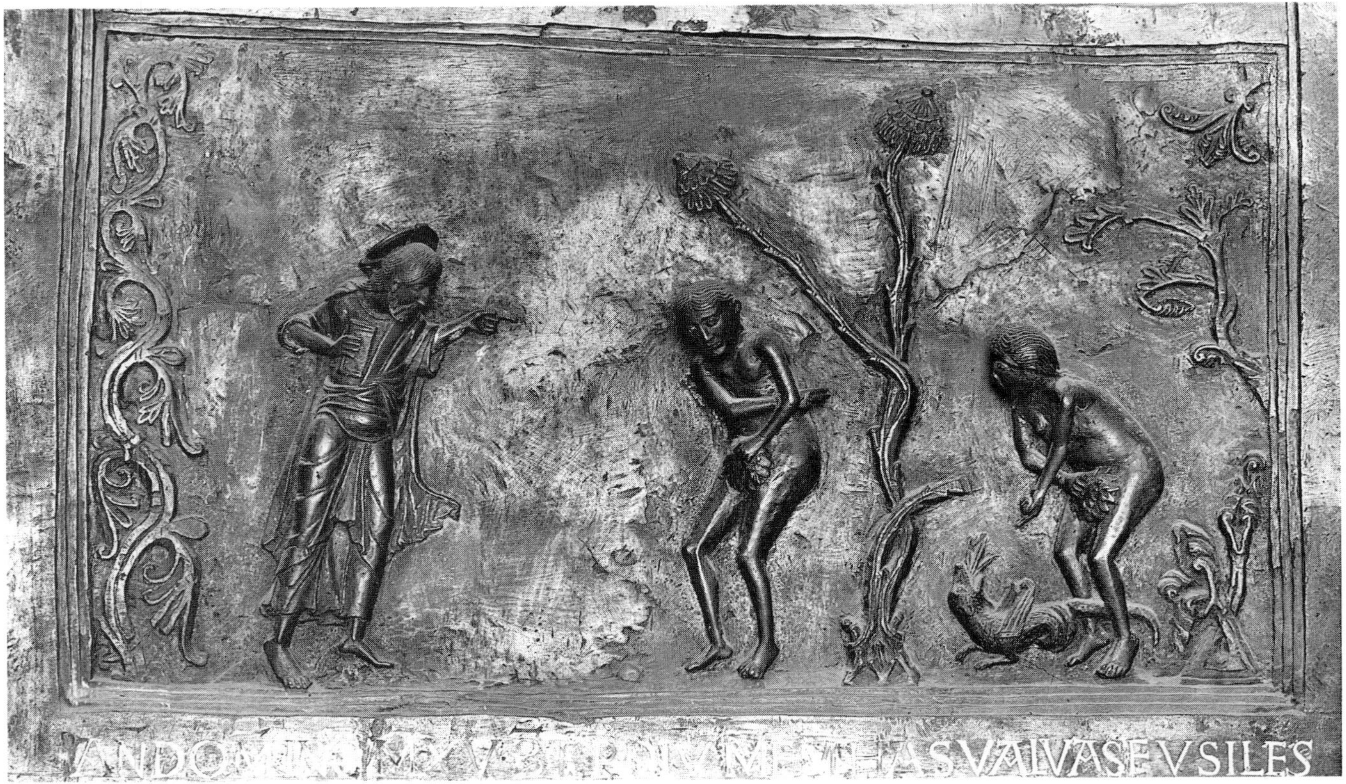

Reproduced by permission of Marburg/Art Resource, New York

helped us to forget: *the body is a situation and as such changes.* The arms of the Magi, which are giving arms, are different from the arms of St Joseph, which are arms of receiving. Arms which give are not, and never can be in real life, identical with arms which receive. Or perhaps we should say from the viewpoint of the body we have invented, which defines for us today the body which is real, that such arms are made identical only when we erase the difference. And indeed, that erasure is part of the tale of invention we are considering. Arms which are neutral and indifferent to what they do — give a gift, receive a handshake, embrace a friend, slap an enemy, etc. — are arms which have become technical functions. Like computers, which are indifferent to the information they process, such arms can do or handle anything. They can just as easily scratch an itch as they can push a button which launches the missiles, because they are detached from a living situation.

I am not, however, proposing any priority of St Joseph's arms over those of the Little Cosmonaut, arms which have become technical functions. Rather, my intention is only to illustrate a difference in order to make the point that the human body is a *mutable* reality. As such, the body changes not only for the individual in relation to the situations he or she encounters, but also culturally, so that the body of one historical place and time is not identical to that of a different historical era. In this respect, the bodies depicted on the doors of St Michael's, Hildesheim, are not less real than our anatomical bodies of today. Rather they are *different* bodies, belonging to a different world. We run a great risk with respect to ourselves, and we seriously prejudice our understanding of our own situation today, if we take this difference as a measure of an increase in our knowledge from the less to the more real. The difference offers no such measure. On the contrary, the difference says 'only' that the human body has changed. Or to be more precise here, since it is we who sculpt the doors, paint the paintings, and anatomize the body, this difference says that we have changed the body. The difference, then, bears witness to the claim that the human body is not so much a given, natural, fact, a matter of nature, as it is a matter of culture, a human cultural invention. Only in the most minimal sense can we consign the human body to a realm of pure nature divorced from history and culture.[6]

The Dutch psychiatrist–historian J. H. van den Berg has written numerous books on this issue of the changing historical body, and he has complemented these works with several volumes concerning the changing reality of matter.[7] The matter of the body and of nature matter differently in different historical-cultural eras, and the physicist no less than the biologist discovers/creates the matter of his or her time. More recently, Jeremy Rifkin has proposed the same point in his book *Algeny*. Writing of Darwinian evolution he says that 'What Darwin discovered was not so much the truths of Nature as the operating assumptions of the industrial order . . .'[8] And most recently, in a *Science 85* article which argues for polyandry as a primate mating system replacing the older view of monogamous animal unions, the author David Abrahamson quotes the biologist John Fleagle, who says: 'You know what's going to be asked. Given that 50% of American marriages end in divorce, is there now a cultural bias toward finding "unstable" primate societies?'[9] We invent the body and the nature that we need. We invent the nature and the body which suit our world.

The body which we have invented suits our time. It is a body which belongs as much to our technological world as the bodies on the bronze doors of St Michael's belong to their world. It is a body which is as inseparable from the images of space flight and the nuclearization of matter as it is from the self of linear perspective vision. If we are to reclaim our continuing participation in and responsibility for the world in which we live and the self we have become, then we also have to remember our invention of this body. To nurture this remembrance, let us add one more illustration to these remarks about the invented character of the body. Through it we shall discover another important difference between the pantomimic and the anatomical body.

Figure 4.4 is Giotto's famous painting *Lamentation*, which dates from approximately 1305. Again, therefore, it is an old reminder, which should not be surprising. These old works stir memories, because it is in these works, predating the space of linear perspective vision, that the pantomimic or gestural body, which we live today forgetfully and which we dismiss as merely subjective, appears. It has not yet been covered over with the body of anatomy, the body which, as anatomical object, we regard as objective, and which, as such, has become for us the only body which is real.

Perhaps the first impression of the bodies of the figures contained in this painting is how *surrealistic* they appear to be. They seem to be caricatures of the body. They seem posed and exaggerated. Indeed, they appear to be like the cartoon figures we are so familiar with today.[10] Recall here, however, Gardner's earlier phrase regarding pantomimic bodies and note her remark that 'the instinct for pantomimic pose and gesture guides the representations and narratives of medieval art from the very beginning.'[11] Giotto's bodies, then, are very much like the bodies which adorn the bronze doors of St Michael's, Hildesheim. They too are pantomimic bodies and that is how we must read them. They are bodies which shape, define, gather, give form to, and/or outline an emotional situation. Or said more directly, these bodies *are* the e-motional outline and form of the situation. If they seem unreal to us, it is because *we* have become accustomed to defining the body apart from its situation. If Giotto's bodies seem unreal to us, it is because within that neutral, abstract, and geometric space of linear perspective vision we have invented a neutral, abstract, and anonymous body to place within that space.

Giotto's figures, however, are not *in* space. On the contrary, they are the genesis of a space, the pivot around which the e-motional space of a situation appears. If they seem unreal to us, it is because we have become accustomed to regarding the body as being *in* a situation and have thereby forgotten that the body *is* a situation. Giotto's figures can remind us of this fact, if we can open ourselves up to and reclaim the experienced sense of an embodied life which still exists for each of us 'beneath' the anonymous and neutral body of anatomy we have invented.

We *live* in the world with others as the pantomimic bodies which we are and not with the anatomical bodies which we have, and our language preserves for us the appearance and presence of the gestural, pantomimic body of daily life. We speak, for example, of people puffed with pride or swollen with rage, of tight-assed and tight-lipped individuals, of those bursting with good will or grasping at straws, of shrinking violets and those weighed down by the cares of the world, of people down in the dumps or higher than a kite. And we speak this way because that is what we see, not with the camera eyes of anatomy, but with living eyes attuned to others and coexisting with them *as* a situation. Giotto's bodies can recall us to the validity of these perceptions. Looking at them we can recover the felt bodily sense of lamentation, its posture, its wrenching agony, and through that specific reminder we can be awakened to the more general theme of the pantomimic body as an e-motional power to generate a situation and to prescribe a world.

To remember the body which one is, to recover beneath the 'official' body of anatomy the lived pantomimic body of daily life, is not, however, an easy task. At the very least it requires a tolerance for ambiguity, a respect for differences. Looking at the bodies of *Lamentation* and the body of the Little Cosmonaut requires that we see a *difference* rather than make a *judgement* about which is more or less real, or true, or accurate. Moreover, such attitudes of respect and tolerance are made even more difficult by the fact that a major difference between these bodies, between the pantomimic body and the anatomical body, challenges a major belief we have about the body as anatomical object. It is a difference which cuts even deeper than the one concerning the relation of the pantomimic body to its situation versus the neutrality of the anatomical body with respect to situations. Giotto's embodied figures, like the bodies on the bronze doors of St Micheal's, Hildesheim, are without an interior. The pantomimic body of long ago — and this is still true of the pantomimic body of today — does not have an interior in the sense of an anatomical and physiological inside which tells about (expresses) the outside. However, because we are so accustomed to the seemingly obvious fact that our bones, muscles, nerves, etc. are not only inside us, but also are what our bones, muscles, nerves, etc. *really* are, our ability to appreciate this *difference* is seriously impaired. Later in this chapter we shall see how we have arrived at this definition of the body as an

Figure 4.4 Giotto, *Lamentation*, Padua

interior space filled with organs which determines our relations to the world, and how this definition so uncritically accepted models, for example, our cosmetically covered, perfectly tanned, muscularly toned health spa bodies of today. For the moment, however, let us just acknowledge that the body, for example, whose muscles are shaped in a gym irrespective of the living situation of the person is a body whose muscles belong to and fit in *every* situation, and, therefore, neither belong to nor fit in *any* situation. Such muscles, unlike those of a construction worker, which in their difference from muscles of a college professor — or from the lack thereof — define the living situation of the individual, belong everywhere and therefore nowhere. Such muscles exist apart from any and every situation. They are in effect anonymous muscles which, having lost their place within the world, must take up their residence *within* the body.[12]

The body which we have invented to fit the space of the world opened up by linear perspective vision is a body of technical functioning. It is an anatomical object whose inside tells us of the outside, an immutable, anonymous body, detached from and indifferent to a situation, a body whose interior space is created and then stuffed with organs, a body whose interior darkness is progressively illuminated as we increase the distance between ourselves and our bodies. The genesis of this body begins with the corpse. The corpse is the first step in our invention or creation of the modern body whose culmination today is the body of the Little Cosmonaut, the body designed and prepared to depart the earth.

III The invention of the corpse

In the space of the world opened up by linear perspective vision there is reason and motive to abandon the body. A spectator self ensconced behind its window has no need for the body, and indeed, in dispensing with the body the spectator with his or her eye upon the world can rid himself or herself of all those extraneous enticing odors and sounds, textures and tastes, temperatures and rhythms which compose the world. In leaving the body behind, the self behind the window can better realize its vision of the world, a vision purified of the flesh, sterilized, if you will, a vision, we might say, without taste.

There is also reason and motive to abandon the body for a spectator self whose vision of the world is fixed upon an infinite horizon. A body whose eyes are drawn out and toward the sensuous world, an e-motional body sensitive to the allure of things, lingering over them, would be a hindrance to the realization of this fixed and infinite vision. Such a body, whose eyes would find the fulfillment of their vision in a movement toward the world, a body whose eyes would also be feet and hands, and nose, and ears, and skin, would be an obstacle. In much the same way, there is reason and motive to abandon the body for a self which, as it approaches the horizon, must shrink from the bottom up towards the head in order to fit within the space of the world opened up by linear perspective vision. The hegemony of the head leaves no room for the pantomimic body, for that body with its power to generate spaces, to create situations. Within the linear, and homogeneous, space of explanation, within that grid where all space has become equal and the same, the heterogeneous pantomimic body has no place.

It is a body, therefore, which we no longer need, a body which has become an obstacle; a body for which there is no place is a body ready to be abandoned. It is also, on the other side of this abandonment, a body ready to be reinvented. The corpse is the most visible image of the abandoned body. It is what the human body becomes in our increasing distance from it. It is what the pantomimic, e-motional body becomes for a spectator self behind a window with a heady vision fixed upon an infinite horizon. The corpse, whose destiny is the astronautic body of technical functioning, is also the most dramatic and historically accurate first step in our re-invention of the body. It is an invention which begins with a certain way of looking at the body, with the anatomical gaze.[13]

A   The anatomical gaze and the corpse

The corpse is an image of the abandoned body and a way of imagining the body as abandoned. It is a vision of the body, a specific way of looking at the body. It is a perspective which, in focusing on the body itself as a spectacle for observation, *isolates* the body from its living context or situation and *fragments* the body which it sees. That vision which isolates and fragments, that vision out of which the corpse is generated, is the anatomical gaze.

We are already familiar with this gaze through our earlier discussion of the grid through which the spectator self veils its vision of the world. Alberti's grid is intended to organize the visible world into a geometric composition, and the consequent geometrization of vision has the effect of decomposing the visible whole into parts. The artist portrayed earlier in Figure 3.2 is already practicing the anatomical gaze. He is the self behind a window looking at a world which has already been divided and subdivided into parts.

The corpse is the consequence of this anatomical gaze, a way of looking practiced within the space of linear perspective vision. That this gaze both *isolates* the body from its given situation by placing it within the pre-established, neutral, and homogeneous space of the geometric grid, and *fragments* the body within this space is already evident in Albrecht Dürer's illustration, *Artist Drawing a Nude Through a Gridded Screen* (Figure 4.5).[14]

The reclining body of the woman in this illustration is clearly the focus of observation. Viewed through the grid, her body is able to be mapped onto

Figure 4.5 Albrecht Dürer, *Artist Drawing a Nude through a Gridded Screen*

Reproduced by permission of Marburg/Art Resource, New York

the geometric space reproduced upon the artist's table. Seen in this fashion, her body now belongs to that space, a space which in its mathematical homogeneity is neutral and indifferent to the body's living situation. This space fits all bodies, as it were. One space suits any and every body, and in this sense it suits no specific or particular body at all. In making the body a focus of geometric vision, in fixing it as a spectacle for the measuring eye, the anatomical gaze depicted in this illustration cuts the relation between the living, pantomimic, e-motional body and its specific situations. The relation of body and world is dis-membered by this anatomical gaze.

Moreover, the body itself which is mapped onto the world created by this gaze is dis-membered. Filtered through the grid, the body enters into the geometric space of linear perspective vision in pieces. Recall here Alberti's words describing the advantages in drawing a body viewed through the grid. He says 'for just as you see the forehead in one parallel, the nose in the next, the cheeks in another, the chin in one below, and everything else in its particular place, so you can situate precisely all the features on the panel or wall which you have similarly divided into appropriate parallels.'[15] The advantage of the anatomical gaze is that the body can be more precisely mapped or scaled if it is broken into parts. And that is precisely what Dürer's artist is doing. The body of the reclining woman enters in fragments into the world opened up by the artist's vision. It is a divided body which is created by the anatomical gaze and which belongs to this world. The anatomical gaze as an inherent feature of linear perspective vision creates a body which, in being dis-membered with respect to its situation, is an isolated spectacle, and which, in being dis-membered with respect to itself, is a fragmented specimen. In short, we can say that the corpse created by the anatomical gaze is a *spectacular, dis-membered specimen*.

Later we will show in detail how the body as corpse is indeed a dis-membered spectacle and specimen. At the moment, however, it is important that we recognize once again that what began as an artistic invention has become a cultural habit of mind. The anatomical gaze inherent within Alberti's invention and intended as a technical advantage for the artist has become a way of knowing. The body of the reclining woman in Dürer's illustration *became* the corpse. To appreciate this difference between the invention and its reception, between Alberti's and Dürer's vision and what has been made of it, between the seed, which they and others planted and how it has been nurtured, consider the illustration, also by Dürer, presented in Figure 4.6.

Here, without any doubt, is the dis-membered body. It is, beyond any question, a body which is a spectacle and a specimen. But as such it is not quite yet the corpse it will become. On the contrary, it is Dürer's projection of the ideal nude. Indeed, for Dürer the power of the anatomical gaze is, in the words of John Berger, inseparable from a belief that 'the ideal nude ought to be constructed by taking the face of one body, the breasts of another, the legs of a third, the shoulders of a fourth, the hands of a fifth — and so on.' And for Dürer, 'the result would glorify Man.' Berger, however, sharply disagrees, because he sees within Dürer's ideal 'a remarkable indifference to who any one person really was.'[16] For Berger, there is already present in Dürer's ideal a prescription for the murder of the body in pornographic vision.

I think, however, that Berger goes too far, because even if there is within Dürer's ideal the prescription for such things, it is others who have come later who have filled that prescription, and we who continue it. Linear perspective vision projects a possible space for the world. Brunelleschi, Alberti, Dürer, and others open up a space of possibility. If, therefore, we can envision within the ideal of Dürer a harbinger of a being like Frankenstein, a creature also composed of many parts, then it falls upon us to understand our participation in, and to acknowledge our responsibility for, the ways in which we have taken up this invention and continue to develop its possibilities. If within the space opened up by linear perspective vision the body does fall apart and does become a corpse, then it is because we have grown indifferent to this spectacle in the way we daily practice our anatomical vision, in the way in which, as a spectator self behind the window, we increasingly practice a distancing and detached vision which fragments the body into a spectacular dis-membered specimen.

B   The corpse as spectacular dis-membered specimen

In the space of linear perspective vision the spectacular nature of the body, its primary identification as a spectacle, is quite evident. Over there on the other side of the window-grid, the body is an object to be seen. Over there, placed within the neutral, homogeneous space of geometrical perspective

Figure 4.6   Albrecht Dürer, *Anatomical Studies*

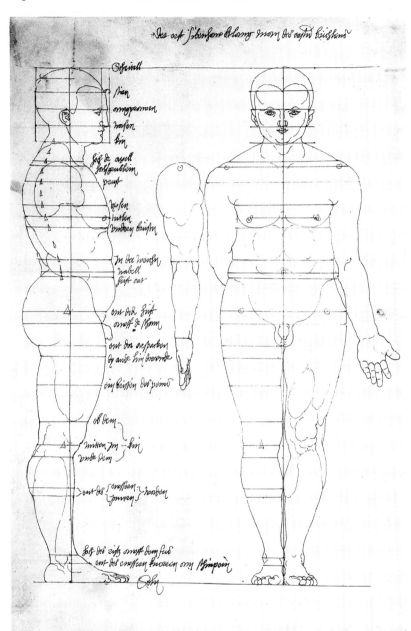

Reproduced by permission of The Harvard University Art Museums (Fogg Art Museum), bequest of Charles A. Loeser

and thereby displaced from its natural context or setting, the body is primarily a matter for the eye alone.

That the body as *corpse* belongs to this same spectacular space, that it too has its primary identification as a spectacle, is attested to by one of those ironic historical connections which weave together the fabric of an age. William S. Heckscher, in a remarkable book entitled *Rembrandt's Anatomy of Dr Nicolaas Tulp*, tells us that formal anatomies, which were primarily annual events, play a significant role in the development of the stage. These 'annual anatomies were spectacles open to the public', he writes, and 'The ordinary citizen, in order to be admitted to the anatomy, had to purchase an entrance ticket.' The first such mention of a ticket, he notes, occurs in 1497 for an anatomy performed at Padua, and Heckscher adds that 'It appears quite likely that the sale of tickets to those wishing to attend public anatomies preceded the sale of ordinary theater tickets by several years and may have even encouraged theatrical confraternities to follow suit.'[17] Whether or not Heckscher is correct about this sequence, the important point for our tale is this cultural connection between the corpse and the stage. How better to illustrate the spectacular nature of the body as corpse, its nature as spectacle, than to recognize this connection between the anatomist's dissecting table and the stage of performance? Within the context of this connection, and quite dramatically, the corpse appears as something to observe, as a thing to be watched. Moreover, placed within the context of theater, the corpse appears not only as a spectacle but also as a dramatic event, as a work of art. In this regard, the corpse is very much a work of invention. The body anatomized as corpse upon the stage of the dissecting table is as much a piece of created fiction as it is discovered fact. The body observed on the stage of the dissecting table belongs as much to the realm of art as it does to science.

A stage is a place of imagination and thus the connection between corpse and stage supports an earlier suggestion that the corpse is a way of imagining the body. The corpse is, if you will, a dream about the body which, as we have said, imagines the body as dis-membered in two ways. On one hand, this dream is a way of imagining the body as isolated or cut off from its natural context or situation. On the other hand, this dream is a way of imagining the body as fragmented within itself, as a specimen.

This dream of the body as corpse is not, however, an illusion and what is dreamed about the body in this way has become fact. By contrasting two illustrations of the body in textbooks of anatomy, one of which lies on this side of the appearance of the spectator self and the space of linear perspective vision, and the other on the further side of this development, we can demonstrate the transformation of this dream into fact. The difference shows the change from a body which even in death remains relational and remains whole to a corpse which is a dis-membered spectacle and specimen.

The first illustration, Figure 4.7, is a woodcut of the physician Andreas

Figure 4.7 *Andreas Vesalius Demonstrating a Dissected Arm*, woodcut

Reproduced by permission of Art Resource, New York

Figure 4.8 Guy de Parc, *Figure d'anatomie*, Chantilly, Musée de Condi

Vesalius in the year 1542. The artist is Johann Stephan von Calcar and the portrait which he offers here of Vesalius is included in Vesalius' revolutionary text, *De humani corporis fabrica libri septem*, published in 1543. Much of my discussion of this illustration (and the next one) is indebted to van den Berg's work, *Medical Power and Medical Ethics*.[18] In addition, I have discussed in an earlier work[19] the significance of Vesalius' text, and here I wish to say only that it is in Vesalius' work that we find the origins of our modern anatomical approach to the body. Vesalius' work, which begins the rupture with the older Galenic tradition of the body, is, therefore, a decisive moment in the invention of the corpse.

The second illustration, Figure 4.8, taken from a work by Guy de Parc, presents a drawing from a fourteenth-century text by the physician Vigevano. While nearly two hundred years separate these two physicians they are in fact separated by more than time. Indeed, they inhabit two different worlds and Vesalius, in spite of the measure of time, is closer to us than he is to Vigevano because we share his world. In the time span between these two physicians, the corpse is invented.

Let us begin our discussion by noticing the differences depicted in their postures, the way in which each figure incarnates his stance towards the body. The earlier anatomist, perhaps Vigevano himself, is looking at the body. More specifically he is looking at the face and, we might even say, at the closed eyes of this body. This in itself is astonishing, because as van den Berg notes, 'here is the first incision in the history of Western anatomy.'[20] The physician who performs this revolutionary act is not, however, looking at the knife which makes this incision in order to open the body. What are we to make of this attitude? Apparently the dissection is *not* the primary matter here. Something else matters more.

That something else is the *relationship* which is portrayed here between the physician and the body. It is portrayed in two ways: first, by the eyes of the physician which look at the closed eyes of the body, and second, by the left hand of the physician which encircles the body from behind, as if to support it. There is in the physician's left hand, as van den Berg notes, 'a certain familiarity in the way it touches the body.' In both of these ways, through eyes and hand, a bond is formed between the physician and the body, and we who view this illustration are, as it were, witnesses to that relationship. Of course, it is true, as van den Berg says, that the relationship 'is not a particularly mutual one.'[21] That would be impossible, since the physician is holding a body which is quite dead. And yet there persists in the relationship, as evidenced again by the physician's look and touch, an echo of mutuality, a dim reminder of a reciprocity that once was there. Perhaps we might say, therefore, that the body which the physician so carefully regards and holds here is a memorial body.

Notice now the posture of the physician Vesalius. Again, it is true that the physician here is not looking at the incision. But it is also true that he is not looking at the body. Rather he is looking at us, the viewers.

With regard to the former point we must say that he is not looking at the incision because the incision has already been made, and in this respect, with regard to the latter point, Vesalius, in looking at us, is inviting us to see what he sees. The bond here is *not* between the physician and the body. It is rather between the physician, who has already observed the incision, and us, who are invited to be observers. The physician has, as it were, already parted company with the body, which becomes now for both of us an object to be seen. The body has been placed over there, within a space equally distant from the physician who has opened it and we who observe it.

It is, however, not quite correct to speak of the body, for there is no body here. Vesalius, as I said above, does not look at the body as the earlier anatomist does, because there is no body to see. There is, rather, a piece of a body, and it is a part of the body which the physician Vesalius holds. It is an arm. In looking at us, therefore, Vesalius is inviting us to observe a fragment of the body. Whereas earlier we are invited to be witnesses of a relationship between the physician and the whole body, here we are invited to be, with the physician, an observer of a part of a body which has become a *specimen*.

The reading of these two illustrations does not intend a judgement. Vesalius is neither more correct about what he sees nor less sympathetic about the body than the physician which Vigevano depicted. On the contrary, they inhabit different worlds and their respective attitudes reflect a change in what the body has become. The body which Vigevano's physician holds still belongs to a world. It is still a relational body, and still whole. It is, if you will, a pantomimic, e-motional body which has died. Vesalius, on the other hand, holds a fragment of a body which has no world. He holds, if you will, a newly invented body, one which he himself has helped to create. He holds a corpse.

Our discussion of these two illustrations has led us to this interesting difference: Vigevano's physician holds a dead body, while Vesalius holds a corpse. The corpse is decidedly different from the dead body. A dead body is a memorial of a relationship which once was and now has been broken, and in testimony to this memory we bury the dead body. We do not, however, memorially bury a corpse. In inventing the corpse, then, we have changed our relationship to death. Our tale of what the body becomes for a spectator self within the space opened up by linear perspective vision is, therefore, also a tale about what death becomes for the self within this space.

Soon we shall follow our story in this direction, but for the moment let us emphasize that the difference between Vigevano's and Vesalius' attitudes indicates that the corpse is invented on the condition that we depart from the dead body. Only in the distance which we establish between ourselves and the dead body is the body opened up to become a corpse. It might very well be the case, therefore, that the distance which the spectator puts between himself or herself and the body is a distance between the spectator self and death. Indeed, it might even be the case that the story of technology as a distance from the matter of earth and body might very well be a story in which our distance from death bespeaks a denial of death. Our astronautic condition, through whose reinvented body we are able to discover a wish or a dream of reincarnation, might very well be a flight from death. Certainly, as we have already heard, images of death and destruction, like the nuclear fires of annihilation, do haunt and shadow our dreams of escape.

C The dead body and the corpse

The difference between a dead body and a corpse is not one which we usually make explicit, and yet this difference makes a difference. It makes a difference in the conduct of our lives and it is a difference whose awareness, so to speak, we carry in our bones. We have no need in life, therefore, to make the difference thematic because it is there in the center of our living. To be a living human being is to know this difference between a dead body and a corpse.

1 Burying the dead body

Whereas Vesalius holds before us an arm for our inspection, the earlier physician is holding a dead body. With his eyes and his hand this earlier physician is maintaining a kind of contact with the dead body. There is, as it were, between them a recognition of a once shared mutuality. There is in his gestures and his attitudes something of a statement which says, 'Here, once, there was a living person who is now quite dead.' These gestures remember that bond and in doing so they acknowledge the memorial character of the dead body.

The dead body is a memory. It is a memory of the person and of the relations of that person to us who now say farewell to his or her body. This is the body that we bury, and the grave that is prepared to receive this body is the place of remembrance. Indeed, the grave may very well be the first instance of memory in the transition to the human species, for we are the only species who bury the dead in a fashion which marks it as a ritual. We mark a site in a special way and we prepare in one way or another the dead body which we lay in the grave for a journey. In doing so we acknowledge a continuing kinship with the person of this body. It is, to be sure, an invisible kinship, or rather, a kinship with what is invisible. Gathered around the grave we acknowledge this kinship. We bury a dead body and we promise to remember.

The promise to remember is, moreover, an implicit act of faith in the future. It is a declaration of hope, as it were, in a future. Gathered around the grave, engaged in the ritual of burying a dead body, we silently declare

124

that as human beings we live in time in a way which is essentially different from all other creatures of the earth. Burying a dead body we implicitly acknowledge a connection between present, past, and future. In the ritual of burial we silently bear witness to a deep-seated belief that in every present moment there is always the possibility to remember the past and to imagine a future.

We bury a dead body; we do not bury a corpse. We bury a dead person because he or she is more than a specimen, because he or she is a memory, perhaps even a haunting memory, and we become memorial creatures, creatures capable of memory and imagination, of promise and of hope, because we bury the dead. In all these respects we are born as human beings at the site of the grave. Memory is kin to death. With the awareness of death comes the power of remembrance and the pain, since every act of remembrance is always a little taste of death. In inventing the corpse, then, do we run the risk of forgetting the dead body and in doing so the risk of forgetting to remember? Does the invention of the corpse betray a wish, unrecognized and implicit, to cut ourselves free of the past, to live without tradition, to overcome the pain of remembrance? Does the invention of the corpse reveal and conceal a wish to forget death? The Renaissance, which is the name which we give to the age which spans the creation of linear perspective vision and the invention of the corpse, means a rebirth. Does the image of the body as corpse indicate a rebirth which would forget death?

What has already been said and what remains to be said in our story, answers Yes to this question. So too, it seems, does the conduct of our lives in a technological world. We are born as human beings at the site of the grave, in the act of remembrance. We are born, therefore, in the shadow of death. Birth and death are the polarities of life. In our age, however, we make life the opposite of death. We pursue life, we hold on to it at almost any cost, and in this respect the corpse, as the body invented to fit the space of linear perspective vision, as the body whose destiny is the neurochemical body of technical functioning, becomes a psychological symptom of our technological age. It is a symptom because, like all symptoms of our psychological lives, it disguises what we wish for and what we dream. The corpse is a symptom which simultaneously reveals and conceals the dream of the spectator self to depart from the matter of earth and body, the wish of this spectator self to distance itself from, to forget, death. It is the guise under which we pursue our hopes for a life without death. Soon we shall see how this corpse haunts two contemporary images of the body in our culture, the medical body and the pornographic body, but for the moment let us close these remarks on the corpse as symptom with an admonition to acknowledge the symptom. If we do so, then we can make a disturbing but necessary discovery: the corpse, in hiding death from us, is our grim image of life. It is the cold, pale reminder of the life without death we would pursue.

2 The corpse hides death

The dead body stinks. It rots and it decays. It putrefies and decomposes. It *smells* of death. It is a banquet table set for worms.

Without a doubt the dead body makes death tangibly present. It announces death in a *sense-able* way. Death here is not only visible to the eye, it is also present in a more intimate fashion. Death enters us through a dead body with every breath we take. We breathe death in. It becomes part of us. Van den Berg, in commenting on the Vigevano illustration, makes this point. 'The dead body beside Vigevano is a decomposing dead body, not a corpse. He exists as a person exists when he has died (we should like to forget it): smelling, rotting.'[22] Is this why Vigevano's incision reveals nothing? Is this why the earlier physician in opening the body does not *see* anything? Is there nothing yet to see because death is still so overpowering in its presence? To *see* the body as a corpse, or perhaps we should say, to transform the body into an object of vision, requires that we first eliminate the smell and the taste of death. It requires that we distance ourselves from its foul odors, and we have, it seems, succeeded quite well. We have deodorized and sanitized death. We have transformed it almost into pure spectacle. Through the medium of the electronic eye of television, for example, one can watch a slaughter from a safe distance, whether it be as news or entertainment. We can watch death, look at it, without being touched by it. It has been removed. It has become unimaginable.

A cultural–historical piece of evidence which confirms the claim that with the invention of the corpse we distance ourselves from the dead body is offered in Phillip Aries' impressive work on the history of death in western culture. It concerns the relocation of cemeteries outside the city, which begins near the end of the sixteenth century, becomes quite apparent throughout the seventeenth century and continues well into the eighteenth. In commenting on this relocation, Aries notes that it is a 'transformation of space, and above all [a] detachment and negligence with regard to the dead [which] has a psychological significance.'[23]

Already in the sixteenth, but especially throughout the seventeenth and the eighteenth centuries, a new olfactory dislike for the smell of cemeteries emerges. Not only is the stench noticeable and newly intolerable, it is also threatening. In a recent article Ivan Illich, citing Aries, says that 'The miasma emanating from graves was declared dangerous to the living,' and he adds that 'During the third quarter of the [eighteenth] century reports that people die directly from olfactory experiences become commonplace.'[24] But this newly emerging sensitivity to the smell of buried bodies can come about only because there has already been a cultural–psychological shift toward a body that is meant to solicit only the eye. This newly formed sensibility points back to an earlier retreat or withdrawal from the body. The smell of buried bodies is the smell of rotting, decomposing bodies, odors which are memories of a body we would leave behind. The campaigns to remove these bodies beyond the city are, therefore, psychological efforts at forgetting. They are, in the political arena, complementary to the psychological act of distancing which marks the anatomical gaze, the gaze which transforms the dead body into a corpse. In removing the dead bodies from the city, we distance ourselves from the smell of death, and in doing so we transform the decomposing dead body into a corpse. In the transformation of space we reveal our detachment and distance from death. The corpse which would hide death is the body now buried in a different and more distant place. The stinking, rotting, decaying dead body which is buried outside the city is a corpse.

Emile Cioran has noted that 'physiology and filth are interchangeable terms.'[25] Death stinks, but so too does life — no, that is too exaggerated. Life has its own smells and we know the difference. The body sweats in labor and in joy. It smells of passion and of pain, and each emotion, like the sweet smell of success, has its own odor. To invent the corpse we have had to distance ourselves from the stench of death, but in doing so we have also distanced ourselves from the smell and the taste of life. The change in burial practices which Aries cites indicates, therefore, another aspect of the corpse. It indicates that the corpse hides not only death but also life.

To appreciate this fact that the corpse hides life as well as death we need only look again at the illustration of Vesalius and notice the arm which he is holding. It is beyond any doubt the arm of a corpse and it is quite without life. 'Yet this same arm, this extremely dead arm,' van den Berg writes, 'lacks every trace of death.' Death is absent here. It has been banished. It is in exile. This arm has not been touched by death. 'Nothing has faded,' van den Berg notes. There are no signs of decomposition. Indeed, 'the arm even has tension, the tension of life', and 'We might be inclined to say: *the arm lives.*'[26] We might be inclined in this direction, but finally we would be unable to do so, because that arm, the arm of the corpse, is quite lifeless. The arm of the corpse hides death but without giving a sign of life. This arm shows no trace of death, but it is also without life.

'With the beginning of anatomy,' van den Berg writes, 'the distinction between life and death became obscure.'[27] The fragment of the corpse held by Vesalius shows the obscurity. The corpse removes the smell of death, and in this respect it departs from the dead body. But it also removes the smell of life, and in this respect the corpse becomes the only thing that it can become: neither a living nor a dead body, but a lifeless thing. As that cold, pale reminder of the life without death we would pursue, as the grim image of life which guides our age, the corpse offers us, therefore, a new and strange kind of life. It offers a life which is divorced from both birth and death, a sanitized life, as purified and cleansed of the smell of death as it is distant and detached from the mess of life. It offers, in short, a life which is destined to become a mechanism, a life in which the Vesalian corpse will soon become a machine.

Our tale of the body will soon take us to a consideration of this and other developments of the corpse. Prior to this consideration, however, let us note just one curious historical example of a distaste for the smell of life which could have arisen only after the invention of the corpse.

In a remarkable brief essay on the history of water, Ivan Illich notes that 'the perception of the city as a place that must be constantly deodorized by washing has a clearly defined origin in history: it appears at the time of the early enlightenment.' It is for the enlightenment consciousness, for a self which, behind its window, has transformed the world into a matter of light (the light of reason), that the city is 'for the first time perceived as an evil smelling place.'[28] It is for such an enlightened self that 'an odorless city' becomes a utopian dream.

This dream, moreover, is born within a cultural–historical 'transformation of sense perception': 'The new interest in scrubbing and cleaning,' Illich notes, 'is primarily concerned with the removal of features which are not so much visually ugly as objectionable in an olfactory sense.'[29] In an age when the world has already become primarily an object of vision, the world's odors become an annoying distraction, a persistent and disturbing reminder. It can be only for a self which has already distanced itself from the body in its retreat to the eye that the nose and the foul odors of the world can become a thematic and disturbing concern. For such a self the odorous quality of the world and the olfactory dimension of existence can be only a *humiliation*, a distasteful reminder of the material (earthy) condition of life. The enlightenment dreams and schemes to wash the city clean of its odors already attests, therefore, to a retreat from the body. They affirm that style of window consciousness which in placing itself as a spectator of the world can only turn up its nose, as it were, at the smell of the world. These dreams and schemes to rid life of its odors can be imagined only by a self which in its wish to distance itself from life and death has invented the corpse.[30]

3 The corpse as a body of interior space stuffed with organs

The corpse is neither a dead body nor a living body. It is neither a body which is buried nor a body with a place within the world. On the contrary, it is a body apart from the world, and a body whose interior spaces are filled with organs which define the mechanisms of life. It is a body which has developed an interior, an inside which now tells about the outside, an interior whose space is progressively mapped and chartered as locations of heart and kidneys, lungs and stomach, bones and blood, muscles and nerves. The dead body, in contrast, has no such interior space. It is, rather, a gelatinous, amorphous mass. There are no organs inside a dead body. There are no bones or muscles in that interior space. Muscle and bone, blood and nerve, organ and location appear when the dead body is made into a corpse. They appear on the condition of our withdrawal or retreat from the dead body, that distance which allows us to become spectators of a body which has become a specimen. They appear, finally, provided that we have taken up the anatomical gaze which in dis-membering the body fragments it into parts whose technical functions are disconnected from and indifferent to a living situation.

We are, however, so accustomed to the view that our bones and muscles, heart and lungs, blood and nerves are on the inside that it is difficult to remember the fact that the organs which we locate in this fashion belong to a special body, a corpse, which has been displaced from the world and whose organs therefore bear no relation to a living situation. To appreciate this difference between the corpse and the dead body, between a body whose interior space is stuffed with organs and a body with no organs on the inside, we need to see it. Let us return once again, therefore, to the illustrations of Vesalius and Vigevano, because simply on inspection it is clear that this difference does exist between these two bodies. Look at the body which Vigevano's physician holds. It is quite clearly a body which reveals no inside. Now look at the body, or the piece of it, which Vesalius holds. This body displays an arm whose interior is known to us all. We know this arm and yet it is an arm which is quite unfamiliar and even alien to us.

The arm which Vesalius displays to us is an opened arm, a dissected limb, whose interior muscles cover bone, and right now at this moment any reader can feel these same muscles within his or her own skin. Such an exercise, however, would be marked by the special conditions already narrated in our story, and it would not represent the usual experience which we have of our muscular arms. For in daily life the muscles of a person's arm are not interior organs but relations to a situation. One ordinarily feels one's muscles not inside the body but in the tasks which are undertaken. They are, for example, in this pen which writes these words, just as later this afternoon they may be in the shovel which will seed the lawn for the coming spring. In this respect one's muscles, like one's bones and blood, perpetually efface themselves before the tasks at hand. They give themselves over to, and perhaps we might even say sacrifice themselves, for the sake of the things which we do. The organs of the living body, like those of its opposite the dead body, are not inside the body. On the contrary, the organs of the living body lose themselves in and co-mingle with the world.

Between these muscles of the living arm and those of the corpse which Vesalius displays there is a world of difference. The former belong to a world, to a situation, and are even defined by it. The latter, those of the Vesalian arm, belong nowhere. They have no living world. They belong, as it were, to any and every situation because they belong to no situation.[31] They are anonymous muscles. Unlike the muscles of the living arm, which in effacing themselves before a world are, so to speak, *pre-personal*, these anonymous muscles of the corpse are and remain *impersonal*. They are, if you wish, muscles without identity or character, and in this respect, and unlike the pre-personal muscles of one's living body, they never give shape to one's character nor contribute to the formation of one's identity. A man, for example, who out of some petty spite or poisonous hatred has held himself rigid and aloof from others, carries the mark and style of this passion as a posture of muscle and bone, and assuredly his muscles differ from those of one who, in a welcoming embrace, has held his arms open and has extended them towards the world. We know this difference. We feel it in our bones, as we say, and we can even see it. We know the difference between these e-motional muscles which, in being solicited by a world, form and give shape to a situation, and those other muscles of the corpse. The e-motional muscles of the living body are drawn out of themselves in relation to the mood, texture, and tone, the feeling, of a situation, and, as such, change so that the arm which embraces a friend is decidedly different from the one which wards off an enemy. Like the humble arms of St Joseph (Figure 4.1) or the figures of lamentation painted by Giotto (Figure 4.4) which we saw earlier, the muscles of a living arm belong to a whole, non-fragmented body whose pantomimic gestures generate the living space of a human situation. Compared with these muscles, we can say that those which Vesalius displays for our gaze are non e-motional: as a fragment of a dismembered body they have been detached from any living human situation and are not capable of being drawn out by the world. As such, these muscles, we might say, have no feel for a situation. An arm, moved by such muscles, can do or handle anything. Its touch, with the connection between body and world already broken, will not register a difference. Its touch will be indifferent to what it touches. It will only perform a function.

In describing this difference between the corpse and the dead (and living) body, I am suggesting that the body develops an interior space stuffed with organs when it is opened, or more precisely, when we withdraw from it and make it an object of the anatomical gaze. It is this condition of retreat, this creation of a distance, which establishes muscle and bone, nerve and blood, as matters of the inside. Van den Berg makes this connection between the anatomization of the body and the creation of an interior space quite explicit. Contrasting the muscles and bones of the living body with those of the corpse, he says that these latter muscles and bones are ' "manufactured" '. These muscles, bones and organs 'only come into existence through dissection.' 'They acquire their shape,' he says, 'when the dissecting knife penetrates the body.' The knife, as an instrument of the anatomical gaze, cuts into the body *and* creates its interior. 'Muscles, blood vessels, nerves, all this crystallizes at the touch of the penetrating metal.' In contact with this knife, muscles which heretofore were lived as e-motional relations with the world contract, condense, and congeal as fibers, as those muscles which Vesalius displays. But before this contact these muscles do not exist. They are, in van den Berg's analogy, as non-existent as crystals in a supersaturated solution are before a probe is introduced. 'Muscles and bones come into existence . . . when the dead person [the dead body and the living body] has become a corpse.'[32]

But is van den Berg's conviction and the story we are telling here correct? Can it actually be the case that the invention of the corpse is co-relative with the creation of a body with interior organs that are anonymous, impersonal, and non-emotional? Were there, as we suggested earlier about the bodies which belong to the world of Giotto and the world depicted on the bronze doors of St Michael's, Hildesheim, no such interior organs before the corpse appeared? Were there no such interior organs before the invention of the corpse, just as there are no interior organs (even today) apart from the condition of our withdrawal and retreat from the body? Again, this is a part of our story which seems too fantastic to believe.

To reply to these questions let us consider again the earlier example of the arm which loses itself in the task of shoveling. It is easy enough to imagine in this instance a moment in time when the shovel, having already been lifted with its weight of dirt many times, becomes too heavy to lift again. At that moment my arms ache and it is quite certain that I feel that ache right here in the muscles within my arms. Is this not proof enough that my muscles do lie *within* the body? Does not the soreness of my aching arms convince me of the correctness of Vesalius' vision?

We are apt to answer quickly here, perhaps even too quickly, and in our haste we would pass over an important consideration. To avoid doing so, let us use a second example before giving our reply.

Imagine that in the act of shoveling an accident of some sort occurs and that as a consequence I cut my arm. The blood flows from the open wound and in that instant when the skin is penetrated it seems once again that the vision of the body as an interior space filled with organs is verified. There is the blood to prove the accuracy of that vision. Should I be so unfortunate as to experience a more traumatic wound so that bone breaks the skin in addition to blood, then I even have a third instance which demonstrates the interiority of the body. Broken bone, bleeding wound, and aching muscles all bear witness to the same reality of my body as an interior space filled with organs.

I have given three examples here because, while they *appear* to confirm the Vesalian vision of the anatomical body, in actuality they bear witness to the fact that this vision rests upon a very *special and specific condition*. In each case there is a *disruption* of my ongoing activity with the world. Either a bone is broken, or an arm is cut, or a muscle is strained, but in each instance my body's connection with the world and with the task at hand is broken. Thus the examples, which at first glance appear to verify the vision of the Vesalian anatomical body, actually demonstrate the fact that this vision rests upon that specific and special condition of the living body's broken connection with the world. It turns out to be the case, therefore, that the anatomical vision of the body as an interior space filled with organs isolates this special condition of the body's disrupted relation with the world and raises it to the level of method. Indeed the invention of the corpse upon the grounds of this specific condition of disruption does even more: it transforms this condition into an epistemology, into a way of knowing which defines what is real. The anatomized body, which displays for the observer bone and blood, muscle and nerve, organ and location as matters of the inside, *is* the living body in its severed relation with the world. It is *that moment* in the living human body's history which is selected, isolated, and emphasized in the anatomical gaze. And it is that body, broken, wounded, and ill, which the invention of the corpse enthrones as the real human body. Anatomy, which, as Barbara Duden emphasizes in a brief but important article on the history of the body, literally means dismemberment, rests upon a disruption of the human body's ongoing relations with the world.[33]

IV Conclusion

The invention of the corpse, the body which as specimen is suited to the spectator within the space of linear perspective vision, eclipses the dead body and the living body. In offering us an image of life as mechanism, as technical function, the corpse hides death and conceals the living body as an e-motional involvement and relation with the world. The living body so concealed does not, however, simply disappear. It continues beneath this concealment a kind of shadow life. Nor does the corpse remain a static invention. On the contrary, it has a history of various disguises through which it enters the stage of the modern world. Indeed, there is a connection and even an interplay between this history of the abandoned body, the corpse, and its shadows, and our tale now turns in this direction.

Chapter five

The abandoned body and its shadows

I Introduction

This portion of the story is a promisory note, for I can do no more here than sketch out in the very briefest way the history of the corpse and its shadows. To tell the full tale would require a story in its own right, a story which would require that we stay together for at least as long as and perhaps even longer than we have so far. Nevertheless, as brief and as incomplete as this sketch will be, it is worthwhile and even necessary to include it, because without it the image of the corpse would remain a pale abstraction. We need, therefore, to get at least a feel for the corpse's descendants, for its family including the shadow side — the skeletons, so to speak, in the closet.

II The corpse and its shadows: a family tree

The chart presented in Figure 5.1 presents a rough and incomplete genealogy of the abandoned body and its shadows. Before I introduce the family members, however, it is necessary to indicate the limit of my analogy of a family tree. Unlike an actual genealogical chart where the relation between predecessor and successor is linear and unidirectional — you are the successor of your parents whose predecessors are their parents, etc. — the shape of this family chart is a spiral. Each member, therefore, continues its presence in the next. Or rather, each member re-figures those who have gone before and pre-figures those who are about to come. Thus we might say that the corpse *begets* the machine, while the machine 're-members' the corpse and further imagines it as reflex. Moreover, I use this rather old-fashioned term 'beget' in order to emphasize this continuing, dynamic relation between all the family members. For example, in being begotten by your parents, you have probably been told somewhere along the line and by someone how very much you resemble and act like your dead grandmother. Indeed, at times this resemblance may even feel to be downright spooky, as if through you grandma has reappeared. A straight genealogical chart misses these emotional, psychological contagions. In the beginning, I want

Figure 5.1 The abandoned body and the shadows of the abandoned body

CORPSE — resurrected as — MACHINE — reanimated via — REFLEX — to become — INDUSTRIAL — as ROBOT — earth as — ASTRONAUT
(1425–   (1628)   (1641)   WORKER   (1928)   depart   (1945)
1543)   (1700s–
                                             1848)

THRESHOLD OF REMEMBRANCE AND BARRIER OF REPRESSION: BODY AS SYMPTOM

- -

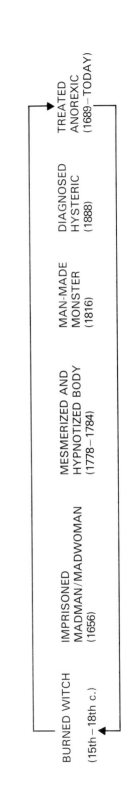

BURNED WITCH   IMPRISONED   MESMERIZED AND   MAN-MADE   DIAGNOSED   TREATED
                 MADMAN/MADWOMAN   HYPNOTIZED BODY   MONSTER   HYSTERIC   ANOREXIC
(15th–18th c.)   (1656)   (1778–1784)   (1816)   (1888)   (1689–TODAY)

to insist upon these continuous and contagious interrelations among all family members in this history. It is a family drama which is presented here, a drama which stretches across many generations.

A second introductory note is also in order. The line which divides the chart in two is a line of silence. Later we will learn more about the dynamic character of this line, but for the moment let us say only that the family members below this line are rather like the black sheep of a family. They are the embarrassing members that no one really wants to speak about, painful reminders of things the official family members have ignored and would rather forget. In presenting the family drama, then, I shall divide the story into two parts, and for descriptive purposes I will speak about the official and the unofficial family.

III The official family's cast of characters

A   The anatomized corpse

The year is 1543. The anatomized corpse lies on a dissecting table, a pale, cold, motionless object of vision for physician and observer. It is not a dead body but it lacks any spark of life. In this same year, when Vesalius dissects the body and thereby lays the foundation for the modern anatomical body, Copernicus sets the earth in motion around the sun. This marks, as I have argued elsewhere,[1] a radical shift in humanity's cultural–psychological life, and this conjunction of moving earth and corpse is most applicable. On an earth in motion the living human body has no place, and we are taught, even today, the difference between what our living enfleshed eyes see, a glorious sunrise, an awe-inspiring sunset, and what is known to be the truth, the earth in orbit around the sun, which itself is in motion in the swirling Milky Way galaxy. Indeed, to set the earth in motion Copernicus had to forget the evidence of his sensuous body, a feat for which Galileo gave him much praise. Copernicus had to abandon his body, he had to leave it behind, he had to become, so to speak, the first astronaut. The body thus abandoned is that corpse which we met in the previous chapter. It is that corpse lying motionless on Vesalius' dissecting table.

B   The corpse resurrected as machine

The anatomized corpse is, however, only a first step in inventing a body to fit the Copernican earth. To keep pace with a moving earth the corpse itself will have to be set in motion. When, in the geometrical space of the heavens, the earth begins to move as astronomical object, the body as anatomical object will have to move in a similar fashion.

The Copernican earth revolves around the sun. It circles it. It circulates through the heavens, and its motion is a mathematically regulated harmony.

In 1628 the English physician William Harvey publishes a text in which he proclaims that the blood circulates throughout the body, pumped by the motion of the heart. Before Harvey's work, the prevailing opinion was that the blood ebbs back and forth within the body like the tides. It was a kind of leisurely motion, rhythmical, periodic, and quite organic. But with Harvey the motion of the blood is changed, and quickened. It moves now in a more or less circular fashion. It circulates throughout the body, its motion generated by an engine which has become a mechanism. The heart is a pump, causing a mechanical rather than organic circulation of the blood, which aptly fits with the mechanically regulated circulation of the earth around the sun. We should say, then, that in order to keep pace with a moving earth the anatomized corpse is resurrected as a machine. In 1628 the cold, pale corpse which has been lying motionless on the dissecting table is changed. The blood is set in motion, color begins to return to the flesh, and a new resurrection, this time one engineered by humanity itself, is achieved.

It is true, of course, that the path of the blood and the planets, including the earth, is not a circle. With Kepler in 1609 we discover that the motion of the planets is an ellipse. But what matters to our story is not the exact geometric shape of the motion, but the fact that the motion as geometric prescribes a movement, a circulation regulated as a *mechanism*. Earth and body obey a new law of circulation, and each begins to move with a mechanically regulated rhythm. A new world is being imagined here, a dynamic world, a world on the move, a world in circulation. In 1492 Columbus imagines a path from the old world to the new which projects a straight line. He sets sail and does not fall off the edge of the earth. Between 1577–80 Sir Francis Drake completes this linear projection motion and circumnavigates the globe. Indeed, from the end of the fifteenth century and throughout the seventeenth century European civilization travels the earth in its epic voyages of discovery, made possible in large measure by the improvements in chart and map making which, as I have shown elsewhere,[2] are tied to the development of linear perspective vision. Moreover, as the people of Europe are on the move, so too is its money. For example, Isaac Newton, whose universal law of gravitation circumscribes the movement of all things under one principle, is charged in 1696 by the king of England with the task of re-minting its entire currency. All the old silver coins, whose value was constantly decreased by being worn down over time, are recalled, and in their place Newton, soon to be made Master of the Mint for his services, substitutes a new currency whose weight and value are as 'homogeneous, stable, uniform, and predictable'[3] as the fall of things under the sway of gravity. As Severson suggests, Newton's achievement in this realm goes a long way toward improving the circulation of money and of goods and services in the English economy.

The regulated, clock-like beat of the heart and the circulation of the blood belong, therefore, to the rhythm of a new age, whose movement, we might say, has become subject to law. Perhaps the clearest and most dramatic illustration of this rhythm is what happens to the movement of things. We have already mentioned Newton, whose universal law of gravitation belongs to the last third of the seventeenth century, but before him there is Galileo, whose studies of falling objects not only prepare the way for Newton, but also radically terminate our earlier sense of things.

Galileo takes a decisive step in a long struggle against the Aristotelian physics of moving bodies. In this older tradition, the movement of a thing was inseparable from its character and its place. Heavy objects, like stones, fell because they possessed the character of *gravitas* (gravity), just as lighter objects, like fire, moved upward because of their character of *levitas* (levity). Moreover, the movement of such bodies was said to reflect a desire to return to their natural places, heavy objects below with the earth and lighter ones above and higher up near the heavens. But when Galileo finally succeeds in subjecting the movement of things to the rule of numbers, all this changes. Things no longer move because of what they are or where they belong or what they desire. Rather, they move simply because they move, and indeed with Galileo there is an implicit sense that a thing will continue to move forever and toward infinity unless impeded by some external obstacle or force. We may say, then, that when the movement of things becomes subject to regulation by number, when movement becomes mechanism, the consequence is that things lose their character, desire, and place.

Probably no one, however, would mourn such a loss. We are today so far removed from this older (Aristotelian) vision of things, that we probably cannot take it seriously enough to reflect upon it. It seems a magical world or perhaps even a childish one. Things possessed of character and of purpose and belonging to a place characterize an animated world and we live, and have lived for many a century now, in a dead world, in a world where nature is a number. The personification of things, their animation, is at best a quaint and amusing view, and it is difficult and perhaps impossible for us now to see anything but progress in this process of de-animation. The life of things barely hangs on, appearing only in vestigial form, for example, in the ways in which we cherish keepsakes, mementoes, and souvenirs. But even here they function only as triggers, as it were, to awaken *within us* echoes and memories of a time or a place, or a relation with another. In themselves they are nothing. In themselves, such things do not matter.

Later we shall consider, however, the price which we pay for this vision of things. We shall consider how the de-animation of things infects us who use them. For the moment, however, I want to note only that there is a kind of echo between this movement of things and the movement of the pumping heart. To appreciate this relation, we have to understand that Harvey's heart, as a pump which circulates the blood around the body, is a heart which is empty, equal and divided.[4]

First, the heart is empty insofar as it is the systolic moment which for Harvey defines the true character of the heart, the moment when the heart discharges blood. It is that moment of emptiness which allows Harvey to isolate the heart as pump. Moreover, other developments of his age indicate that a heart which is empty of blood also becomes a heart empty of belief. Second, the heart is equal insofar as its function of circulating the blood is the same in all the species which Harvey considers. From the perspective of function all hearts, including those of men and women, are equal. Third and finally, the heart is divided insofar as the septum cordis, the tough, fibrous tissue in the center of the heart, is a wall without holes, rather than a sieve with small holes allowing the blood within the heart to percolate back and forth.

The resurrection of the corpse as machine begins, therefore, with a pumping heart which is empty, equal, and divided. It seems appropriate that this heart should appear when it does. A heart, divided within itself and the same for all, which moves without belief, seems a fitting response to things, which having lost their character and the specificity of their place, now move without desire.

C From resurrection to reanimation

The corpse resurrected as machine still needs, however, more than a pumping, mechanical heart. This heart moves the blood, but the body itself must move. It too, in addition to the blood, must be set in motion. Its movement, however, needs to fit the world of which it is a part. It must be, therefore, a movement which is like that of things and that of the heart. In short, it must be a movement without the stamp of character, a movement empty of desire, purpose, or intention, a movement somehow divided within itself, a movement without reference to or indifferent to place, and a movement which is the same for all bodies. And indeed such a movement is achieved with the notion of the reflex, in which bodily movement brought under the rule of law is translated into physical motion. The corpse resurrected as a machine is reanimated via the reflex.

The history of the reflex is far too long, complex, and detailed to include within our story. We can, however, briefly highlight a few of its major details and indicate how it satisfies the above criteria for a movement subjugated to mechanism.

Let us begin our discussion of the reflex with an example. You are descending a small hill when suddenly you lose your footing. You begin to fall forward, and it seems as if you are about to introduce your face and chest to the rocky ground. But before such painful, and perhaps dangerous, contact is made, your arms, raised up near your head and chest, thrust out in front of you and your two hands absorb the impact of your fall. You are unhurt, save for a few minor bruises on the palms of your hands.

I take this example, which is readily familiar to all of us, from a small but profound work entitled *Reflex and Revolution* written by the Dutch psychiatrist J. H. van den Berg. In presenting it as an illustration of the body's reflex action, he notes that while a person does not know all the efficient movements of the body which spare him or her injury in this situation, that person nevertheless does know that he or she fell and was unhurt. It is, moveover, within this context of a person in a situation falling without injury that this reflex is a meaningful condition of action. Without the context of a person situated in a world the reflex has no meaning. Indeed, imagine someone performing this action while sitting at the dinner table. Not only is it ludicrous, it may also be indicative of severe disturbance. Our example suggests, therefore, that the reflex action of the body is inseparable from a personal body's tie to the world.

Van den Berg notes, however, that 'the history of the reflex . . . is the history of the mechanistic interpretation of the human body.' It is, he says, '. . . the victory of a concept of the body in which there is no place for principles or forces other than those in the lifeless matter open to physical and chemical investigation.'[5] It is important to note this intimate connection between the reflex and the concept of mechanism, because it indicates not only that the reflex body historically belongs to the tradition of the abandoned body — the anatomized corpse resurrected as a machine and reanimated via reflex — but also that in belonging to this tradition the reflex is already perceived and understood as being separate from the personal body's connection to the world. Indeed, van den Berg's example is aptly chosen to demonstrate this broken connection, because it is the same example used by Descartes in 1641. Descartes, who belongs to the early speculative phase of the history of the reflex, meditates on the situation of a falling person and concludes that the automatic character of the action shows that the person who falls in this fashion has nothing to do with his or her own reaction. Although Descartes does not use the term reflex, his view anticipates its use and some of its features.

With Descartes we have the description of an action which is *divided within itself*. It is an action which gives evidence of a split between the person and the body. It is the action of a depersonalized body, the abandoned body, an anonymous body. It is the action of any body and every body, and indeed all bodies act or, more accurately, react in the same fashion from this perspective of reflex as mechanism. Just as the divided heart which pumps the blood is the same for all, this reflex action, which divides the person from his or her body, is the *same for all*. At the level of this divided action, at the level of reflex, there are no differences between bodies. At this level all bodies are equal and react the same. The reflex body, we might say, is the democratic body, the body, as van den Berg clearly shows, of the masses fused together in spasms of group reaction.

Because we are part of this history of the abandoned body we are apt to miss the significance of Descartes' view. It is surely correct to note the efficient and automatic character of reflex action and to acknowledge that such action does occur without the necessity of personal awareness. Indeed, if *I* had to think about the placement of my arms before a fall, I would certainly long ago have suffered serious injury. But I do not have to think about this action any more than I have to think about the rhythm of my breathing. And yet it is certainly true that *I* belong to this rhythm, that it is mine, and that how I breathe in a situation is an index of how I belong or fail to belong to that situation. In other words, between me and my body there is a whole range of relations linking the pre-personal and the very personal, and only in the most extreme situations, like severe injury or illness, or under pre-established conditions, like in a laboratory setting, can and does my body become detached from me to function as a piece of machinery. Indeed, the fact that I can, so to speak, lend my body to pre-established situations, like an experimental arrangement, to demonstrate a reflex, or the fact that after an injury or illness I can recognize the functioning of my body at that time as out of the ordinary, is proof enough that I belong to my body. No, that is not quite the way to put it, because it still smacks of that split about which Descartes speaks. Rather, we must say that these extraordinary circumstances are proof enough that the most ordinary but also most primary fact about a person and his or her body is that the person *is* his or her body. You *are* your body and because you are you also *have* a body at varying degrees of distance.

It is, therefore, quite a different thing to change what is an automatically efficient action of my body in a specific situation into the action of an automaton. But this is precisely what Descartes' vision achieves, primarily because he brings to this situation a certain way of looking at the body. This view is made quite explicit in his work *La description du corps humain*, written in 1648 but never published by Descartes in his lifetime for fear of the Church. In this work he offers an explicit formulation of the body as machine which has become famous. The difference between a living body and a dead body, he says, is like the difference between two watches, the one with the spring wound and intact and the other with the spring relaxed and broken. The difference, then, is a matter only of mechanism, and it is from this perspective, and because of this perspective, that Descartes envisions the reflex as he does, as a bodily action divorced from the person. Descartes' reflex belongs to a body which in fact is neither a dead nor a living body. It is inscribed within that body which, as an anatomized corpse, has been resurrected as machine. Small wonder, then, that Descartes withheld publication of his views. In seventeenth-century Catholic Europe the human body is still a symbol of the divine incarnation and still a promise of a glorious resurrection and transformation. There is a world of difference between this body and the body as a mechanism, and, while they are not strictly incompatible, there is a certain amount of friction between the two views. In seventeenth-century Catholic Europe it would have been difficult to imagine, let alone accept, this glorious divinely promised resurrection of a mechanical body. It is difficult even today for us to accommodate these two views — as witness, for example, the clash between fundamentalist views of creation and the theory of evolution. Descartes, therefore, was a prudent if not courageous man. Perhaps, who knows, he even surmised that the terms of the body's resurrection would have to change, that the resurrection would have to be engineered in a new way, through the genius of man.

Descartes died in 1650 at the age of 54, but before he did he completed another work, in 1649, entitled *The Passions of the Soul*, in which he continued to elaborate the relations between the conscious person and the estranged body. Another example which he uses, this time the automatic blinking mechanism of the eye, further elucidates the nature of the reflex. In the example, Descartes notes that this mechanism will occur and the eye will automatically close even if the person knows that the hand which moves toward him belongs to a friend and not to a foe.

There is within Descartes' treatment of this example the same depersonalization of action previously described. Moreover, this example, like the other one, also indicates that with the split between person and body there occurs a split between the body and the situation. As Descartes' discussion makes clear, the protective eyeblink happens regardless of the known intention of the advancing hand. This automatic bodily reaction does not distinguish between friend and foe, and in emphasizing the automatism of the action over everything else, Descartes affirms again his view of this body as belonging to anyone and everyone and therefore to no one, as well as his view of this body as belonging anywhere and everywhere and therefore nowhere. This eyeblink, this piece of functioning mechanism, is not only de-personalized, it is also de-contextualized. The automatically functioning body behaves without reference to the situation. The reflex is an action which is *indifferent to place.* Indeed, the prior commitment to the abandoned body, to the anatomical corpse resurrected as machine, already of necessity displaces the reflex from the world, where it is a condition for action within the world, to a circuitry within the body, where it can become a cause of action and an explanation for it.

A body, moreover, which is insensitive to its situation, a body whose actions are displaced from the situation, is also a body acting repetitively. Friend or foe, once or a hundred times, the eye blinks again and again, and in the same fashion. Such a body can learn, therefore, only in a limited way. Its capacity to learn by remembering the past is bounded by the circuits of action already inscribed within it. Ordinarily, to remember is to perceive differences, to perceive in a situation the similarities and differences with other situations and to vary and shade one's actions accordingly. But a body which has become indifferent to, and detached from, the situation can no longer carry its memories in this fashion, in relation to the world. This body must now bear its memories alone, by itself, without the support of the world. Small wonder, then, that its capacity to learn will be restricted to the arena of conditioning. The conditioned reflex will be the way this body of repetitive action bears the weight of memory without the support of the world. The conditioned reflex will be the way of inscribing the memory within the body regardless of its situation. Indeed, in anticipation of our computer language today, the conditioned reflex will be the way in which a body prescribed by reflex is programmed for action.

We might say, then, that the reflex body is not only a depersonalized and decontextualized body, but also a body whose memories have lost their place in the world. Displaced from the world, they are carried by the body itself as conditioned reflexes. But the body itself cannot bear the weight of memory alone. At almost the same time as the conditioned bodies of Pavlov's dogs move onto the stage of history, the hysteric bodies of Freud's patients also make their appearance. Pavlov's dogs, which in the absence of meat repeat a salivary response conditioned to the sound of a bell, and Freud's hysterics, whose neurotic symptoms betray how they suffer from reminiscences, from memories which have no place in the world, make their appearance respectively at the very beginning of the twentieth century and at the end of the nineteenth. This coincidence suggests that the body forced to bear the burden of its memories alone, apart from the world, breaks down. It suggests that the neurotic body is the shadow side, the other side, of the conditioned body. Between Descartes' repetitively blinking eye, Pavlov's salivating dogs, and Freud's suffering hysterics there is, therefore, this connecting thread of the reflex body and its shadow.

The discovery–invention of the reflex body in the mid-seventeenth century translates human movement within the world into physical motion in space. This change has two significant consequences.

Ordinarily, the way in which a person moves through the world marks who he or she is. One's posture and gait are not merely physical events. They are also symbols, indicative of one's history, of the way in which one has, for example, borne up under the cares of life, or shouldered one's responsibilities, or repeatedly been willing to lend a hand, or repeatedly turned one's back on the problems of life, or courageously faced them. In each and in all of these respects, one's movement within and through the world bears the stamp of a character, and, as David Levin has pointed out in a recent and remarkable book, the ethical and moral foundations of a person's life are truly, deeply and most fundamentally rooted in this organic fashion.[6] One's character is, so to speak, one's muscles and one's bones, not however *in* them as organs of anatomy but given *through* them as gestures and styles of movement and conduct in the world. When we translate, therefore,

142

movement into motion, when the gesture of a person becomes the motion of a machine, we shift the terms of what it means to be a person living in the world. In place of issues like the moral and ethical dimensions of character, which give style and substance to how a person moves through his or her life, we substitute, for example, questions of efficiency, which are more suited to the domain of physical motion in the space of the world. The reflex body becomes, then, the harbinger of a new being, a creature not only empty in heart of blood and belief but empty in soul as well, a creature whose motion in the world is filled with efficiency but empty of character. It might very well be the case, therefore, that our invention–discovery of reflex man and woman is largely responsible for the progressive erosion of values which has marked our age since at least the end of the nineteenth century. It might very well be the case that reflex man and woman are incapable of anything but a kind of destructive nihilism. To pursue these concerns, however, would take us too far afield, so I will settle for simply noting again that David Levin gives full and profound treatment to them. In comprehensive fashion and in a language of rare beauty and eloquence, he traces the cancer of nihilism to our denial of the body, and he shows how we need to reintroduce the gestural body into our systems of education if we are to recover the organic, fleshy foundation of our moral, ethical character.

The way in which a figure moves within the world is also indicative of his or her desires. One's posture and gait reflect not only the character and style of one's history, but also the character and intensity of one's purposes and intentions. To move within the world is not simply to change one's position in space. On the contrary, a person moves within the world because he or she has found within the world a reply to his or her desires, and/or because he or she has been called out in one fashion or another by the world. To move within the world, then, is to acknowledge that one is inseparably tied to the world and that in the most fundamental way, at the level of action, this bond is between one's flesh and that of the world — an erotic tie between sensuous flesh and the sensible world, a bond of desire. Moreover, when we recognize that in its root sense desire, as I have indicated elsewhere,[7] describes the most fundamental experience of how we as human beings situated between earth and sky take up the task of making a world into a home, then one's movement within the world reveals in most graphic and dramatic fashion how one is engaged in the task of making and finding, of leaving and returning home. The invention–discovery of the reflex body, then, will also alter the character of human desire. In designing a body displaced from the world, in creating a body indifferent to its situation, we will sever the relation of desire between body and world, and desire, like memory, will move inside, to be borne alone by the body itself without the support of the world.

We are not at all surprised to discover, therefore, that within fifty years of Descartes' speculations about such a body, the English philosopher John

Locke, in 1691, makes desire a matter of interior uneasiness, a restlessness carried on the inside. We are also not surprised to discover, as we did with memory, that a body whose desires have lost their place within the world casts a shadow. The reflex body forced to bear its burden of desire by itself, apart from the world, becomes the mesmerized and hypnotized bodies of the eighteenth century. As we shall discover, these two bodies, with their dramatic indifference to the situation, symbolize a body which has fallen asleep to the world. The mesmerized and hypnotized bodies sleepwalk onto the stage of history, and in this condition of sleep they call attention to the body which has lost its home. In their dazed postures they haunt and shadow as homeless bodies the reflex body of our invention.

We are at a point in our brief history of the abandoned body where the anatomized corpse has been resurrected as machine and reanimated via reflex. This body is now in motion in the space of that world opened up by linear perspective vision. We are roughly in the middle of the eighteenth century, and the earlier speculations of Descartes and others are soon to give way to numerous experiments which isolate and demonstrate the reflex nature of the body's action, and which clearly indicate the electrical character of the reflex. In 1791 Galvani will demonstrate the electrical character of the animal's body. The reflex body will become an electric body, and electricity will become the new animator of life. Set in motion in the world, this body will disperse in many directions and exfoliate in many careers. Of the many paths which we can follow we shall, however, choose two which, I believe, remain the most faithful incarnations of the reflexive body.

D   The body of the industrial worker

Of the many features of the reflex body, the ones which need to be emphasized here are its divided and mechanical characters. The body reanimated via reflex is a machine, and hence its motion has a mechanical, repetitive character. In addition, insofar as the motion of this body is divided within itself, it can be said that its motion has a fragmented character as well. Or perhaps it is closer to the truth of things as they develop in the course of history to say that the motion of the reflex body is in principle capable of division. It is a motion which lends itself to being broken into its parts — a motion, then, which allows or invites fragmentation.

In 1776 Adam Smith, one of the founders of our modern science of economics, publishes his epochal work, *Inquiry into the Nature and Causes of the Wealth of Nations*. The significance of this publication to our story lies in the fact that in it Smith proposes that a piece of work can be made more productive and efficient by dividing it into its parts. In his famous example of the pinmaker, Smith demonstrates that by dividing the work into eighteen parts, each pinmaker can considerably increase the number of pins produced. Two direct consequences of this division, however, are that each worker completes only a fraction of the whole task, and that each worker is continuously engaged in repeating this particular fraction over and over again. Smith's division of labor is in effect the anatomization or dismemberment of work, a fragmentation of it which converts the worker into a mechanical performer of repetitive functions.

The intimate connection between the character of this anatomized work and the body which performs it is, I think, quite clear. Work and body are both divided and mechanical in character. Perhaps what is not so clear, however, is that this eighteenth-century anatomization of work could not have occurred unless and until the body of the worker had been prepared to perform it. In this respect, therefore, the industrial worker, who is heir to this invention of the division of labor, is the consequence of the anatomization of the body resurrected as machine and reanimated via the reflex. Or stated in another way, the worker on the assembly line has been one of the most predominant incarnations of the body discovered and invented to fit the space of linear perspective vision. Moreover, the things produced by this work also reflect or complement the worker who produces them. Mass produced, they are anonymous things, interchangeable things, things which are equal and the same, much like the reflex body of the worker is anybody or everybody and therefore nobody, a body which is the same for all. Later we will consider the price we pay for such things, the effect which their mass production has upon the value of things and our sense of them, but for the moment we should note in one more way how the worker is indeed the incarnation of the reflex body, or what van den Berg calls 'spinal man'.[8] In 1848, Karl Marx and Friedrick Engels wrote, 'The working men have no country',[9] a phrase meant to describe how all workers belong to one and the same class, despite national boundaries. Within the context of this brief history of the abandoned body, however, Marx's words take on an additional meaning. We are all equal and the same at the level of the reflex, working body. And, at the level of this body, we are all equally without a home.

E From worker to robot

The industrial worker is an explicit incarnation of the reflex body and the robot is an image of this worker taken to its full degree. The idea of the robot is, of course, older than the industrial age, but the specific sense of the robot in relation to labor, and the word itself, belong to the time frame of this history of the abandoned body. John Cohen shows, for example, the presence of this idea of a humanly created automated creature in Greek mythology, and the history of the golem is perhaps even older. Cohen rightly points out, however, that these earlier searches were very much tied

145

to the context of the gods and to humanity's search for the secret that would reveal the source of life and bring the knowledge of creation.[10] The robot itself, however, and the coining of the term, belong to a different context. 'Robot' is a Czechoslovak word meaning 'forced labor', and the robot as such enters the stage of history in 1928 as a dramatic character in a play by Karel Capek entitled *R.U.R., Rossum's Universal Robots*.[11]

It is of interest to our story that the author of this play has indicated that the idea for it came to him while he was riding in a car and looking at the grim faces of people on their way to work. The car, as van den Berg argues so persuasively in *Reflex and Revolution*, is an instrument designed for reflex man and woman, since in driving we must, in large measure, trust in and give ourselves over to the automatic reactions of the body. At 55 miles per hour on a crowded expressway a person has little or no time to think about his or her next move. On the contrary, the car in this context fairly well invites the driver to divorce himself or herself from the body, leaving the car and its motion in relation to the other cars in the hands (and eyes and feet) of the body, while the driver either projects himself or herself further up the road anticipating what may occur, or wanders off in daydream and fantasy to another time and place. The car, then, as an instrument of technology, actually does epitomize reflex man and woman. It is the vehicle through which and within which the person and his or her body are divided. Moreover, insofar as the car invites the presence and performance of the reflex body, this body which is the same for all, is a symbol of equality. It is an instrument of technology which is perhaps even more pervasive than the camera, and as such emblematic of mass, democratic society. In principle at least, the car makes us all equal and the same. But I say in principle, because in fact a Mercedes is different from a Ford. And yet do not such differences reaffirm that in principle the automobile does have a leveling equality? Do we not have to display and show off our differences precisely to escape the way in which the automobile reminds us that in the most fundamental way, at the level of the reflex, anatomical body, we are all the same?

The robot, then, in its modern sense of 'forced labor', is the industrial worker in his or her car. That is in any case how the robot is born. It (since we cannot say he or she) is conceived in a car through the grim faces of early morning laborers. What Capek saw that morning and in that setting, he tells us, was the mechanization and dehumanization of humanity. And what he described in his drama was the robot worker, efficient, free from the distractions of memory or desire, with the body of man or woman remade and now superior to nature — a body designed to work, a body whose death would simply mean the absence of motion. In all these ways, Capek's robots gather together and restate many of the features of the anatomized corpse resurrected as machine, reanimated via reflex. They also anticipate, however, a later theme, one which at this point in our story is on the immediate horizon.

Near the beginning of his drama, Capek has the manager of the plant where the robots are made explain Rossum's original intention in creating them. Built to work, they were intended to free humanity from the necessity of labor. Moreover, in designing them, Rossum wanted to create a being more perfect than man or woman. He wanted to make a creature which would never tire of its labor, a creature which would never be distracted by the pains and pleasures of the flesh. Through Rossum's intention, therefore, Capek also reveals the motive of this creation. The robot would be a being which would transcend nature. It would rise above the flesh. In designing his robots, then, Rossum was redesigning humanity. He was building into the robots an image of a new man or woman. He was realizing through them a dream of humanity to depart from the body. At one and the same time, therefore, the robot, by taking upon itself the drudgery of a laboring body, would free humanity from the yoke of necessity, and in doing so, tirelessly, it would incarnate the dream of a body more perfect than nature, the ideal of a body which had escaped the needs and demands of the flesh. That Capek ends his play, however, with the robots in revolt, suggests that our dreams of escaping the body cannot so easily be fulfilled. The body we would abandon re-appears, and it seems with a vengeance. The robot runs amok. It becomes, as it were, a monster.

In a moment we shall explore the monster as a shadow of the abandoned body. Before doing so, however, we need to finish the official side of the story. We need to meet one more cultural–psychological incarnation of the abandoned body.

F The robot and the astronaut

The robot as a body more perfect than nature, as a body which has escaped the needs and the demands of the flesh, anticipates the final figure of the astronaut, and with this figure the dream of transcending the body is realized in the specific fashion of a flight into space. It is true, of course, that the astronaut takes his or her body along on this flight into space, but it is a body which has been radically transformed. It is the body of the Little Cosmonaut which we have already met, that body in which all human activities have been transformed into technical functions. That body is the present culmination of the history of the abandoned body.

The anatomical corpse is a body which was invented–discovered at that moment when, with Copernicus, we transformed the earth into an object in space; at that moment, then, when, psychologically, humanity abandoned the earth to take up its place in the stars. The figure of the astronaut only transforms that psychological journey into an actual fact. The dream of distance from the living body, which has animated the discovery–invention of the anatomical corpse and all its variations, has become the event of departure. What we first imagined we have now enacted. Technology, including and especially this technological reinvention of the body, is the psychological dream of flight from matter become reality. Poised on the launchpad, prepared to leave the earth, the figure of the astronaut sums up the dreams of reincarnation and departure which have animated the discovery–invention of the abandoned body.

Before this figure departs, however, we should note two final facts. On one hand, we should note again that this history of the abandoned body is our history, the history of our bodies, of the bodies we have become, bodies of technical functioning which lie at a great distance from the bodies of everyday life. We are, therefore, all astronauts. On the other hand, we should note the date 1945 assigned to the figure of the astronaut in Figure 5.1. It seems, perhaps, too early by about twenty years or so. But I choose this date intentionally to underscore the notion that our psychological dream of departing the earth may have become a nightmare. With the explosion of the atomic bomb we have set in motion events which today imperil the earth. It might very well be that in 1945 we added newly compelling but dangerous motives to our dream of escaping the earth.

IV The unofficial family's cast of characters

In the chart presented in Figure 5.1 there is a line between the figures of the abandoned body and the shadows cast by these figures. It is not, however, a line of separation which is intended here. On the contrary, that line actually symbolizes a cultural threshold which is at one and the same time a place of remembrance and a barrier of repression. As a barrier of repression, it is the place where the body of everyday life, the pantomimic, gestural body of lived situations, is forgotten or left behind in our discovery–invention of the abandoned body. As a threshold of remembrance, it is the place where this body nevertheless continues its presence, refusing, as it were, to be silenced and left behind, insisting that it be remembered. At this cultural threshold, then, the pantomimic, gestural body of everyday life, the body which is always more than an objectified technical function, is forgotten and remembered, and as such it is present as a cultural symptom. For just as an individual symptom, like anxiety or depression, both reveals and conceals a conflict of emotions, these shadows of the abandoned body reveal and conceal the animate flesh of daily life, the body of desire, memory, and movement, the individual, personal body of character in relation to the world, from which we have taken flight. As symptom, then, these figures of the body haunt and shadow our cultural dreams of escape and reincarnation. They are, if you will, the unconscious side of our technological age made visible. They are the cultural unconscious made flesh.

In relating the brief history of these shadows, I remind the reader of what was said earlier with respect to the figures of the abandoned body on the other side of this threshold. These cultural figures are no more linear stages in a historical trajectory than the previous ones. On the contrary, they too overlap each other and each figure simultaneously refigures those that have preceded it and prefigures those that are to come. Thus the anorexic, for example, refigures in a fashion the witch, while the witch prefigures in a fashion the anorexic. It is not surprising to discover, therefore, that the first diagnosis of anorexia occurs in 1689 but that the figure does not become culturally prominent as a symptom until much later. The anorexic is already present throughout this shadow history, but her specific moment awaits our own time.

In addition, however, the connections among these figures of the shadow body are less visible and immediate than was the case with the figures of the abandoned body. Whereas earlier we were able to establish some sequence of action between figures — saying, for example, that the anatomical corpse resurrected as machine is reanimated as a reflex, no such sequence can be established here. These figures have not been officially created on some putative line of progress, as it were. They are shadows. They are cultural dream images, and their connections are as much as or even more with the figures that they shadow than with each other. In telling this side of our story, then, we shall, more or less, be speaking the underside of what we have already spoken. Through these shadows we shall hear echoes of the abandoned body.

A The body bewitched

We begin with the figure of the witch, who, as Norman Cohn has pointed out, has haunted the consciousness of European humanity in many forms and disguises.[12] The specific figure of the witch, however, generally makes its appearance in the fifteenth century. It is then that the witch becomes a prominent, dangerous, and hunted figure. In 1486 two Dominican priests, Jacob Sprenger and Heinrich Kramer, publish their manual *Malleus Malificarum, The Hammer of Witches*, which diagnoses signs of witchery, prescribes methods of interrogation, and indicates forms of punishment, torture, and death. The great witch hunts, which appear in conjunction with the Catholic Church's inquisition against heretics, begin here, continue with increased intensity throughout the fifteenth century and into the sixteenth and seventeenth, reach their peak in Europe and America in the late eighteenth century, and then begin their decline toward disappearance in the early part of the nineteenth century. As an early shadow of the abandoned body, then, the witch is an enduring figure, haunting much of the history of our efforts to leave the body behind.[13]

A cultural figure endures in this fashion because it is a powerful symbol. Of the many things which might be said about the reasons for this power, perhaps what is most pertinent to our tale is the connection which can be made between the body of the witch and the anatomized corpse. The anatomized corpse is a vivid symbol of the abandoned body. Lying motionless on the dissecting table, this body is more than a mute witness to the flight we have taken from the body in creating a Copernican earth. Departing the earth to take up its place on the sun, Copernican humanity necessarily discards the body which is tied to the earth, and that body with its weight of living flesh is left behind.

The witch's body, however, rises up, as it were, out of this dissected corpse, and in her flight she is the other, forbidden side of our dreams of escape, a figure propelled through the heavens by demonic powers. She is the dark, shadow side of our flight from the abandoned corpse, a frightening image of the underside of our dreams of departure.

Moreover, the ways in which the witch's body is imagined indicate a continuing, disturbing, and frightening presence of the body we would discard and the earth from which we would depart. The witch's body is a carnal body. It is a body which belongs to the earth, a body so filled with flesh that it is imagined primarily in sexual terms, since sexuality is the most potent and insistent reminder that our bodies matter, that we are material beings with needs, desires, and hungers which return us, with our soaring ambitions and intellectual dreams, to the earth. In her vigorous and flagrant sexuality, a sexuality which is imagined in relation to the figure of the devil, the witch carries what we would deny and overcome in our flight from the body, *and* continues to remind us of this denial. Overloading the body of the witch with the weighty demands of the flesh, we would fix that pernicious body with its corrupt and stinking sexuality over there, and thus distance ourselves from it and be rid of it. But however much the witch is punished, tortured, and burned, she continues her haunting presence, and indeed, the more she is repressed the more insistent, horrible, and frightening she becomes.

The witch is also a body which belongs essentially to the darkness of the night, and in this respect her shadow is the other side of the light of reason, the infinite, visionary eye of spectator consciousness which, in its detachment and distance from the world, would become primarily its observer. The witch as a creature of the night reminds the spectator that the light of consciousness does cast a shadow. In her disturbing presence she reminds us that a world which would become a matter of light, a matter primarily for the eye alone, forgets and denies its darkness only in peril. In that darkness, witches, demons, and devils grow. In that denied darkness they are nurtured and appear as our nightmares. The body and the earth to which it belongs become a body of the night embedded in the darkness of the earth under the too brilliant gaze of the eye of distant vision, and the night and the dark out of which the witch will emerge are the same night and darkness in which the other shadows of the abandoned body are unsuccessfully imprisoned and out of which they too will emerge. The madman will be shut away out of sight; Mesmer will work his miracles in a darkened room; Mary Shelley's monster, Frankenstein, will first appear to his creator as he wakens from sleep; and Freud's hysterics will dream: Each of them will be born in darkness and in night, and each in turn will enter the lighted stage of historical consciousness out of darkness and from the dream.

Dark, sensual body of the earth, painful, disturbing reminder of the other side of our dreams of escape, devil's consort in the night, the witch is a figure who is hunted, punished, tortured, and burned. She is also, as our language has indicated, essentially a feminine figure. Each of these aspects will be repeated throughout the shadow history of the abandoned body. For the most part each of the shadows will carry the feminine form and each in its turn will be tortured, killed, confined, diagnosed, isolated, cured, treated, or otherwise silenced. This treatment is perhaps not difficult to understand. We would silence what disturbs us. The feminine character of the shadow is, however, a more difficult issue, and any efforts at interpretation would take us far beyond the limits of this brief history. It should be noted, however, that insofar as the shadows of the abandoned body are predominantly feminine in character, we might venture the notion that the discovery–invention of the abandoned body is, psychologically speaking, a masculine enterprise. In other words, we should note the very strong possibility that the dreams of departure and escape from matter are dreams of the masculine psyche which have had as their correlate the repression and subjugation of the feminine. In this respect, the identification of nature and earth with feminine qualities in the early history of science, a fact which Carolyn Merchant notes, is not surprising.[14] The earth we would leave behind is Mother Earth, the earth imagined as soft, warm, nurturing, dark, and inviting, qualities and features to be disowned by a spirit which, in its zeal for departure, would be a hard, cold, distant, piercing vision. Nor is it surprising that since the late nineteenth century there has been a growing and increasingly vital reappearance of feminine consciousness in the midst of our technological culture. What we would abandon, forget, disown, discard, and destroy, reappears, making its claim upon us to be remembered, owned, embraced, and lived.

B The body of madness

Since the fifteenth century, according to Foucault, the face of madness has haunted the imagination of western humanity.[15] In the context of our story, this timing is most appropriate. So too are the reasons for this haunting.

The grinning face of madness mocks the vanity of life. In madness life itself is seen to be 'only futility, vain words, a squabble of cap and bells [and the] head that will become a skull is already empty.' Mocking life, the madman as the fool becomes the messenger of death. 'Madness,' Foucault writes, 'is the déja-là of death,' and 'From the vain mask to the corpse the same smile persists.'[16]

Between the madman and the corpse there is the connection of death. For Foucault the connection is an effort on the part of humanity to replace and subdue death. Our history of the abandoned body fits with this motive. The corpse, as we saw, is neither a living nor a dead body, and in being resurrected it is resurrected as machine. In itself and in its resurrection, then, the corpse would take the place of death. It would be a measure of our distance from death, of our flight from and denial of it. Death denied, however, *is* a foolish mockery of human life. Death denied *is* madness. The madman and madwoman, who begin to haunt the imagination of western humanity in the fifteenth century, are, therefore, most appropriate shadows of the corpse. In their foolish mockery of life, they would remind us of the spectre of death we seek to avoid.

The madman and madwoman, however, are more than grinning fools. Both are also a raging passion, an animal fury. The body of madness is perceived as an animal body which has not yet been tamed to fit the controlled, mapped and mathematical space of linear perspective vision. Madness is an animal metamorphosis of the human being.

Unlike in earlier ages, however, this metamorphosis is not, according to Foucault, a possession by other powers. On the contrary, it is a dispossession of reason. The madman and madwoman are an animality which has not yet been subjugated by the powers of a reason which would tame the body from afar. The body of madness in its animal fury is still too close to nature, too much a part of it, as judged by a reason which would distance itself from nature and the body and depart from them. As such, in its passion and fury this body is the shadow of that other body, the machine, which in its regulation and control is the antithesis of an animal body, of a body that belongs to nature. The madman or madwoman is a body out of control, and the grinning face of the fool is a mockery not only of a life which would deny death but of a kind of reason that would leave the body behind.

But whether as grinning fools or animal passion the madman and madwoman are finally confined and shut away by that reason which would distance itself from the body. In 1656 the first hospital specifically established to house madness is opened. It is the Hôpital Général, and in its charter we find another shadow of the abandoned body.

The chief concern of this house of confinement is the condemnation of idleness, and its primary task is to prevent 'mendicancy and idleness as the source of all disorders.'[17] For Pinel too, who in 1795 frees the madmen and madwomen of Saltpetrière of their external chains, madness is rooted in idleness and laziness, and the prescription which he advises is repetitive, mechanical work. Placed in this light, the madman and madwoman are the obverse, the underside, of the industrious worker. Perceived and judged from the perspective of a body whose reflexes have been honed for work, a body which does not fit the mold of productive, useful, efficient labor, a body which in its idleness as well as in its animal fury cannot work, be prudent, sober, industrious, and controlled, must be mad. In diagnosing, condemning, and confining this body, we reaffirm the efficient, productive body of the industrial worker. In imprisoning this madness, we contribute to the industrialization of the body. In shutting away this animal body, we take another step toward the body's mechanization. The madman and madwoman in their cells are the shadows of the workers in their factories, and the factories, with their assembly lines, are the social counterpart of the asylum. Indeed, the asylum institutionalizes the same moral values of bourgeois society as does the factory — patriarchal authority, industrious labor, and obedience — and in neither place do the disorders of the human heart have a place. In the factory, these moral virtues establish, as it were, a socially sanctioned, controlled form of madness, while in the asylum morality allows itself 'to be administered like trade or economy.'[18] But the creation of these spaces, which either allow no time for disorders of the human heart or confine such disorders in an effort to change them, is to be expected, since the human heart itself has already entered the space of practical labor. It has become a pump, a machine, of which it can only properly be asked whether it works or not. The madman and madwoman have a different heart, a heart of passion and of fury, a heart which can still be characterized in terms of harmony and disharmony, of order and disorder, and not simply in terms of disfunction. The body of madness, then, is also a shadow of the body with a pumping heart, of the body of technical functioning. It is a shadow, however, imprisoned and shut away in the asylum, the place where the mad person is confined until there is a change of heart.

The body of madness, like the body bewitched, is a shadow of the abandoned body. It is, if you will, a return of the repressed body of everyday life, a return from that distance through which the discovery–invention of the abandoned body is achieved. But the distant gaze which has banished the living flesh and made its return necessary also prohibits the return, and indeed the asylum itself becomes the primary place for the practice of this distant vision.

In its early appearance, madness is at first everywhere. It is, as it were, in the midst of the world. Look again at Figure 2.5, a painting by Hieronymous Bosch entitled *The Temptation of St Anthony* and dating from 1500. The demons of maddening temptation surround St Anthony. They fly through the air and rise up from the waters of the earth. But with increasing precision, this madness which is everywhere, which surrounds us, as it were, is further removed, until, mastered by the very same gaze of distant vision which has produced it, madness is confined over there in the asylum. Imprisoned there on the other side of the bars, the abandoned body as specimen has become the shadow body of madness as spectacle. The madman and madwoman are something to see. Foucault notes this intimate connection between madness and distance. Commenting on its confinement, he writes of madness that 'if present, it was at a distance, under the eyes of a reason that no longer felt any relation to it . . . Madness had become a thing to look at . . . an animal with strange mechanisms.'[19]

The asylum, the place where the shadows of madness are shut away, is, then, an institutional incarnation of the spectating eye, the eye of distant vision. It is the social consequence of that distance which humanity has put between itself, its reason, and its body. The asylum is created in that space of linear perspective vision to house and to spy upon the body which haunts and shadows the abandoned body. Brought into being by this vision which would observe the world and the body from afar, which would transform all into spectacle, the asylum is also the place where this vision reigns supreme. Observation and naked visibility inform the structure of the asylum, and in that place the body of madness is not only put to work, it is also observed.

Under the steady gaze of this observing eye, the madman and madwoman, like the figure of the witch, are silenced, and the body of which they would remind us is forgotten. Observed, the madman and madwoman are diagnosed and treated, but in such a way that the distance established between us and them is increased by placing a distance within the madman and madwoman themselves. In the asylum they are not only observed, they become their own observers. Through observation, and in the very idea and structure of the asylum, the madman and madwoman are driven further away from us and deeper into themselves. Pinel, who was mentioned earlier, can strike the external bonds from the bodies of these madmen and madwomen, therefore, because internal bonds have been put in their place. Confined and judged, watched and observed in distance, and even alienated within themselves, the madman and madwoman are controlled by the bonds of guilt that are forged in the eyes of the other and by the bonds of shame forged in the eyes of the self. Moreover, insofar as the asylum carries out the same moral program as is carried out in the space of industry and trade, these same bonds of shame and guilt are inscribed into the body of the industrious worker. As internal moral reflexes, as it were, shame and guilt are primary ways of programming the body of industry; and in the space of the asylum, under the pressure of observation, they become ways of reprogramming the body of the mad person to become the productive body of the industrial worker.

The eye of distant vision succeeds, therefore, not only in confining madness away from the world in the asylum, but also in hiding it within the madman and madwoman themselves. Something of this shift can be seen in a comparison of the earlier painting by Bosch and the painting by Goya shown in Figure 2.6. Dating from approximately 1794 and entitled *The Dream of Reason Produces Monsters*, it shows, among other things, that

154

madness has now become internalized. The maddening demons which haunt Goya's landscape haunt a dreaming, sleeping figure. They have been moved from the face of the world and have been hidden in the darkness of the dream.

Goya's painting, and especially its title, offer, however, another interesting speculation and as my final comment on madness I offer it here. It is the dream of reason which produces the monsters of madness. We dream when we sleep, and thus it is also the *sleep* of reason which produces monsters. As modern men and women, we know that and we agree. Madness, judged and perceived from the side of the abandoned body, is the animal body dispossessed of its reason. Madness is the loss of reason. It is, as Goya himself suggested about this etching, a madness produced by an imagination deserted by reason. But the phrase 'dream of reason' can also be heard as a vision, and in this sense Goya's etching can be viewed as the dark side of a vision, the night side of a vision about reason which dreams of purifying itself of the body and its passions, the excess of a reason which would negate imagination. Goya's painting, then, becomes a beautiful illustration of madness as the shadow of a reason which would forget its darkness, the nightmare of a reason which in creating the abandoned body would depart the flesh.

C   The body that falls into sleep

The year is 1778 and a physician, Franz Anton Mesmer, has recently arrived in Paris from Vienna. He is already both famous and infamous for his medical cures, which consist essentially in moving a magnet or even his hand over the diseased part of the body. In Mesmer's view all elements in the universe are connected together with a very fine, invisible, ethereal substance — a fluid — which manifests itself, for example, in phenomena like gravity, electricity, and magnetism. Even within the body there is such a fluid, which Mesmer describes as animal magnetism. The body itself is a magnet, and disease, understood as a disturbance in the flow of this fluid, can be cured through the application of a magnet, or even by the influence of a magnetically balanced body. Invariably, however, what occurs in the process of cure is a strange kind of sleep into which the patient falls. Not quite awake or asleep, the patients appear rather to be in a dazed condition. They are, in the apt phrase of van den Berg, 'Sleepwalkers by day.'[20] They are, in a phrase which has become commonplace for us today, mesmerized.

In Paris, Mesmer hits upon the idea of group treatment. Van den Berg offers a detailed description of this treatment and in it we shall discover another shadow of the abandoned body.

A large, round, oak tub, called a *baquet*, is filled with chips of wood, splinters of glass, and flasks of magnetized water. Patients gather around this tub and either take hold of iron bars which project from the cover of the *baquet*, or contort themselves in such fashion that the diseased parts of their bodies touch these bars. A rope wrapped around each patient connects all the patients together into one magnetic loop, as it were. Mirrors line the room, which is semi-dark, and a silence, upon which Mesmer insists, permeates the room. Some time passes as the patients wait and then music is heard. Mesmer, himself an accomplished musician and friend of Mozart, plays softly on a glass harmonica. The effect is astonishing. In this room of darkness, silence, music and mirrors, most of the patients are, according to an eyewitness account, thrown into 'fits and convulsions, accompanied by odd contortions of their limbs while they [are] laughing, crying or singing.' All of this behavior, according to the same account, ends 'in a swoon and a general feeling of faintness.'[21] For patients not quickly affected in this manner, Mesmer himself would enter the room and touch the patients in order to quicken the flow of the fluid. Sitting knee to knee with the patient and placing his hand on the patient's stomach, he would stretch his fingers in the direction of the navel and with a slight pressure he would slowly move his hands down along the abdomen and the groin. According to accounts of the day, Mesmer would at times touch and rub the body in this fashion for hours. Figure 5.2 illustrates this rather intimate relation between the mesmerist and the mesmerized body. The reader should particularly note the posture of the two participants. The man, who is the physician, is quite close to the woman, who is the patient. His hands have either already touched her or are about to do so. And the woman, touched or about to be touched in this way, strikes a curious pose. She appears neither asleep nor awake. Is she inviting the touch or refusing it? Perhaps she is doing both simultaneously. Perhaps she is inviting the touch without knowing it.

Summarizing this description of Mesmer's technique, we can say that in the darkness and silence of a music-filled, mirrored room, bodies swoon and faint while others erupt in laughter, tears and song. That body which swoons and faints is, I would suggest, the anatomical body, while the one shaken with fits and convulsions, and overflowing with symptoms, laughter and tears, is the e-motional body now long buried beneath the abandoned corpse. There is another kind of resurrection here, one, however, which is spontaneous, unplanned, and not engineered by the eye of distant vision. It is the resurrection of the animate flesh, the resurrection of the e-motional body. This body arises, moreover, within the same medical context which created its disappearance. But unlike that earlier context in which the body as an object of vision is discovered—invented as anatomized corpse, the medical context of the mesmerized body emphasizes a body with which the physician is in touch. The physician as mesmerist replaces eye with hand. We might say, then, that the abandoned body, created in the distance opened up in the space of linear perspective vision in Florence in 1425, is reclaimed from distance in Paris in 1778 by the hand with a mesmerizing touch.

Figure 5.2 *Practicing the Animal Magnetism*, from *Divided Existence and Complex Society (Leven in meervoud)*, by J. H. van den Berg

Reprinted by permission of G. F. Callenbach N. V., Nijkerk, The Netherlands

We need to say more, however, about this touch which awakens the e-motional body. In his consideration of these matters, van den Berg notes that with Mesmer's technique 'A new erotic announces itself,'[22] a description which seems quite appropriate in light of the account of Mesmer's method and the illustration in Figure 5.2. The touch which awakens the e-motional body is a special kind of touch. It is definitely *not* the touch with which we are familiar, the touch of the physician whose hand quite naturally remains detached and distant from the body which he or she touches. Quite the contrary, the mesmerist's touch closes this distance in opening up a space of intimacy, and indeed the intimacy of this touch was one of the things which scandalized the physicians of the abandoned body in Mesmer's own time. Perhaps, however, in focusing exclusively on Mesmer, on the touching hand of the physician, these physicians of the abandoned body did not recognize that the body asked to be touched in this way. In darkness and in silence, did the abandoned body fall into sleep in order to allow the e-motional body to reawaken? And did the form of this awakening, a trance-like state between sleeping and wakefulness, and the style of it, an emotional catharsis of convulsions, fits, tears, symptoms, and laughter which, under the touch of the mesmerist physician, reveals a strong erotic and even sexual character, only indicate how deeply the body had been abandoned and thus how vigorous and dramatic its awakening had to be?

We are today perhaps too far along in a psychoanalytic age to be anything but doubtful of the mesmerist's intentions, and perhaps it is true that this physician's touch concealed hidden motives. But even if that is the case, the physician's hidden motives, if there were any, could not on their own have created this erotic body, any more than his touch alone could have done so. The body could refuse such a touch. It could pull away. But it did not. The body of the patient in Figure 5.2 conspires, albeit ambiguously, with this touch. The patient's body lends itself to this touch even while the patient herself seems distant from it. Her body, we might say, is there to be touched, but she is not. It is a strange kind of presence, a presence which is also an absence, a presence which is incarnated in the trance-like state between sleeping and wakefulness which this patient and the others manifest. Is not this kind of presence, however, precisely to be expected? A bodily presence in the absence of the person is exactly the kind of body reanimated via the reflex and described by Descartes. Whereas, however, the reflex body is a body without desire, the mesmerized body is a body full of desire. An ironic twist is at work here, for what better way for the body of desire to return than via a mimicry of this reflex body. The separation of person and body, which in the creation of the reflex body exiles desire from the body, becomes the means by which desire returns. I think we must say, therefore, that the intimate touch of the mesmerist's hand, regardless of any hidden motive, awakens the body of erotic desire, and even a sexually erotic body, because the body asks and needs to be awakened in this fashion. The mesmerized body is the shadow of the reflex body, the way in which this body, cleansed of desire, reappears.

In this description, however, we should not make the mistake of seeing the woman as conspirator in this drama. The woman's body lends itself to this touch and not the woman. If the physician as mesmerist cannot be judged by the standards of hidden and improper motives, neither can the woman. She is neither guilty of a hidden wish to be touched in this way, nor the victim in any simplistic fashion of the hidden wishes of an unscrupulous physician. It is not a question of individual neurosis here. On the contrary, each of them is part of a cultural, historical psychology which neither of them has brought into being. In this drama, the physician as mesmerist lends a hand and the woman a body. We can and we should note, however, that again, as with the witch, it is the figure of the woman which carries the shadow of the culture, and in this larger context of a cultural psychological drama it is appropriate to speak of the woman as victim. Earlier the witch, who carries a denied sexuality, is persecuted, tortured, and burned. Now the mesmerized patient, carrying another shadow of this denied sexuality, is destined simply to be cured. When we realize, moreover, that in the history of hypnosis, which parallels and belongs to that of mesmerism, the hypnotized body is, for the most part, the feminine body *and* the uneducated peasant body, we recognize that the shadow of the abandoned body is carried by those figures in a society who are without power, by those figures whom society in one way or another has already dismissed. The woman's body and the body of the lower-class peasant share the periphery and as peripheral, marginal beings they can carry the shadow.

I should add here, if only for the sake of completion, that the structure of the hypnotic situation weds the hypnotist, as a man of power, dominance, and authority, to the woman or the peasant who, in their weakness and simplicity, are not more than children. As van den Berg points out in his study of these matters, it is sufficient in some cases for the physician simply to walk into the room to have his patients fall into a hypnotic sleep. His presence itself is filled with authority, and his touch is like the hand of a father upon a child. In this respect, the child too is destined to become a figure to carry a shadow of the abandoned body. The polymorphous perverse body of childhood sexuality, which Freud will encounter, is waiting outside Mesmer's darkened room.

The mesmerized patient is, I said, destined to be cured. To be cured, however, she must first be transformed into a neurotic — a transformation, however, which assigns to her only a negative value. The shadow, then, has nothing to teach. Its darkness is lightened. That the shadow has to be lightened is, moreover, quite clear in the destiny of Mesmer himself. In March 1784 the King of France, Louis XVI, advised by the medical faculty of the University of Paris, appoints a commission of investigators which includes among others the American Benjamin Franklin, a man who himself has dabbled with invisible forces, the forces of electricity. They find nothing to substantiate Mesmer's claims for the force of animal magnetism and Mesmer is dismissed as a quack and charlatan. Although Mesmer himself is able to retire to a quiet, comfortable life as a country gentleman, the dismissal of his claims amounts to a dismissal of the mesmerized body. The shadow which it carries, then, will have to make another appearance and in such a fashion as to force the culture of the abandoned body to take more serious and prolonged notice of it. And it will do so. The body of erotic desire as mesmerized body fades, to reappear in the guise of the hysteric, and in Freud's hands the hysteric will bring together the shadows of the child, the feminine body, desire, and sexuality, and thus will intensify their darkness. Between the mesmerized body of 1778 and the hysteric body of 1888, however, there stands another cultural shadow, the body of the man made monster, the body of Frankenstein, an electrical body conceived in 1816 by Mary Shelley. It is to this shadow that we now turn.

D   The monster's body

On a summer night in the year 1816 Mary Shelley, young wife of the poet Percy Bysshe Shelley, is sitting with her husband and their friend, the equally renowned poet Lord Byron. Their talk centers around recent scientific theories, especially, as Mary Shelley informs us, galvanism and the possible reanimation of corpses via electricity. The talk is lively and before the evening is over a proposal is made that each should write a ghost story to be shared with the others. What, if anything, the poets wrote, we know nothing about. But what Mary Shelley wrote has become an enduring legend, a mythic cultural theme. Out of that context and through the imagination of that young woman, the monster Frankenstein walked onto the stage of history.

Mary Shelley's novel has been so popularized, especially through film, that we are apt to disregard the original tale. In doing so, however, we run the great risk of forgetting that the monster Frankenstein is the double of his creator, Dr Victor Frankenstein, and that he is the offspring of the doctor's desire to be the creator and the source of a new race of beings, a race which would never know the pain and agony of death. The animation of lifeless matter, the resurrection of the corpse, is motivated by a wish to conquer death, and in this respect Victor Frankenstein is nothing if not the epitome of the gaze of distant vision which in creating the anatomized corpse would distance itself from death. His achievement, however, is a nightmare, and in this respect the monster Frankenstein is the disfigured shadow of the resurrected corpse. In his grotesque and hideous form, the monster is the frightening shadow of the abandoned body.

What distinguishes the monster Frankenstein from so many earlier monsters of the human imagination is that he is so explicitly crafted by the mind and hand of man. He is *made* by man and he is *man*made. As *made* by man the monster is the product of a human vision which would master, tame, and even remake nature. Victor Frankenstein would '. . . pioneer a new way, explore unknown powers, and unfold to the world the deepest mysteries of creation.'[23] In this context the monster is the other, dark side of his creator's dreams of creation, a disturbing reminder of the hubris of a reason which would distance itself too much from nature. Victor Frankenstein himself seems aware of this danger, but he does not heed its warning. Near the beginning of his work, he expresses some doubts about exceeding the limits imposed upon humanity by nature and by God. But he quickly brushes such doubts aside in his decision to make the monster large so as to increase the efficiency of his work. In this decision he indicates that beyond his doubts he is little concerned with what he is doing, and rather more concerned with how well and how quickly it can be done.

As *man*made, the monster's creation is a most unnatural genesis. He is, as Joyce Carol Oates points out,[24] a creature born of Victor Frankenstein alone, a monster-son born exclusively of the masculine spirit. In this context, the monster is the darkest reminder that the discovery–invention of the abandoned body as predominantly a psychologically masculine enterprise has destructive consequences. The witch, the mesmerized patient, and even the body of madness all indicate the psychologically masculine character of humanity's dreams of departure and reincarnation. But in each of these instances, the force of the feminine remains, even if only as a shadow. With the monster, however, all connection with the feminine is severed. As imagined by Mary Shelley, the monster is created by Victor Frankenstein alone, completely removed from the feminine principle, and in this respect the monster Frankenstein dramatically suggests that a cultural enterprise which not only continues the subjugation of the feminine but actually excludes the feminine courts death and destruction.

This theme of destruction is thematic in the relation between Victor and the monster. Victor, the creator, abandons his own creation. He refuses to take responsibility for what he has done. This denial of responsibility is evident in the first encounter between Victor and his creation. Exhausted by his labors, he falls asleep, and while dreaming a horrible dream in which Elizabeth, his bride-to-be, becomes the rotting corpse of his dead mother, the monster awakens him. Victor is horrified by the pale yellow skin and the cold lifeless eyes, and he flees in terror. Apart from the Oedipal character of Victor's dream and the suggestion that the fruit of such a dream would be a monstrous offspring — a suggestion made by Oates which would make Mary Shelley an interesting forerunner of Freud — the scene of this first encounter becomes a warning of destruction. The abandoned body abandoned by its creator becomes the bearer of death, and in this respect the monster as shadow warns that unless we are responsible to and for our creations the death we would escape will become our own destruction.

As a tale told quite early in the history of technology, Mary Shelley's *Frankenstein* seems prophetic. Our Frankenstein today is, we might say, the bomb. If we refuse to take responsibility for its creation, if we make it into a monster by fleeing from it, do we create the destruction and death we would escape through the wizardry of our technology? In Mary Shelley's story Victor Frankenstein, the creator, dies. The monster Frankenstein does not. The last we see of him is in the far reaches of the Arctic wastes. He has retreated to the cold and the dark. In the threat of a nuclear winter our own monster promises much the same conclusion. Joyce Carol Oates sums up and confirms this aspect of the shadow as prophetic warning. The Frankenstein story is 'a parable for our time, an enduring prophecy, a remarkably acute diagnosis of the lethal nature of denial: denial of responsibility for one's actions, denial of the shadow self locked within consciousness.'[25]

Much more could be said of how the manmade monster Frankenstein is a cultural shadow of the abandoned body, but two final images will suffice. One returns us to the corpse which figures so explicitly in the genesis of the story by Mary Shelley and within the story itself. The corpse is the anatomized body and anatomy means dis-memberment. The corpse, then, is a dis-membered body. Frankenstein the monster is a corpse. Or it is more accurate to say that he is the fragments and composition of many corpses. In this respect, we might say that Frankenstein is the dis-membered body *re-membered*. He is sewn together and he is, as shadow of the abandoned body, a monstrous reminder of the living body we would forget.

The second closing image concerns the way in which the re-membered monster, the corpse now stitched together, comes to life. He is reanimated through electricity, and in this respect the monster is the shadow of the reflex body with its circuitry of action. In Frankenstein's monster, however, the corpse reanimated by electricity does not result in the industrial worker or the robot; rather it is a monster of destruction who stalks the streets. We might say, then, that the electrified corpse is a shadow of the robot or industrial worker run amok.

In any of its guises, however, the monster, like all previous shadows of the abandoned body, is the other side of who we are and who we have become in our technological dreams of departure and reincarnation. In closing our remarks on the monster it may be well to keep this relation between ourselves and the shadows in mind. We need the monster, the witch, the madman and madwoman, and the others, to see ourselves more fully, and perhaps even to see ourselves at all. As Joyce Carol Oates writes, 'The monsters we create by way of an advanced technological civilization are ourselves as we cannot hope to see ourselves — incomplete, blind, blighted, and, most of all, self destructive.'[26] We need the shadows if we are to survive.

E   *The hysterical body*

In an earlier section of our shadow history of the abandoned body, we indicated how the reflex displaces action from the world into the body. The reflex body is a body which has lost its place within the world. As such, moreover, this body is forced, as we saw, to bear the weight of its memories and desires alone, without the support of the world. The mesmerized body, on the other hand, is a body back in touch with the world, and as a shadow of the reflex body it is a body which remembers desire, the reappearance of the body of desire. The mesmerized body, however, is in touch with the world in a peculiar fashion. Like the hypnotized body, it is neither actually asleep nor fully awake. The desire to be back in touch with the world is muted, we might say. The mesmerized or hypnotized bodies are 'sleep-walkers by day.'[27]

The mesmerized or hypnotized body was, if you will, a reluctant shadow of the body of memory and desire, and its first contact with the world was somewhat cautious and hesitant. As such, its shadow character did not have to be taken as seriously as it should. This body could be and was dismissed. With the hysterical body, however, the caution and hesitation were gone. The hysteric patient, unlike the mesmerized one, was *eventually* fully awake, and in her wakefulness she was an insistent reminder that the body displaced from the world and forced to carry its memories and desires alone breaks down. In this insistence, moreover, she demonstrated another feature of the shadow history of the abandoned body. The shadow as carrier of what we would deny demands our recognition and attention, and if it is ignored or too easily dismissed it returns, perhaps in an even more intense fashion. Indeed, the shadow is a continuous presence until we hear what it has to say.

The hysteric body reached its full ripeness in the work of Freud, whose publication in 1895 of *Studies on Hysteria* with Josef Breuer marked the birth of psychoanalysis. Her appearance, however, pre-dated Freud, and it was actually the French physician Charcot who gave the hysteric a prominent place on the stage of history. In the late 1870s and throughout the 1880s, Charcot's clinic in Paris was the center for the hysteric's dramatic presence, and indeed, as Drinka points out in his rich history of these women, they achieved a kind of celebrity status in their day.[28] It will therefore serve us well to linger for a moment with Charcot before moving on to Freud.

For Charcot hysteria was a neurotic condition primarily of women and marked by fainting, convulsions, and a host of other symptoms. These symptoms, which were present between seizures, included anaesthesia or the loss of sensation and feeling, tremors, paralysis, catalepsy, astasia—abasia or difficulties in walking and standing, tunnel vision, and the presence of hysterogenic points on the body, which, when touched, either produced a seizure or stopped one. Certainly in each and all of these respects the hysterical body was re-presenting the mesmerized body, but because, unlike Mesmer, Charcot was an eminent and respected physician of his day, a member and true believer, as it were, of the brotherhood of the abandoned body, these symptoms were attended to more seriously. But although Charcot did take the hysteric and her symptoms seriously, she remained primarily asleep insofar as Charcot tended to equate hysteria and hypnosis. In doing so, Charcot could still silence the speaking of this shadow body on its own terms. Under hypnosis he could still exercise his measure of control. Figure 5.3 demonstrates this power of the physician and this early submission of the hysteric body.

We should note, however, that despite Charcot's domination of the hysteric body, the symptoms remained a persistent and dramatic shadow of the abandoned body. In her anaesthesia the hysteric mimics the body without feeling, the corpse, while in her tremors, paralysis, astasia−abasia we are given the symptomatic side of the body whose movement in the world is more like the motion of a machine. These disturbances of movement are, as it were, exaggerated expressions of the motion of the reflex body, calling to our attention through their exaggerated display the darker, problematic side of this invention. And lest this message be missed, the hysteric body offered another symptom, not found in the earlier appearance of the mesmerized body. This body suffered from tunnel vision. In other words, it saw the world almost precisely as it had been mapped out for the spectator eye in the space of linear perspective vision. It presented a vision of the world in which sight tends to converge toward a vanishing point, but it did so now as part of a complex of symptoms.

Perhaps, however, the most dramatic way in which Charcot's hysterics shadowed the abandoned body was through the presence of the hysterogenic points on the body, which if touched by Charcot either produced a seizure or terminated one. Figure 5.4 illustrates these points, and what we should immediately notice here is how diffuse the erotic character of the shadow body has become. Most of these points center around the genitals and related erotogenic areas, but in comparison with the mesmerized body, the body of desire here is a veritable chorus inviting the hand of the physician to free it from its imprisonment within the abandoned body. 'Do more than sit knee to knee with me and place your hand on my stomach,' the body cries. 'Touch me here and here and here,' it says 'and the life of desire will be restored.' And indeed it is, dramatically. Touched by the hand of the physician, who is not now a mesmerist too easily dismissed, the body falls into a seizure, and in this state it explodes in a delirium of erotic or religious passion. Figure 5.5 illustrates this wild delirium of erotic and religious frenzy. The body of desire released in sexual excitement or religious ecstasy is quite apparent.

Again, however, we must note that there is a kind of margin of safety

Figure 5.3 A. Brouillet, *Clinical Lesson of Dr Charcot*

Figure 5.4 Hysterogenic points on the body of an hysteric

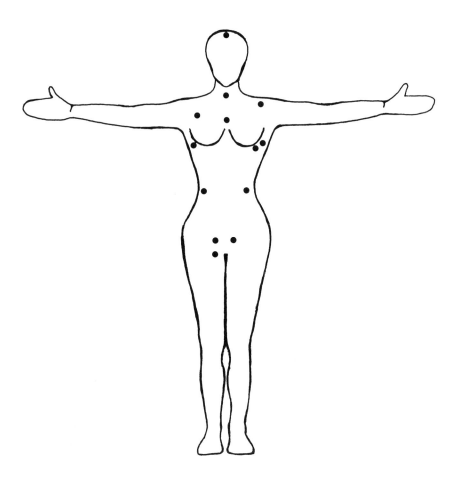

Drawing by Liota Odom from *The Birth of Neurosis*, by G. F. Drinka, courtesy of the author

between the shadow body of the hysteric and the culture of the abandoned body represented by the physician. Charcot's hysteric presents the body of desire, like the hypnotized and mesmerized bodies do, ambiguously. In a state of seizure, her body betrays desire but she does not do so. A shadow of the reflex body is appearing here, a body whose action is separate from the person. In its state of seizure, the hysteric's body is simultaneously reminding us, through mimicry, exaggeration, and distortion, of the reflex body, and offering us a distance from it. With its automaticity the seizure presents the reflex body short-circuited, as it were, by passion, but it is a passion

Figure 5.5 Passionate attitudes: crucifixion, erotic posturing, ecstasy

From *The Birth of Neurosis*, by G. F. Drinka, courtesy of the author

which no one owns. The body of desire is here but no one need be responsible for it. We should not hear in all this, however, a disparagement of the hysteric, for this presence by absence is only what the cultural dream of the abandoned body will allow. Only in a kind of sleep or in a state of seizure can the body of desire make its shadowy claims. Charcot's understanding of these seizures, released or terminated by touch, demonstrates this restriction. For him they are consequences of anatomical functioning, and in this respect Charcot aligns hysterical seizures with epilepsy and thereby reaffirms the primacy of the abandoned body. The hysterical body as a shadow body of desire is a disturbing reminder. Appearing in the guise of a seizure, it can be interpreted as belonging to the seizures of epilepsy, and in this way it can be safely disguised again beneath the abandoned body.

What Charcot, however, could not hear was better heard by Freud. Or perhaps we should say that what the hysteric body whispered to Charcot it shouted at Freud. In any case, the shadow history of the hysteric body does take a new turn with Freud, although here again the difficulty which the shadow body has in being recognized is demonstrated throughout Freud's career. An instance of this difficulty, at the beginning of his career, can be the place to start our discussion of Freud and the hysteric body.

In 1895 Freud and Breuer published five case histories of hysteria. At the time Freud, having already returned from Paris where he had studied with Charcot, was 39 years of age, while Breuer was past 50. Since they were presenting a subject which was still marginal in German psychiatry and medicine, despite the Frenchman Charcot, Freud was quite understandably pleased at this association with an older, respected colleague who also happened, like him, to be Jewish. In the Vienna of the time Jewish origins were not a big advantage. The association, however, was not destined for longevity, primarily because of Breuer's hesitation. Earlier, in 1882, Breuer was seized by a panic in conjunction with his work with one of his young hysteric patients. As she began to improve under Breuer's caring hand, she confessed to him that she was pregnant with his child, and to prove it, she developed the symptoms of pregnancy. Breuer was horrified, and in shock over this development which he could not explain, he hurriedly fled Vienna for a vacation in Paris with his wife. At the very beginning of Freud's work with the hysteric body, then, there was, through his colleague's departure, another instance of escape from the body of desire. Breuer's patient was not quite in a hypnotic sleep nor was she in a state of seizure when she confessed her pregnancy. She was there with Breuer, as van den Berg makes clear in his telling of the story.[29] The body of desire spoke there, but in person, as it were. What else was Breuer, who like Charcot was still the physician of the abandoned body, to do? How else to keep a safe distance between this body and the culture of the abandoned body? Breuer did what we would expect. He ran away.

Freud, however, stayed, and the hysteric body of desire which Breuer abandoned gave birth to psychoanalysis. The history of the relations between psychoanalysis and the hysteric body is filled with ambiguity and ambivalence, oscillating as it does between the twin poles of embracing this body on its terms and denying it. We cannot, however, even sketch that history here, but we can note that in eventually abandoning hypnosis Freud, most probably without recognizing it, allowed the hysteric body its place while awake. Psychoanalysis does not silence the hysteric body by obliging it to sleep, although it does so in other ways. We shall consider this issue as well as some of the things spoken by the body of desire in the final chapter of our story. To complete our current discussion, however, we need to say a few more things about Freud and the hysteric.

In his collaborative effort with Breuer,[30] Freud demonstrated that the hysteric in her bodily symptoms behaves as if she knows nothing of anatomy. Her bodily symptoms, whether they be a motor paralysis, a loss of speech, an inability to see, do not reveal or betray any anatomical connection, and in this respect Freud quite explicitly accepted the hysteric body on its own terms. The hysteric body is not the body of anatomy. It is its shadow, and in recognizing the symptom in this fashion Freud went a long way toward accepting this shadow of the abandoned body. Indeed, he did more than accept it; he began to develop its meanings. In his case history of Dora,[31] for example, Freud's analysis of her hysterical symptoms led him to an awareness that the body speaks a symbolic language, which is neither reducible to the mechanisms of the abandoned body, nor able to be distanced from the flesh as a pure meaning of a spectator's mind. On the contrary, the hysteric's symptomatic body is between these categories of machine and mind, behind the abandoned body, which as anatomized corpse belongs on the dissecting table, and the self behind the window, a consciousness which has removed itself from the body and the world. For Freud every hysterical symptom 'has a psychical significance, a meaning' which, however, necessarily involves a certain degree of 'somatic compliance.'[32] The hysteric body is a compliant body, a body which is bent on meaning, as it were, and as such quite different from a dumb, brute mindless mechanism.

Moreover, insofar as the shadow history of the body has been so much a shadow history of the body of desire, we should not be surprised that Freud 'discovers' that the hysteric body bent on meaning is fired with desire.[33] In its symptoms the hysteric body betrays an erotic, sexual history, because this body, especially in the wake of the mesmerized and hypnotized bodies, is so very much the shadow of the reflex body, that body whose automatic motion in the world has been purified of any movement of desire toward the world. Indeed, we could even say that the hysteric's body is re-membered by desire, and for Freud that is precisely what the hysteric's symptoms are. They are her memories. The symptomatic body is the memory of a desire, of a sexuality, which has been displaced from the world. Moreover, when we recognize with Freud that 'hysterics suffer mainly from reminiscences,'[34] we realize how eloquent a witness the hysteric body is to the fact that the body forced to bear its memories and desires alone and apart from the world breaks down. Indeed, the hysteric body dramatically draws attention to how much the living, e-motional human body is the movement of desire toward the world, how very much the flesh of the body and that of the world are, as Merleau-Ponty says, intertwined.[35] Freud himself recognized this connection between the human body and the world, for the symptom reveals not only a body bent on meaning and fired or re-membered by desire, but also a body which is radically social. The hysteric's symptoms, Freud noted, are identifications with and substitutions for relationships with other people. Thus, for example, a hysterical loss of voice for which there is no physiological basis can very well be mute testimony to a broken relation with a significant other. In the absence of voice this symptom can very well bespeak the silence of estrangement.

As much as Freud was able to appreciate the shadow character of the hysteric's body, however, he was not able to appreciate it as a shadow cast by the character of an age. The hysteric, unlike the witch, was not tortured and burned. She was not imprisoned as a madwoman. Nor was she otherwise silenced and dismissed like the mesmerized and hypnotized patients who preceded her. On the contrary, she was simply diagnosed and treated. In the diagnosis and treatment of the hysteric, however, the shadow of the abandoned body was once again placed at a safe distance from the culture of the abandoned body which made its appearance necessary. First the symptom was removed to the past and located in a traumatic event of seduction between father and child, and then, as if this distance were not yet far enough, the event of seduction by the father became the child's wish for seduction. But whether it was a case of an actual event or a wish, the hysteric body as a shadow of the abandoned body nevertheless lost its power to comment upon our cultural dreams of departure and reincarnation. Psychoanalysis at the turn of the nineteenth century had the opportunity to open up the shadow, symptom, dream side of technological culture. It had the chance to show how the symptomatic body, the neurotic body, is the underside of the technological body. It had the possibility to reveal that technology is psychologically a culture of the abandoned body and the departed earth. But it did not do so, although as we shall hear in the final chapter of our story, the opportunity to do so remains. That it did not do so, however, has had the consequence of making another return of the shadow body necessary, and it is to this shadow that we now turn.

F   The starving skeleton

No one has ever died of hysteria. People, however, do die of anorexia. I take this difference to be a rough index of how far along the path of the abandoned body and its shadow we have traveled. And I take it, too, to be an indication of the circular character of the journey, of an ending which returns us to the beginning before the circle spirals to a new level. In the beginning, with the figure of the witch, the shadow body brings the presence of death. Now, in our own time, anorexia casts its shadow of death over our increasing perfection of the abandoned body, over that body through which we would escape death. In the beginning, the shadow body which would remind us of the dark impossibility of this dream of escape is forced to die, since no one cares for such a reminder at the beginning of a dream. Now, however, that we are deeply into the dream and are beginning to sense something of its nightmare, the shadow body itself is the harbinger of death, the insistent, dramatic reminder that the dream of escaping death through the discovery, invention, and perfection of a technological body is the pursuit of death itself.

The anorexic body is, among many other things, a ghostly witness of the extent to which we have failed to nourish the living flesh with our dream of abandoning the body and departing earth. In dreaming this dream we have in effect declared that matter no longer matters. Small wonder, then, that in the midst of plenty the anorexic starves. Indeed the more we try to force-feed her, to put flesh back on her bones, the closer she comes to death. It is as if through her battle with food we are given a symbol that the material world we have created is a dead matter, a world which cannot sustain us.

We cannot, however, view the anorexic's refusal of food as only a negative sign. To do so would be again a refusal of the shadow. In her remarkable book, *Starving Women*,[36] Angelyn Spignesi consistently attends to the anorexic and her symptoms, and in so doing she helps us to appreciate what the anorexic would have us remember. Her refusal of food, for example, and her obsessive counting of calories, mockingly imitate and caricature our objectification of food. On the other hand, the ritualization which accompanies the preparation and eating of food reanimates food and the human activity of eating it. The anorexic's rituals display in symptomatic form the forgotten value that food matters, that it is not just a consumable thing but a vital potency, that it is alive, not of course with calories but with a power to sustain life *and* to bring death. The starving body of the anorexic, then, dramatically awakens us to the fact that the preparation and eating of food belong to the circle of life which includes death. The anorexic body is not a corpse, equally distant from the living and the dead body, but a living body dying of starvation, and in this respect she calls us to remember that food is always communion and that in eating it we enter into union with others, into community.

The anorexic's refusal of food in the pursuit of an airy thinness is often complemented by a manic zeal for exercise. She diets and she runs, seeking, as it were, the image of a perfect body. Hilda Bruch, who is a recognized authority on anorexia, cites this theme of perfection as a predominant issue in the lives of anorexics. As she notes in her work,[37] the anorexic is often seen in the eyes of parents and teachers as the perfect child, obedient, well mannered, and controlled. Taking upon herself the burden of this image, the anorexic seeks to achieve it, regulating her life by transforming ordinary, natural activities into technical, measured functions. Food is weighed and records are kept of eating and exercise. But in all of this, the anorexic caricatures to the point of exaggeration an image of the body as machine and reminds us that the dark side of this pursuit of perfection is the shadow of death. Indeed, in her manic zeal to exercise the body to the point of perfection, the anorexic appropriately casts her shadow upon the exercised, properly toned, well muscled bodies so visible in our health spas and our television advertisements. If you imaginatively introduce the figure of the anorexic into this space, and if you see these bodies through the eyes of the anorexic, then perhaps you can see how these bodies, whose muscles protrude from the inside, like the bones of the anorexic, are bodies which fit everywhere and anywhere and hence belong nowhere. Earlier in our tale of the abandoned body we showed how such bodies, with an interior space stuffed with organs and which belong nowhere, characterize the corpse. In her dramatic ritualization of exercise, then, the anorexic becomes a stark commentary on the corpse, on those bodies which in exercising for exercise's sake pursue a perfection which has become detached from the specificity of any living situation. She becomes, in her haunting presence, with her haggard features and tired eyes, the other, exhausted side of this anatomized corpse resurrected as machine and exercised to death. Imaginatively installed within this space of the perfected body, the anorexic shows us how our health spas, like our attitudes toward food, can be inimical to life, gymnasiums of death. In that space, she shows us the curious, ironic, but terrifying fact that our manic pursuit of health may actually be a loss of life.

So much more can be made of the anorexic's symptoms. So much more can be learned from this shadow of the abandoned body. I will, however, restrict myself to one final comment.

Although in rare instances some male cases of anorexia do occur, the anorexic is essentially a woman. Again, therefore, it is the feminine figure who carries the shadow and in this particular instance, as Spignesi again so poignantly argues, the anorexic makes the feminine character of the shadow quite clear. The refusal of food, the pursuit of thinness, and the cessation of her menses all focus our attention on the ways in which we have tradition- ally bound the woman to the material earth. In the refusal of food, she shows us how in assigning to her the tasks of purchasing, preparing, and serving food, we have exiled her to the kitchen. In the pursuit of thinness, she indicates how we have imprisoned her within a masculine ideal of the beautiful body. And in the cessation of her menses she calls our attention to how we have objectified her generative capacities as the functions of repro- duction, how we have chained the woman's body to the categories of gynecology, or as Mary Daly even more forcefully argues in her startling, disturbing book *Gyn/Ecology*,[38] how we have actually tortured, maimed, and murdered the woman's body in the practice of our medicine. Through each of these symptoms the anorexic, I would suggest, vividly calls our attention to the masculine character of our dreams of departure from the earth and escape from the body. We are all astronauts in this technological age, but the astronautic body of technological functioning there on the launchpad prepared and ready to depart the earth, is a masculine figure. And the shadow of the abandoned body, the body left behind, exiled, imprisoned, and enchained, is the figure of the woman. What the shadow history of the abandoned body shows, then, is that technology as a cultural- psychological dream of departing earth and remaking the body is not only a dream of escape from matter but also a flight from the feminine. Perhaps it is even a flight from the maternal, as Susan Griffin suggests in her work. She writes: '. . . it is not easy to forget the real shape of our mother's body. The memory of her powerfulness haunts us; our bodies remember her.'[39] Such a reminder can only weigh down the spirit that would soar, a mascu- line and manly spirit that would forget its dependence on the maternal and on nature while ascending the heights. Out of this denial, then, it becomes necessary to create 'a dualism between culture and nature, intellect and emotion, spirit and matter', and to make of women carriers of the negative side of these dualisms, 'symbols of feeling, carnality, nature, all that is in civilization's "unconscious" and that it would deny.'[40] Thus the woman is made into a witch to be burned at the stake, or driven mad and imprisoned in the asylum, or made to carry our denied carnality in a mesmerized or hypnotic state, or imagined as a monster exiled to the desolate landscapes of a frozen world, or diagnosed and treated as a hysteric and thereby dismissed as hysterical, or finally exiled, imprisoned, chained and abandoned as anorexic to the material earth from which we would depart. In closing our history of the abandoned body and its shadows, I would, therefore, suggest that the anorexic is truly antipode to the astronaut. The astronaut and the anorexic are the soul of technological culture, its psyche split into the departing masculine self and the abandoned feminine. As we take leave of the earth, then, in a body newly created and designed for space, we might pause, turn back, and catch a glimpse of who and what of ourselves we leave behind. There on the departed and perhaps fully deadened earth stands the anorexic, starving skeleton who mocks our 'ideal of "mind over body." '[41]

V Our ambiguous inheritance: a final word

In this story of the body as specimen I have concentrated on the discovery– invention of a body to suit the space of linear perspective vision, and I have presented a brief history of this abandoned body and its shadows. I have told the story in this fashion in order to indicate that the body of today, the body in which almost all of our human activities have been understood and re-made in terms of technical functions, is a history. If we realize that there is a history of the body, a cultural history of the flesh, we are less inclined, I believe, to take our specimen body too literally, less inclined to assume that this objectified body is the real body, the way the body is and must be, the only body that there is. For in fact it is neither the only, nor even the most real, way in which we are embodied. On the contrary, the body of technical functioning, which has been symbolized in our story by the figure of the astronaut, is the most general and most minimal way in which we are incarnated. Moreover, as Barbara Duden reminds us in a brief but insightful article entitled 'Historical concepts of the body', a profound difference remains between this objective body of knowledge created in distance from oneself and one's living body, between the body which one has and the body which one is. Indeed with respect to this specimen body she says, 'I feel anaesthetised because the categories I was educated to describe myself [in] cannot be felt.'[42] Each of us may know, for example, that his or her heart is a pump, but no one, except in extreme circumstances of illness or accident which disrupt the flow of one's life, experiences the heart in this fashion.

Our tale, then, has attempted to show that the human body is primarily and essentially a matter of culture and history and that as such it changes. Nothing in this tale, of course, either negates or challenges the fact that the human body is also a matter of nature, a matter of physical corporeality which over the long course of human evolution is more or less constant rather than changing. Indeed, in discovering–inventing the specimen body, we have, as a culture of science and technology, emphasized the natural, constant, and physical aspects of our embodiment. But we have done so in such a way as to virtually exclude the body's cultural–historical character and to obscure even the fact that our discovery–invention of the specimen body is itself a cultural–historical achievement.

It would not do, however, to conclude this story without at least mentioning the body today. I end my tale of the body, therefore, with two images.

The specimen body, the body of technical functioning, today has many guises. Of all those that could be indicated, however, it is, I would propose, the medical body and the pornographic body which anchor the range of its expression. Each of them epitomizes the objectification of the body, and each of them creates its body through a distant gaze, through a vision which transforms the body into an object of vision. Moreover, each of them owes its ancestry to the corpse: the medical body insofar as our knowledge of it is at least in part the consequence of the anatomical corpse, and the pornographic body insofar as the pornographic eye, as Susan Griffin so clearly demonstrates,[43] seeks through the humiliation and subjugation of the flesh the reduction of the body to an inanimate thing.

These bodies, of course, also differ, and we rightfully regard the medical body as an illustrious example of our technology. I do not wish to dispute this achievement. But in singing its praises we cannot forget that the medical body is an ambiguous inheritance. It is ambiguous because the very same attitude of distance and objectification which realizes the medical body also realizes the bomb. We need to ask, therefore, if and how our practice of medicine, and perhaps our too easy acceptance of modern medicine's pervasive influence on our society, might contribute to our becoming desensitized to our responsibilities. To the degree that we can so easily hand over our bodies to medicine and thereby take leave of our bodies, we might too readily and unknowingly fall into this habit of mind, and to the same degree, therefore, hand over other dimensions of our living to those whom we perceive as experts. In the small acts of distancing ourselves from ourselves we may very well encourage a more fatal and final surrender of responsibility.

The medical body is an ambiguous inheritance in yet another way. Are we, for example, really so sure that the increasing medicalization of our society reaps only positive benefits? Apart from the increasingly obvious fact that the medical body which we are continuously improving with our machines, diagnostic techniques, drugs, and surgical procedures is fast becoming a body few if any can afford, there is the disturbing possibility that our health has really not improved all that much under these conditions. Indeed, Ivan Illich has indicated that our overall health has in fact declined as a result of the medicalization of society, and he may very well be correct. Certainly his book *Medical Nemesis*[44] makes for disturbing reading, and we cannot afford to ignore the data which he cites. Our research and our cures — apart from the fact of their increasing expense — might very well be worse than the disease, or, as Illich points out, might even be the spur to new problems. But just as we cannot disinvent the bomb, we cannot disinvent the medical body. It is not, therefore, a question of cancellation. It is rather a question of learning how to live with the knowledge which we have — a question which requires some closure of that distance which has already moved us too far from ourselves, our bodies, and the earth.

I close, therefore, with these two images of the medical and the pornographic bodies to remind us of the ambiguity of our inheritance. Together these two bodies might help us to remember not to forget that the abandoned body casts a shadow.

Chapter six

World as spectacle

I Introduction: a window on the world

Linear perspective vision places a window between ourselves and the world and establishes the hegemony of the eye as the world's measure. In doing so it has established the conditions for an emotional and attitudinal shift toward the world. It creates a psychological distance from the world which makes possible an emotional retreat or withdrawal from the world. It gives birth to the self as spectator and transforms the body into a specimen, an object of vision and observation. Out of that attitudinal, emotional distance we have realized actual distances. Within the space opened up by linear perspective vision, we have realized the dream of a technological world. Within that dream, all of us today are astronauts, embarked on spaceship earth for a journey to the stars, with bodies which have been remade for space in terms of technical functions. Abandoning the body as it is lived, we have refashioned it, discovered–invented it as anatomical corpse. Departing earth, we have discovered–invented it as a Copernican ball in space.

But what we have done with (to?) ourselves and our bodies we have also done with (to?) the world. The window of linear perspective vision is after all a window on the world, and if there is a spectator behind the window looking at the world it is because there is a world in front of that window for the spectator to see.

A world to see! That is precisely the point. When the world is viewed through a window, the world is well on the way to becoming an object of vision. Complementing the spectator self behind the window, and the specimen body, the window of linear perspective vision has effectively transformed the world into a spectacle. Spectator, specimen, spectacle belong together. They are, so to speak, the codes of a technological civilization, the signatures, as it were, of self, body, world. When the self becomes a spectator and the body a specimen, the world becomes a spectacular place.

In this part of our story we shall consider how, in the space opened up by linear perspective vision, the world becomes a matter of explanation and a matter of light. We shall also consider how, within this space, the things of the world are changed.[1]

II World as story and as fact

The reader might recall that within linear perspective space the horizon line sets the limit for the height of any object to be depicted within its space, and that this line is fixed at the eye level of an observer imagined to be standing on a horizontal plane, staring straight ahead at the world. In effect, linear perspective vision establishes a homogeneous space where all objects and viewers of such objects are placed on the same horizontal, level plane. As a direct consequence of this condition, depth as a matter of levels becomes depth as a matter of spatial distance. Moreover, this transformation of the world's depth is an indispensible element in the rise of the modern scientific world of explanations. Figure 2.4 previously illustrated these themes and can do so again, should the reader wish to return to it.[2]

The transition from a space in which the world's depth is a matter of levels to a space in which its depth is a matter of spatial distance, to a horizontal space where all objects lie on the same plane, was and is a profound cultural–psychological shift in the history of humanity. With that change we opened up a new world. Inventing that space, we made a space for the invention of modern science. Making that space, we made room for the world to become an arena of discoverable facts. Creating a space in which everything was arranged on the same plane, we created the space within which everything could be explained.

In its root sense, to explain means to make level or plane, to flatten out or to smooth out. When we explain things, then, we level things out, often by reducing one thing to something else. We level out the differences, as it were, and in doing so we make such things equal or the same, at least within the space of the explanation. If, for example, I am inclined toward a psychoanalytic interpretation of behavior and motivation, I might, in response to your request for an explanation of your husband's stinginess, explain that such a tight-fisted attitude with money owes it origins to a tight-assed disposition toward feces in the anal stage of development. Such an explanation, of course, would be a crude oversimplification, and I do not intend its use here as a caricature of psychoanalysis. Rather I want only to illustrate with a simple example how explanation is a process of equalization, a process of seeing one thing in terms of another by relating or even reducing one thing to another, which often also includes a sequence of cause and effect. The cause–effect character of explanation does not, however, concern us here. For our purposes, it is sufficient that this example indicates only that explanation places seemingly dissimilar things on the same plane. Thus in terms of our example, current stinginess with money and the earlier retention of feces, two quite different phenomena, are placed within the same epistemological space. In the explanation their differences are erased.

In the early history of science, Galileo proceeds in much the same fashion. He establishes his law of falling bodies, according to which all bodies regardless of their weight fall equally fast, by experimenting with small wooden balls rolling down an incline plane. He does this and he also, according to popular legend, drops stones of unequal weight from the tower at Pisa. Now whether the latter actually happened is not at issue here, and I cite it only to indicate that Galileo's explanation applies to all kinds of falling objects in all kinds of situations. Whether the objects are small wooden balls or stones, and whether the situation is a constructed incline plane in a laboratory or a tower in a busy square, does not matter. The explanation gathers together under one law all falling objects in all conceivable situations, and in this respect it establishes an equivalency between them. In effect, the explanation creates a mental space into which all of these falling objects and their situations are gathered, and in that space their differences disappear. These differences are, if you will, smoothed out, which is only another way of saying that these objects are placed on the same level or plane of existence. Outside this space of explanation, the differences matter, and different objects and their falls matter in different ways. They belong to different levels of existence. For example, if I drop a ceramic coffee cup which my wife has made as a gift for my birthday, its fall to the floor is not equivalent to the fall of a glass of milk dropped by my son. The objects differ from each other and each of them has a different meaning. Each of them lies on a different level or plane of existence, and their falls do matter. Moreover, we should even probably say that they fall in different ways. With respect to what each of them is and in relation to my life, they do not fall equally fast to the floor. Indeed, to establish the fact that they do fall equally fast, I must remove and distance myself from their differences, detach myself from their respective situations and situate them in that neutral space where they and their falls are the same. If and when I do that, then, and only then, are the falls of these objects ready to be explained.

When we create a world where all objects lie on the same plane, we are ready to make a world where all objects can be explained. Linear perspective vision creates such a space, and in doing so it prepared the way for us to create the world of scientific explanations. In that space and in that world we go about the business of smoothing out the differences. Moreover, things which do not fit into that space, things which are different and which properly belong to different levels of existence, are destined to disappear.

One early example of something which did not fit within this newly created space of explanation was the angel. Indeed, the angel, who is above ordinary life, began to find less and less space in the world of linear perspective vision. Already by the late fifteenth century, for example, angels were being painted standing on and supported by clouds, because they had lost their place in the world. But what was and is true of angels was and is true of the demons below ordinary life, and if heaven and matters of the spirit increasingly ceased to make sense in the world of scientific explanations, so too did hell and its demons. These levels of reality and all that belongs to them were destined to become only private, subjective, interior fictions, perhaps to be dreamed and imagined, but certainly no longer to be seen as part of the objective, measurable world of facts and explanations. They were destined to become, I would suggest, the unconscious of our age, the unconscious of that spectator self installed in his or her space of explanation.

In a recent issue of *American Scientist*, Bert Hansen offers an illuminating insight into the issue we are discussing. The theme of his article concerns the eclipse of magic with the rise of the scientific revolution, an eclipse which has been so thorough that today we find it nearly impossible to hear the word 'magic' without thinking 'illusion'. He begins with a discussion of 'The Franklin's Tale' from Chaucer's fourteenth-century *Canterbury Tales*. In the story Dorigen, while awaiting her husband's return, is forced to withstand the proposals of an unwanted suitor. To gain time and, hopefully, to defeat his proposals, Dorigen challenges the suitor to remove every rock from the coast of Brittany. The suitor, not to be thwarted, enlists the aid of a young cleric with reported magical powers. Together they return to Brittany. Hansen, quoting Chaucer, writes:

> The skilled cleric . . . worked night and day, doing all that was possible to arrive quickly at the results of his astrological computations; that is to say, to bring about an illusion by some juggling appearance . . . so that Dorigen and everyone would think and say that the rocks had either gone away from Brittany or else that they had sunk underground. At last he arrived at the proper time to work his tricks and magic in that cursed superstitious manner. He brought out his astronomical tables from Toledo, carefully corrected. He lacked nothing, neither his tables for short periods of years nor those for longer periods; nor his roots and other mathematical gear, such as his centers, his quantities, and his tables of proportions for all sets of equations . . . He calculated all these things very expertly. He was quite sure that the moon's motion was favorable for his operation and he knew all the other details to be observed in order to purchase such illusions and evil tricks as the heathen people practiced in those days. Therefore, he waited no longer, but as a result of his magic, it seemed for a week or two that all the rocks had disappeared.[3]

Hansen, in considering this story, notes that in the Middle Ages, in that world space preceding the space of explanation created by linear perspective vision, 'the power to create illusion and the power to produce physical change are not easily distinguished.' Thus, Hansen asks, 'Did the cleric . . . simply calculate the coming of an unusually high tide? Did he somehow affect the expectations and perceptions of the relevant observers? Or could he really make the rocks disappear?' The three questions offer three possibilities. Hansen, however, correctly notes that for us today only the first two questions can be taken seriously. But wisely he adds, 'That people today would seriously consider only the first two possibilities merely reflects the modern assumptions that magical effects cannot be real and that what is real cannot be magical.'[4] In short, Hansen notes about magic what we have already noted about angels and demons. In the space of explanations magic has no more place than either demons or angels do, and thus without question and by definition they are all unreal. Hansen himself puts it this way: 'In the scientific revolution the realm of the natural widened to become coterminous with the real and squeezed the rest out into the nothingness of being unreal, fictitious, and fantastic, or magical'.[5]

Heaven, hell, and magic were not, however, the only things destined to be discarded in the space of explanation: so too was the value of history. In the space of explanation, we turned our eye toward the future and turned our back on the past. Progress and not history was destined to matter. Indeed, the geometry of linear perspective vision already prescribed it. Within that space not only are all objects situated on the same plane, but also they are arrayed before us as a spectator staring straight ahead at the world. Hence, insofar as this geometry became a cultural habit of mind, not only were the things of the world which belong to different vertical levels of existence, above and below life, as it were, reduced to the same horizontal level of existence or destined to disappear, but also the things behind us, matters of the past, as it were, were eclipsed in favor of what lies in front of us, matters of the future.

Descartes understood this issue well, and in comparing the value of mathematical knowledge and historical knowledge of the world he unequivocally chose the former. History, he thought, was rather useless, since all the patient work of a historian on ancient Rome, for example, could produce a knowledge merely equivalent to what a maidservant of the time might have had. The study of the past was ambiguous, mere opinion, while the mathematical study of nature offered certainty and the promise of progress in increasing knowledge. Indeed, Descartes was so certain of the progressive character of science and its power of explanation that he felt that in time one man would be able to gather together all that could be known of the world. Needless to say, Descartes also thought that that man could very well be himself!

But if we are inclined to be amused by Descartes' naïvety, we should not ignore the fact that this optimism about science and its explanations of the world went hand in hand with a firm belief in the progress of science and the future betterment of humanity. Indeed, this coupling of science and progress was something of a credo in the early history of science which lasted well into the late nineteenth century, and anyone who has read, for example, Francis Bacon cannot help but marvel at this firm belief in, and commitment to, the future. Francis Bacon, who in many ways can be regarded as the founding father of the modern scientific method of experi-metation, died from a chill he caught while stuffing a dead chicken with snow in an attempt to find another way for preserving food. We know of course that the achievement of this aim had to await the work of Clarence Birdseye in 1925, but if nothing else Bacon and his method did indicate that firm belief in the future as progress, and his experiment with the dead chicken does seem to earn him the appellation of 'The Man Who Saw Through Time.'[6] It fits him and all those who, standing within the space of explanation, view the world head on.

The space of explanation is the landscape of our world, and in that space the world's depth as a matter of different levels has been eclipsed by depth as a matter of spatial distance on a plane which progresses toward infinity. We believe in progress and in facts and we are uncomfortable with mystery and imagination. Indeed, any sense of the world as a reality of multiple levels simultaneously coexisting is the stuff of fancy and of dream. Consider, for a moment, the painting by Marc Chagall illustrated in Figure 6.1. It is called *Paris through the Window*, and it is obvious that the *window* has changed and that it looks out on a new landscape. It is a landscape of the dream, and from the perspective of waking life where linear, single-plane reality is a cultural habit of mind, this landscape is quite unbelievable. We simply do not see the world in this fashion, except perhaps in our dreams and in art — the safe confines of the imagination. Using the word as an adjective rather than as the name of a historical artistic movement, Chagall's landscape is *surreal*. Multiple dimensions and levels of reality are superimposed one upon the other, and in the presence of that kind of land-scape we are in the midst of a depth which simultaneously reaches below and above the surface plane of our waking reality. To put this all another way, Chagall's landscape is not the subject matter of explanation. It evokes and requires a different kind of response from us, because it presents a different world.

The works of the contemporary photographer Jerry Uelsmann do the same thing, but it is worth our while to mention him here because he never-theless uses a camera to break the hold which linear perspective camera vision has had upon our consciousness and perception of reality. For Uelsmann, the camera does not merely reproduce the world of visible facts. On the contrary, it displays the world as a visual metaphor, a world of juxtapositions, contrasts, and multiple images. In speaking of his own work, Uelsmann says, 'I am involved with a kind of reality that transcends surface reality.' This reality, he adds, is 'More than physical reality, it is emotional, irrational, intellectual, and.psychological.'[7] It is the reality of

Figure 6.1 Marc Chagall, *Paris Through The Window*, 1913

Reproduced by permission of Solomon R. Guggenheim Museum, New York; photograph by Robert E. Mates

the depths, and, in this respect, I would venture to add that Uelsmann's photographs present the unconscious landscape of our age, that landscape of coexisting multiple levels of reality which was exiled to the shadows of the night in the clear, daylight space of explanation, the space within which all the things of the world became situated on one and the same plane.

That there has been a movement like surrealism in our time not only in the plastic arts but also in literature (as exemplified by the symbolist poets and the works of Poe and Kafka); that there are photographers like Uelsmann and Hockney; that there has been a place made by psycho-analysis for the presence of these shadows of the night, for symbol, image, dream; that all this and much more has occurred within our time indicates that there has been a *breakdown* of our linear perspective vision of reality, and the *breakthrough* of another vision and a new world. In the final chapter of our story we shall take up this theme and consider its implications for the cultural–psychological story of technology. At the moment, however, it is important to indicate that such instances as we have mentioned above have remained, for the most part, encapsulated within the reigning space of explanation. Our reigning vision of the world as a space where everything, lying on the same plane, is a matter of objective fact has been able to appropriate virtually all of the above, either by confining it to the world of art, which, it is assumed, has little if anything to do with real life, or by indexing to it the adjective 'subjective'. In these ways we can safeguard and preserve the factual, unidimensional character of our levelheaded world. But in doing so we miss the all-important truth that these landscapes are the unconscious of our age, symptoms in need of our attention. Moreover, unless we somehow learn to attend to these symptoms, to experience the world in a fashion which welcomes metaphor, image, symbol, and dream in addition to fact, we may very well create monsters out of these shadows.

To attend to the symptoms is, however, always difficult, and that shadows can easily turn into monsters is all too obvious. Moments of breakdown and breakthrough are filled with danger, because old visions die hard while new ones struggle to be born. As an example, consider that moment, captured in the landscapes of Bosch, where the medieval world was being eclipsed by the new world of linear perspective values and vision. Recall his painting, *The Temptation of St Anthony*, illustrated earlier in Figure 2.5. What is depicted there is a world of multiple symbolic resonances, a world whose depth was not one of spatial distance but of vertical levels. By Bosch's time, however, that world was fast disappearing beneath and above the visual homogenous space opened up by linear perspective vision, and Bosch's paintings depict the nightmarish, monstrous, chaotic quality of a world being cast into the shadows. As McLuhan notes, 'Bosch injected the spaces of the medieval dream world into the new Renaissance spaces,'[8] and the result was that the depths of the medieval world took on the face of terror. Looking at Bosch's paintings, we might wonder what faces of terror will mark the breakdown of the world of linear perspective vision, if and when we attend the symptoms of breakdown. We might also wonder, however, what dreams of destruction might be realized if we fail to heed the symptoms.

The medieval world, with its vision of a reality of multiple and simultaneous levels, was long ago, and the world of someone like Chagall seems at best amusing, and most probably strange. And yet, even if only in our dreams, we know these worlds and share these visions. Whatever a culture's vision of a world, the world at large remains our home, and that home embraces both the vision and its shadows. The world as our home is always multi-leveled. Like a house, it has many *stories*. We need to attend to this more holistic view of the world, to a view which embraces surface and depth, to a view which allows us to experience the world not just in terms of facts to be discovered and known, but also in terms of stories to be imagined and heard. Indeed, we need to do so not only because we live our lives through stories, but also because we need stories to make the living of life a human reality. Facts alone are not enough, and in an age like ours, linear in its vision, literal in its cast of mind, and factual in its attitude, we will invent stories commensurately with the degree to which we become technical and managed in our living. In a society as highly technological as ours has become, we see, for example, the proliferation of games like 'Dungeons and Dragons', television shows like *Star Trek* and *Starman*, and films like *E.T.* and *Star Wars*, all of which point to a kind of hunger for the more mythic dimensions of life, for those things that elude and lie outside the rational and the explained. For in the final analysis, we need something larger than the space of explanation in which to live, something deeper and higher to reach for, something in addition to the facts we may describe and know. We need stories to guide us and show the way, two functions which are contained in the very meaning of the word 'story'.[9] To survive and to live a human life we need more than facts which we can get hold of. We also need, in the sense that James Hillman's works indicate, myths that take hold of us.[10]

III Energy as the light of the world

Linear perspective vision lays stress upon the visual sense and de-emphasizes the other ways in which the world makes sense. When the window of linear perspective vision has become a primary cultural metaphor, a habit of mind, the world has become primarily a matter for the eye alone. It has become primarily a visible matter, well on the way toward becoming a bit of observable, measurable, analyzable data, readable as a computer print-out, for example, or perhaps as a blip on a radar screen. Indeed, so many of our technological instruments emphasize this feature of visibility — microscope, telescope, camera, television — that we might venture to say that our sense of reality has nearly become identical with our ability to render something visible. Seeing is believing, we say, and in our technological environment this old cliché has taken on a weighted meaning. It is, for example, the microscopic cellular evidence which often convinces a patient that he or she is ill, even when the experience of illness is at best ambiguous or perhaps absent. We live in a diagnostic age and to diagnose something is literally to know something through seeing it.

But perhaps the most persuasive indicator of our commitment to the belief that what is real is what can be made visible is the pervasive presence of television in our lives. Indeed, we might even say that our window on the world has become a television screen, and that the world as spectacle has in this respect become *programmed*. Surely television news coverage often leaves the impression that world events have become something like a soap opera, insofar as the line between fact and fiction often seems dimmed. How close the reporting of news comes to the making of news is a real issue in our society today, as witnessed, for example, by the media coverage of events like hijackings and hostage situations, or even so called prime time sporting events. We do not like to think that such things are *staged* for the television camera (a metaphor which emphasizes the role of vision), but the notion of world events as media events does raise the issue. And although the increasing presence of television at world events probably does serve the positive purpose of increasing accountability by injecting into every event which it covers a large dose of public opinion, a legitimate concern remains.[11] Indeed, we are apt to say that something is real because we saw it on television, and in this respect a television society inverts and thus intensifies its belief that what is *real* is what is visible. Television almost brings us to the point of saying that everything *visible* is real. When television viewers, for example, send gifts to the bride and groom of a soap opera marriage, Alice is in Wonderland and we have all begun a descent down the rabbit hole.

Marshall McLuhan's work[12] on the medium of television is certainly relevant to this discussion. Since, however, the discussion is headed in another direction, I will simply mention that in his description of television as a medium which invites the viewer to participate with more than a distant eye, McLuhan indicates how this medium challenges the long-standing hegemony of the eye so appropriate to the culture of the reader and the book. Television, therefore, simultaneously elaborates further the rule of the eye, at least insofar as it extends the equation of visibility equals reality as we have just discussed it, and challenges that rule. Or as Donald M. Lowe puts it, television has created a new sur-reality. On one hand, it has 'extended sight and sound, [but] without reference to the other three senses.' In this respect an eclipse of the body, this time in favour of eye *and* ear, remains. On the other hand, it *superimposes* this new reality of the eye and ear over the older reality of the eye, creating quite literally a *surreality*, and in this respect it does break the rule of the singular eye of distant vision. 'The electronic surreality [of television and film] is multi-perspectival and environmental, whereas the typographic reality is uni-perspectival and objective.'[13]

Of all that can be said of television, of its power to break the reign of linear perspective vision, and/or of its power to solidify the presence of the window in emphasizing that visibility matters, the one feature which is central to the idea and the actual workings of television needs our emphasis. On the television screen the world, broken down at its source, is re-assembled as dots of light, and in this respect the television screen is everyone's personal converter of light back into matter which originally has been decomposed into light. The television screen, then, is very much our technological elaboration of the window of linear perspective vision, because in each instance the world dawns as a matter of light. Indeed, of the window and the television screen we have to say, with the full power of the pun intended, that *light matters*. On one hand, light is the issue. It is what matters, what is central, what counts. On the other hand, with the window and the television screen, the world matters as a matter of light. With the window and the television screen the matter of the world has become a matter of light. In fact, however, it has become something more, something already suggested in the notion of the television screen as everyone's personal matter–light converter.

Amidst all the events, images, inventions, and instruments which belong to our technological world, the one item which is perhaps the most fundamental is the equation $E = mc^2$. Nothing, perhaps, has had more of an impact on our lives, or indeed on the history of humanity, than this mathematical formula, which has become the symbol of our age. Expressing the relation of identity between energy and mass, this equation is the code by which the cosmic energy of the stars is released from the ordinary matter of the earth. It is a kind of magic formula which transforms the earth itself into a sun. It is the metaphor which prescribes the words (and actions) by which matter is energized.

This formula, I want to suggest, is the supreme achievement of the spectator self behind his or her window, and the supreme realization of the world as spectacle, of the world as a matter of light. Here in this equation our enlightened world is put to use. Through the window the world matters as light, and now with this equation this light of the world becomes the factor through which the world's mass is converted to energy. Light, or more accurately its characteristic speed, c, squared is the factor that tells us not only that mass is energy (and energy mass) but also by how much. Energy is mass exponentially enlightened, as it were, and this formula, symbol of our age, amplifies our recognition of the world as a matter of light. Not only is the world a matter of light, but also this light of the world is energy. With this formula we say, in effect, that the way in which the world matters as light is as energy. We say, in other words, that the world is a matter of energy and that energy is the light of the world.

Having experienced energy crises and still facing dwindling energy supplies, and living amidst continuing public debate over the advantages and dangers of nuclear energy, we find that the truth of this statement lies at the center of our lives. For some, energy truly is the light of our world, the promised savior and redeemer; for others it is the threatening spectre of either its absence or eruption in the fires of nuclear annihilation. Moreover, we know the truth of this statement in another, directly 'hands-on' way, for each time we turn the knob or touch the button which switches on the television each of us enacts this equation. Television is everyman's and everywoman's participation in this equation $E = mc^2$, insofar as the television screen is, as noted earlier, the place where the world, broken down at its source, is re-energized as light.

We are energy producers and consumers, and it is energy and our need for it which most characterize our age. Loren Eiseley, the naturalist who writes with a poet's soul, calls the western industrial human a 'world eater'[14] who has consumed nature itself. We have fed upon the earth, converting it into a resource to serve our energy needs, making it a 'gigantic gasoline station', in the vibrant image of Martin Heidegger.[15]

The history of human civilization has been a history of energy and its consumption, and again it is Eiseley who offers us a memorable image of this history. It is the ice in its cycles of advance and retreat against which humanity has built its fires. Huddled against the long dark night of winter, we wait, as we have always waited, with some dim apprehension of a final moment when the cold and the dark will have outlasted the light of our fires. That image of the last dwindling fire, of the dying light against the cold, frozen background of the distant and indifferent stars, has ensorceled the soul of humanity.

Against that moment, Eiseley says, we have constructed our civilizations. To stave off that moment, we have climbed the fiery ladder of energy production and use, and with increasing frequency we have had to consume the resources of our world. Until this century, however, the resources of the earth which we could transform and use as energy were limited. They were limited *and* non-renewable. They were also a gift, a friend from the past. Our energies were won from a heritage of fossil fuels, and against that final winter night '. . . we extracted hundreds of millions of years of stored sun . . . .' The 'long-silent burial grounds of the Carboniferous Age' fired our civilizations, and we built upon 'the corpses of the past'[16] a haven against the icy dark.

It could be said, therefore, that until this century our production and consumption of energy, based as it was on the limited and non-renewable sources created by the sun, were constrained by the yoke of necessity. What was limited would one day be absent. Scarcity and the promise of this eventual and inevitable absence of resources were Nature's way of setting limits and of enforcing limits. It could also be said that within this context our production and consumption of fossil fuels always had about it some dim, potential reminder of death. Our energies were funded, as it were, by death. The civilizations we built upon the earth were supported by the remains of the past. In our production and consumption of energy, present and past were linked. So too were life and death. The fires we built to warm us against the advancing night, to sustain and advance our life in the present, were kindled by the life which had preceded us.

In this century, however, we have broken the yoke of necessity which heretofore had marked our production and consumption of energy. With the splitting of the atom we have freed ourselves of that dependence upon resources both limited and non-renewable. Breaking into the atomic heart of matter, we have re-created here upon the earth the processes which naturally occur only in the heavens. Like some modern Prometheus we have stolen the secret of heavenly fire, and with this secret we have unleashed from the very matter of the earth the energies of the stars. The earth as repository of the sun's stored energies — wood, coal, natural gas, oil — has itself become a small sun.

But the earth as a sun is not an inhabitable place. Having become the creators of a seemingly unlimited supply of energy, having progressed, in the words of Jeremy Rifkin,[17] from a pyrotechnology to a nuclear technology, we have gone from the condition of receiving energy as an inheritance to the condition of making it ourselves. To do so, however, we have had to provoke nature in heretofore undreamt of ways. To become the authors, creators, of our own energies, we have had to discover–invent a way to break down the ancient differences so rooted in our daily lives between energy and matter. And we have done so. Splitting the atom we have overcome the split between energy and matter. We have made them one and the same. Like Dr Frankenstein, however, we may also have succeeded in producing a 'monster': the threat of nuclear conflagration. The fire of the sun, re-created upon the earth, threatens our destruction and even motivates our departure from the earth. That long, cold, wintery night of death we would escape in releasing energy from matter comes back to haunt us in the image of a nuclear winter.[18]

That matter has been reduced to energy is perhaps not immediately apparent in the equation $E = mc^2$, since m in the equation refers to mass. But the meaning of mass in physics leaves no doubt that through the equation it is matter which has been exponentially enlightened and that as such energy is the light of the world. In the context of our present discussion, it will serve us well to consider the notion of mass in some detail.

'The mass of a body,' Capra says, 'is a measure of its own weight: i.e., of the pull of gravity on the body.' In addition, he says, 'mass measures the inertia of an object: i.e., its resistance against being accelerated.'[19] In the first description 'the mass of a body' refers to its connection to the earth. The pull of gravity on a body is, as it were, an index of the strength of that body's tie to earth. Indeed, to move a body with a certain mass away from earth requires enough energy to sever that connection, and in this respect the first description of mass indicates the opposition of a body to having its connection with the earth destroyed.

The second description, moreover, has an analogous meaning. Mass as a measure of resistance to acceleration implies that a material body prefers, as it were, to stay in its place. A material body, then, is not only tied to the earth, but also is a place upon the earth, and in this respect we might say that mass refers to a material body's resistance to being displaced, either with respect to the earth as a whole, or with respect to its specific place on the earth. Or to say all this in another way, physics acknowledges that mass is a measure of a body's tie to the earth and, at least implicitly, recognizes it as a measure of a body's tie to its place. It recognizes, at least implicitly, that a material body *is* a place.

Later we shall discuss how each of these recognitions finds its support in our daily experience of things, but for the moment I want to indicate another aspect of mass contained within these two descriptions. As a measure of the earth's gravitational pull and as an index of inertia, the mass of a material body is a *resistance* to be overcome. In this respect, we might say that a material body in its tie to the earth and to a place is something to be overcome. To overcome mass is to overcome things. Physics, we might say, invites us to get over things.

We are invited to get over things with a promise. Look at the equation $E = mc^2$ again, while remembering the relation of mass and things, and you cannot fail to hear the promise. The equation says that mass, exponentially enlightened, is energy. The promise, then, is that if we let go of things, if we overcome them, they will become energy. In short the equation says that we can become creators of energy if we overcome things, if we overcome their mass, which is their resistance to being accelerated. And indeed, that is precisely what we have done. Mass, which is an index of a material body's tie to the earth and to a place, and as such a measure of its resistance to being moved from its place, a measure of its resistance to acceleration, is converted into energy at very high speeds of acceleration.

The promise, however, works both ways. If we can convert mass into energy, the equation also promises that we can convert energy into mass. Notice, however, that to do so requires that we divide our energies. It requires that $E = mc^2$ become $E/c^2 = m$. The equation, then, as a symbol of our age, contains an *attitude*. It describes not only a physical event, but also a psychological disposition which inclines us toward energy and away from matter. The equation, taken as an index of our psychological attitude toward matter, says in effect not only that energy is more enlightened mass, but also that mass is less enlightened energy. Indeed, it repeats at a cultural–psychological level what is already stated in the equation about the physical level. As Harold Fritzsch[20] makes so clear, galaxies, stars, planets, things, matter are the condensation of cooling energy. As the universe cooled and darkened, energy condensed and matter formed. We cannot help but hear in this description of the physical events echoes of a cultural–psychological dream: matter as less enlightened energy is cold and dark. It may very well be the most ironic and tragic aspect of our stay upon the earth that in our pursuit of enlightened matter, in our dream to escape the coldness and darkness of matter, we may bring about the cold and the dark of a nuclear winter.

Our cultural–psychological preference for energy over matter is, more-over, no mere fairy tale projected onto the equation. Indeed, the physicist himself professes this same inclination. As Capra notes, the equation $E = mc^2$ is an acknowledgement that 'mass is nothing but a form energy.'[21] Mass is an appearance of energy, a form which it takes. Thus, even while the equation allows two possible conversions, one of mass into energy and the other of energy into mass, emphasis is placed upon the identification of mass as already a form of energy. The equivalence between mass and energy which the equation establishes is in effect an identification of mass with energy, a reduction of the former to the latter. Through the equation mass is energized, making mass, as an index of a material thing's tie to earth and to a place, a 'vapor and a fallacy.'[22] With mass converted in principle as well as in fact to energy, things, if not as a matter of fact then as a matter of principle, no longer have anything to do with the earth. The hold which the earth has upon things — mass as the pull of gravity — is broken by this conversion, and the place which things have with respect to the earth is lost. Energized in this fashion, the materiality of things, the material world, is overcome. We might even say that things are de-materialized in this con-version of mass into energy.

Perhaps, however, our way of reading the cultural–psychological sense of this equation is too extreme. Does this equation, which refers to the physical world, harbor a cultural–psychological dream of de-materializa-tion, which refers as much to us as it does to the things of the world? Lest we end in doubt let us note Capra's words one more time.

Engaged in showing the perfect harmony which exists between the views of modern physics and Eastern mysticism, Capra states: 'Like modern physicists, Buddhists see all objects as processes in a universal flux and deny the existence of any material substance.'[23] While the Buddhist denial of substance is quite probably a very different cultural dream from that of the physicist, Capra sees them as the same, and that equivalence is psycho-logically significant. The conversion of mass into energy which $E = mc^2$ allows is not only an identification of mass as energy and even a reduction of mass to energy, but also ultimately a denial of mass, of matter, itself. Capra's way of viewing the equation, then, suggests that there does lurk within it a dream of departure from the material world.

The equation $E = mc^2$ is, we said, a symbol of our age. As such it describes for us what we believe the world to be: the world as a matter of light is a matter of energy, and energy is the light of our world. In speaking of the world in this way, however, we also speak about ourselves. This belief about the world mirrors or reflects who we, the believers, are. In his works on the historicity of matter, van den Berg persuasively notes that 'the physicist and chemist discover *the matter of his time*, or rather, *his time* and *himself*.'[24] I would suggest, therefore, that the energizing of matter described in the equation $E = mc^2$ mirrors the distance we have already placed between ourselves and the world in retreating behind the window. Indeed, the material world could not radiate with the energies of an exploding sun until we had removed ourselves from the world in this fashion. It could not be energized until we had broken our connections with the world, lost touch with matter (and with what matters), and made the world a matter of the eye alone. We should say, then, that it is only within the space of the world opened up by linear perspective vision that the world is and can be a matter of energy. We should say that energy is the light of the world when the world is envisioned at the vanishing point.

Throughout the discussion I have strongly indicated that the energizing of matter, described in $E = mc^2$, is a danger. Indeed, in the shadow of our discussion stands the bomb, and perhaps this is as it should be, since the bomb stands in relation to our efforts to energize matter as Frankenstein's monster stands in relation to our attempts to energize the body. Each is, as it were, the dark and terrible reminder of the distance we have placed between ourselves and the world, of our cultural−psychological abandonment of the body and departure from the earth. Each is the shadow side of our efforts to reanimate a deadened matter. The corpse resurrected as machine, reanimated via reflex, and charged with electricity becomes a monster. The earth set in motion as a planet around the sun, explained in the space of linear perspective vision, and energized with the fires of the stars becomes a bomb.

Perhaps, however, there is also another side, another way of understanding this equation, this energizing of matter. After all, the shadows of the abandoned body are, as we have seen, reminders in a double sense. They are reminders of what has been forgotten and indicators of what can, and needs to be, recovered. In this respect, then, the shadow of the bomb may very well be a symptom inviting us to acknowledge that we cannot energize *dead* matter, and that if we begin to attempt this we will end only in destruction. Perhaps, as a symptom, the bomb is calling us to begin again, asking us to recognize that our equation requires of us a new perception and understanding of matter, a new attitude toward it, a new cultural psychology. Perhaps this shadow of the bomb is asking us to discover that matter, like the body, is primarily and essentially alive with energy, and not simply, like the corpse, a dead thing to be energized. In the final chapter of our tale we shall take up a consideration of this issue.

IV A few words about things

In the space of linear perspective vision the size of things is a function of their spatial distance from a viewer. Thus as things approach the vanishing point they appear smaller and further away. Figure 2.4 in the second chapter of our tale illustrates this phenomenon and it may be well for the reader to look at it once again before we continue.

We are quite used to the law of perception according to which the further something is the smaller it appears, and indeed it is almost impossible for us today to recover the sense in which the size of a thing is an index of its significance in our emotional lives, and not just a measure of spatial distance. It is equally difficult to recover the way in which the size of a thing is related to its place and is not just an indication of its position in space. Earlier, however, with Figure 2.8, we illustrated these points, and in the context of that illustration we discussed several examples of how the size of a thing is an index of its meaning in relation to us and not simply, or even primarily, a measure of its physical distance from us. Perhaps, again, it would be well for readers to familiarize themselves with that discussion, although our present discussion takes us in another direction.[25] Our concern here is not specifically with this issue of things and their size, nor with the rescue of things from the space of linear perspective vision. Rather our concern is with what happens to the things of the world as a consequence of being situated in that space where their size is a function of their spatial distance from us.

In a sense we already know what happens to things within this space of linear perspective vision. They are energized and they are explained. We have already seen, however, that in each of these instances a displacement of things takes place. To explain things is to move the things to be explained into the same neutral, homogeneous space and onto the same plane, and indeed it is only in this move that the size of things can be reduced to a measured comparison as a function of spatial distance. But to move things into the space of explanation is to move things out of their given place. To explain things is to displace them. Things, however, seem to have a resistance to being moved, which in terms of the physical sciences is called their 'inertial mass', an idea which, at least implicitly, suggests that things have a tie to, and perhaps we might even say a preference for, a place. In this respect, therefore, the energizing of things which overcomes this resistance is also a displacement. We should say, then, that what happens to things in the space of linear perspective vision is that they lose their place. They lose their place insofar as they are moved into the same space and onto the same plane, and they lose their place insofar as their inertia to being moved is overcome. In short, we should say that in the space of linear perspective vision things are displaced insofar as they are energized and explained.

In our century of wars and revolutions we are, perhaps, quite used to speaking of displaced persons, but what is the sense of speaking of displaced things. Things, after all, are only things. They neither have their place nor a place in our lives which really seems to matter. Or do they? Even today, when things have been so thoroughly explained and energized, have they completely lost their place? Or are we still able to recognize the displacement of things and be affected, and even troubled, by it? To consider these questions we need an example.

It is late evening and you are preparing to go to sleep. As is customary for most of us, you follow a kind of pattern, perhaps turning off the lights in one room and then another, checking the front door to see that it is locked, and setting out your clothes for the morning in one corner of your bedroom. The room is quite ordinary, a bed, a chair and writing desk, a bureau, a clothes closet, and perhaps some photos or posters on the walls. Beside the bed there may also be a small night table with room for a lamp, the book you are currently reading, and your alarm clock. All of this is quite familiar, and for countless nights you have entered the space of this room and, situated amongst these things, you have surrendered yourself to sleep without either worry over or even much thought about these simple, quite ordinary things.

Now it is morning. The alarm has awakened you. You open your eyes and you notice the light. A bright sun is beginning to fill the room. The day also smells fresh in the breeze that enters through the window. You think to yourself that it promises to be a good day, and with this thought you get out of bed. The slippers which you left last night at the side of your bed are there to greet you, as is your robe which perhaps you rather carelessly threw last night across the bottom of the bed. The night table with lamp, clock, and book are still there, as is the bureau, chair and writing desk. The photos, which perhaps you hardly ever notice any more, still hang in their places on the wall, and the clothes in your closet remain in their place. All is as it was last evening and on countless evenings before. Without any reflection at all, for in truth none is ever required, you leave this room and the things within it and begin your day. And when you return in the evening the room and these simple things will greet you again in the same fashion, marking another ending, preparing for another beginning.

But, of course, all of this is as it should be, and no one ever really expects the things of his or her world to change or to disappear when asleep. Indeed, to entertain such expectations would make sleep impossible. It would also point to a rather deep and serious disturbance in one's life. We count on things to keep their place, and our trust in them runs deeper than our knowledge that things are inanimate and hence are incapable of being other than how they are. Indeed, if it were only a question of this knowledge, our trust in things would always, at least in principle, remain shadowed by doubt, because what we know is always partial and incomplete. But there is no doubt here, and we trust in things to keep their place because we have lived our lives with them in this fashion. They have always been faithful sentinels in this way, always silent witnesses to our presence and to our needs.

Indeed, things are perhaps the most faithful witnesses of all, and in their fidelity to us they function as extensions of ourselves, reflections and echoes of who we are, were, and will become. Those things in your room, for example, those simple, ordinary things mirror who and what you are, and situated in that room they give a shape to its space, they form it into a place, they outline a world. That is why most of us do find it difficult to fall asleep, especially the first few nights, in a new place. The things there are not ours; they are not us and we sense no guarantee of their fidelity. Furthermore, it is also why the loss of such things, of those things which bear witness to our living, is always something of a tragedy, for in losing them we lose something of ourselves, we lose something of our world. The crime of theft always involves more than the loss of physical things. It is always more than an economic loss. It is also, and most deeply, a loss of one's self. Finally, it is because of this that things are often the most poignant and painful reminders of someone's death. Even after a long time, the absence through death of someone you have loved can be brought home sharply upon discovery of one of their things. The pipe he smoked in the evening found now beneath the chair, or the necklace which was always her favorite, attest in their patient waiting to the depth of the loss. At such times it is as if the dumb faithfulness of things intensifies our emotions and through them we enter more profoundly into our grief.

Our example would suggest, then, that things do matter in our lives, that they do have their place, that they are the places around which aspects of our world are gathered together, held there, and preserved. Moreover, our example would also suggest that therein lies the importance and worth of things. Staying in their place, they give us our place, and without such things in our lives we would have no place at all. What happens to things in the space of linear perspective vision, therefore, happens to us as well. If they are displaced, then so too are we. Indeed, technology as our cultural–psychological dream of distance from matter and our departure from the earth is only the other side of this displacement of things. Things can no more stand in their place without us remaining mindful of our place than we can stand in our place without things. Moreover, in their displacement the things themselves suffer and, like the abandoned body casts its shadows, displaced things also shadow our lives. Things, too, begin to haunt us, and in their symptoms they too remind us that a life which has lost touch with things is a life which has become too distant and detached from the world. In the decay of our inner cities, in the pollution of our air and water, in the congestion of our highways, in the spirals of inflation and depression of our money, in the breakdown of our machines, like at Three Mile Island in 1979 and more recently at Chernobyl, the things of our world bear our suffering, making visible, as it were, what we would disguise, calling us back from the distance we have placed between ourselves and them, reminding us that *we* have departed, that we have abandoned them. In their symptoms and their sufferings they look to us and to us make an appeal for our mutual salvation. The poet Rainer Maria Rilke knew such things and loved them.

. . . These things that live on departure
understand when you praise them: fleeting, they look for
rescue through something in us, the most fleeting of
all.[26]

We could end here, with the poet Rilke, with his words about things, and at least we would have glimpsed a difference between things that are a place and do matter in our lives, and things that have been displaced into the space of linear perspective vision. But to end here would leave us with only half of the story. Something more, therefore, needs to be said. In being displaced, things are moved out of the context of our lives *and* moved into another space, the space of explanation. We need to return again to that space, because it is within that space that another, more familiar, kind of displacement of things occurs.

The space of linear perspective vision is an homogeneous space, a neutral space, a space within which all places are like all other places, a space within which everything is equal and the same. It is the space of explanation and within that space all things are leveled and reduced to the same plane. Differences, in other words, are erased within that space. A democracy amongst things is established within that space, and things, as it were, lose their character for the sake of a faceless anonymity.

We have already indicated that our modern sciences are generated within this space, and that for them the reduction of things becomes on one hand the equalizing vision of the anatomical structure and physiological functioning of the human body, and on the other hand the equalizing vision of the sub-atomic energy forces which form the atomic structure of the universe. But our modern science of economics is also generated within this space. To give but one example, it is, as Randolph Severson points out, Isaac Newton who, as Master of the Mint under King William III in 1699, applies the features of the scientific world to the task of reshaping the English currency. The chief consequence is that money takes on the same identity that things have within our scientific vision of the world. Money too becomes 'homogeneous, stable, uniform, and predictable.'[27] Moreover, this economic vision of money, like the scientific vision of things, is destined to become the primary measure of the reality of things, a fixed and stable measure of their worth. Indeed, combined like the two lenses of a pair of glasses, the scientific–economic vision of reality is destined to persuade us that the truth of things is found in their explanations, just as the worth of things is found in their price.

The convergence of economics and science into one vision of reality, the convergence of truth as explanation and worth as price, the convergence of money and things, is perhaps the most obvious way in which we have lost touch with things, in which things have lost their place. When things, within the space of explanation, have become so identical one with the other, so equal to each other, so anonymous that all trace of their characteristic differences — of those differences amongst even similar things which give them their character — has been erased, things can become only a matter of money, because money is all that is left to mark their differences, because money is all that is left which makes a difference. Gloria Vanderbilt or Calvin Klein jeans certainly cost more than a pair of Penny's Plain Pockets, but this difference is a manufactured one, an artificial one. Between the former and the latter there are no real differences, and what I buy at the higher price is a fantasy of difference, a fantasy perhaps of being in fashion, or of youth, or of my success. There is, of course, nothing wrong with such wishes in themselves. I can purchase those dreams and perhaps I need to. What is so disturbing, however, is how small and how dismal such modern dreams are, and what is so tragic is that these things, so anonymous in their production and consumption, cannot bear the difference. These things, mass produced, are commodities for mass consumption, and it is not the jeans themselves (the thing in itself and as itself) which register the difference. It is the price. When I buy them and I wear them it is not the jeans that I want you to notice but the label, which is an index of the price. It is the price which makes a difference, and it is this difference which has to generate the fantasy of other differences. The jeans themselves, the things themselves, nearly disappear, and in this reduction of the characteristic worth of things to their economic value we are most exposed to the displacement of things. When things have become only or primarily a matter of money, they become primarily a calculable matter, which severs the emotional bonds between us and things.

Lewis Hyde, in a sensitive and beautiful work entitled *The Gift: Imagination and the Erotic Life of Property*, speaks eloquently of the pervasive presence of displaced things, of these things which have become primarily and essentially matters of money. In discussing the notion of usury, a practice which most clearly indicates the reduction of things, including money itself, to a matter of money, he notes that when things have become commodities 'the objects of the outer world can no longer carry the full range of emotional and spiritual life.' 'Feeling and spirit', he adds, 'mysteriously drain away when the imagination tries to embody them in commodities.' Things whose worth has been revalued in terms of money cannot support us. The interest, meaning, and even desire of our relationships with things are broken, and we find ourselves in a landscape of commodities and consumer goods subject to the laws of supply and demand. One of the major contributions of Hyde's book is that he shows how this landscape, in being too thin to nourish the life of the imagination, has influenced the poets of our time. The landscape of things as commodities, as matters primarily of money, is the wasteland of the imagination, and 'certainly this is part of the melancholy in those poems of Eliot's in which men and women are surrounded by coffee spoons and cigarettes but cannot speak to one another.'[28] Things which have become a matter of money have been displaced and we lose our place with them and with each other. We cannot gather together with one another around such things. Commodities can neither generate nor sustain a sense of community.

We would be in error, however, if we were to regard money itself as the problem. It is not the exchange of money for things which is at issue, but the way in which money is used to empty things of all but their monetary value. The psychologist Robert Sardello has written some very wise words about this difference, and in his article 'Money and the city' he reminds us of the positive and necessary place which money has in our lives. Money is a relationship between me and things, between me and you, and between us and the community. With a simple example he invites us to imagine that moment when one buys an apple for a quarter. This moment of exchange is a ritual, he says, which gathers together 'the relationship to the store in which I stand, the clerk whom I face, the employer who paid my salary, the family budget which portioned the earnings, the desire which brought me to the store, the company which owns this store and the employees which it retains, the produce merchant who brought the apples in, the farmer who grew the apple, the tree from which it came, the earth from which it sprouted, the rain which moistened it, the clouds which shaded it, and the sun which reddened it.'[29] It is only when this moment of exchange has been quantified, only when the worth of the apple, which is the fullness of all these relationships, has been reduced to a monetary value, to the price, that a displacement occurs. Then the apple is severed from all these relationships, distanced from me. Then it becomes a commodity. And if at this moment we change that apple to diamonds or gold and increase the number, then it is true to say that money is power, that money talks, and even to say that time is money, because money is all that matters. At such moments we may want to affirm that 'money talks, but it don't sing and dance, and it don't walk,' but it is an empty gesture.[30] The problem does not lie in the fact that money talks. On the contrary, it is what we ask it to say and how we hear it which matter. When it says only that things are money matters, we have furthered the displacement of things.

Earlier, when we came to a place where these few words about things could draw to a close, we invited the poet Rainer Maria Rilke to speak. Now we repeat the invitation at this closure. It is a passage from a letter dated November 13, 1925, and written to the Polish translator of the *Elegies*. Perhaps it has too much the tone of lament, and perhaps it is too pessimistic in its conclusions. Nevertheless, it captures the difference we have been speaking of between things which keep their place and things which have been displaced. In any case, it is our final word about things.

Even for our grandparents a 'House,' a 'Well', a familiar tower, their very dress, their cloak, was infinitely more, infinitely more intimate:

almost everything a vessel in which they found and stored humanity. Now there come crowding over from America empty, indifferent things, pseudo-things, DUMMY-LIFE . . . A house, in the American understanding, an American apple or vine, has NOTHING in common with the house, the fruit, the grape into which the hope and meditation of our forefathers had entered . . . The animated, experienced things that SHARE OUR LIVES are coming to an end and cannot be replaced. WE ARE PERHAPS THE LAST TO HAVE STILL KNOWN SUCH THINGS. On us rests the responsibility of preserving, not merely their memory (that would be little and unreliable), but their human and laral worth.[31]

V Conclusion: the world as our home

In all his works J. H. van den Berg has persuasively and eloquently demonstrated the many ways in which the world is 'our home, our habitat, the materialization of our subjectivity.'[32] The transformation of the world into a spectacle has, at the very least, changed our sense of home. Technology as a dream of departure from the earth has made the issue of home into a question. We began our tale of technology at this place with the claim that we are all astronauts. Do we belong to the earth? Does the distance we have placed between ourselves as spectators and the world as spectacle and the body as specimen condemn us to a homeless condition even in the midst of our wanderings through the stars?

Technology is a journey and if we have so far concentrated on technology as departure it is not because we do not recognize that it is also the possibility of return. To answer our questions, if they can be answered, we need to turn to this moment of the journey. We began with lift-off and now we are at the apogee of our journey. It is time to turn around and look back. In doing so, moreover, we shall be making a place for the symptoms which shadow the dreams of technology, for those symptoms and shadows which have haunted our dreams of abandoning the body and departing the earth.

Chapter seven

Re-entry: paths of return

I Return and re-entry: a story, an image, and a dream

On June 13, 1983, *Pioneer 10*, a spacecraft launched in 1972, passed the orbit of the planet Neptune and left the solar system. Traveling at a speed technically called 'solar system escape velocity', a speed which exceeds that necessary to escape the earth, it was the first man-made object to depart the solar system for the universe beyond. Although the odds that anyone will ever encounter *Pioneer 10* and decipher its messages (which include among other things drawings of a man and a woman, and sketches of the earth and the solar system) are quite small, it is estimated that in about 32,000 years the spacecraft will come closest to the star Ross 248 and that it will pass relatively close to a star every million years. Those two facts may be astonishing, but it is even more astonishing to realize that this spacecraft 'will last longer than the life of the universe has been.' Yet even that is not the whole story. *Pioneer 10* will also outlast the earth itself. 'Everything that's in the solar system will get gobbled up when the sun explodes and turns into a red giant, but this [spacecraft] will still be going.'[1]

This spacecraft, child of our technological ingenuity, is the epitome of our dreams of departure and escape. In a sense, however, it is also a symbol of return. It is true, of course, that this vehicle itself will never return, but in carrying messages of who we are and of the earth it carries the slim hope, and the deeply rooted need, to be remembered. That this hope of and need to return, even if only through remembrance, are in fact a vital part of our dreams of departure and escape is attested to by an incident prior to the launch of *Pioneer 10*. It was reported that 'before *Pioneer* was launched, the last test crew wrote their names on a piece of paper and stuffed it into the spacecraft.' In the dark, cold, empty reaches of outer space, 'Someday, someone may find those names.'[2]

I begin with this story because its cosmic scope suggests the mythical dimensions of our technological dreams. Mythical motifs of the journey and immortality are apparent in this story, and the dreams of technology do indeed embrace these themes. In abandoning the body and refashioning it as technical function, something of the fear of death and the wish for immortality lies hidden, and in our distance from matter something of the wish to depart and the need to escape the earth shows through. Heretofore in our tale of technology, however, we have not given much consideration to the theme of return, and we need to do so, here at the end of our tale, because return belongs to this tale. It belongs to the cultural psychology of technology and to the phenomenology of it, to the way in which technology reveals itself in our world.

Return belongs to the cultural psychology of technology insofar as it shadows our astronautic condition. We are in orbit, as Walker Percy notes, up on things and high on hope and perhaps even high on uppers, and cheerful too about our progress from the frontier of early America to the high frontier of space. There is, however, a 'psychic law of gravity'[3] which marks return with the index of necessity. The high and up are shadowed by the low and down, our cheerfulness by depression, and the high frontier of space by the deep frontiers of soul. In this respect, the shadows of technology may habor in their message of return an end to optimism. They may signal by their presence that return means the end of the Enlightenment dream of reason, the end of progress, and the end of dominance and control of nature through a detached, distant spectator self, a figure whom Percy says is lost in the Cosmos, a wraith in a machine, 'a ghost with an erection.'[4] Return may also mean a new awareness that there are limits to growth[5] and that small is beautiful.[6] Return may even be the genesis of a new cultural psychology, the birth of a new woman and a new man.

Moreover, nothing about this return is fanciful. The fact that return is a psychological matter does not mean that it is less real, or that it does not matter in the world. Indeed, throughout our tale of technology, we have been at pains to show that what is psychological about humanity is a cultural matter. Our collective psychological life is a matter of culture. It is embodied in the things we do, in the world we build, and the technological world is no exception. Technology is a world event and a psychological dream, and thus if return belongs to the dream of technology we can rest assured that it also belongs to the technological world. Return is as much a part of the phenomenology of technology as it is of its psychology.

The image presented in Figure 7.1 illustrates quite vividly the issue of return in the technology of departure. It is the ascent stage of the *Apollo 11* lunar module making its docking approach to the command service module during a rendezvous in lunar orbit. There is a lift-off here, a departure, but it is from the surface of the moon toward the earth that rises above the lunar horizon, beckoning, as it were, the astronauts home. The journey depicted here is in its moment of return after departure. It is a journey toward re-entry into the embracing atmosphere of the earth.

On its technical side return is a question of re-entry, and re-entry is fundamentally a matter of attitude. For the spacecraft to re-enter the

Figure 7.1 Apollo 11 Lunar Module Ascent

Source: NASA

earth's cloudy embrace, it must present itself in the right attitude, which means that its angle of penetration into the earth's atmosphere must be neither too shallow nor too sharp. With too sharp a re-entry the capsule would burn up, whereas with a re-entry too shallow the earth's atmospheric embrace would become, as it were, a wall of rejection, sending the spacecraft bouncing off into the heavens. Re-entry is a matter of attitude and attitude matters at the moment of re-entry.

But, of course, we have to turn around again and remember that technology as an event in the world is also a cultural–psychological dream. Return as re-entry is, therefore, also a psychological issue. To put this another way, re-entry is more than a technical matter. Re-entry is also a cultural–psychological work.

The technical language of re-entry tells us, therefore, that the cultural–psychological work of re-entry, of return from dreams of departure and escape, requires the proper attitude. If, on one hand, our desire to return is too sharp we may be consumed. If it is, in other words, too much a passion to return to things as they once were, or as we imagined them to have been, we may be destroyed. Such intense desires of return may take the form of nostalgic longing for a pre-technological edenic world; for a simpler, more innocent time in which, as we fancy it, we lived more harmoniously with nature. Or such desires may take the form of negativity, finding in technology the reason and cause for all our present ills. In either case the earth which rises on the horizon does not simply call us home. Rather, it calls us to restore a lost order, to set things right again, to negate what is and what will be. Return in this attitude is rooted in the fear of technology and works in the service of denial.

On the other hand, if our desire to return is too shallow we may lose the earth. The attitude in this instance is rooted in a false optimism concerning technology and in an uncritical acceptance of its style and its claims. Here our desire to return is rather weak, because technology promises us a future which will one day dispense with the earth, which will one day free us of its bonds in much the same way that it may liberate us from the necessity of death by freeing us from the body. In this attitude, too soft on and uncommitted to return, technology is our savior, the fulfilment of our destiny to quit this nursery planet, the means by which we will take 'the inevitable next step in evolution',[7] our departure forever from the earth. Viewed in this light the earth itself becomes for us a rather casual matter, not to say a casualty of our neglect, either immediately in terms of our pollution of it or later in terms of our destruction of it, while the earth which rises on the lunar horizon becomes less a call to return home and more an image of some final farewell.

But in spite of the possibility of a re-entry either too sharp or too shallow, return remains a dimension of the cultural–psychological dream called technology. Technology is as much a dream of return as it is of departure and escape. Or perhaps we should say the dream of technology is shadowed by the opportunity of return. Moreover, the language in our description of re-entry again informs us about the attitude of return. The language carries an erotic connotation, in spite of its more or less clinical sound, and in this respect we might anticipate that technology as a journey of return will involve a reaffirmation of our erotic tie to the earth, and perhaps even a rediscovery of the erotic character of the earth itself. Already, through technology, we are on this path insofar as it is now possible for us to consider the entire earth as a living ecosystem, to acknowledge it as a whole earth, greater than the sum of its parts, like a body of living human flesh, an organism. What steps are necessary to link our awareness of the earth's vitality to a recognition that we are drawn into the orbit of its life through desire, that life here calls to life, that our flesh and that of the earth are knit together into a larger whole by the power of Eros itself? This remains, I believe, an open question.

Technology is the opening of that question, or at least the opportunity for the question to be opened. In realizing our cultural–psychological dreams of distance, even to the point where distance can become departure forever or perhaps destruction, a curious event, perhaps unexpected, has occurred. In leaving the earth, we have, it seems, become more aware of it. Seen from outside the envelope of its protective atmosphere, seen from space, the earth can be *seen*, for the first time in the history of humanity, as home. And perhaps that is the most radical meaning of return: technology as homecoming. For it is only in leaving one's home, in departing from it, that the possibility of return arises. It is only in our distance that the possibility of remembering home takes place, the possibility of taking up in a new way what was, the possibility of recovering as a destiny what was heretofore a heritage.

For countless millennia we have stood upon the earth gazing at the stars, and in all that time the earth has stood under us, supported our stand, *stood under* our dreams of departure, and our desires of escape. For all that time the earth has 'under-stood' us. Now we have, at least to some degree, realized these dreams, and at the moment when our farewell to the earth (and let us not forget here that it is also a farewell to the body weighted as flesh which ties us to the earth) seems possible, we turn around and see the earth there before us: one, whole, and luminous as depicted in Figure 7.2. We are tempted. The bonds of desire, erotic bonds, reach further than the pull of gravity. We are called across the distance to return, to understand finally the earth which for so long has understood us, to remember it as home, to take up with understanding this heritage of earth as home as a destiny of homecoming, to take up the task of truly making the earth and nourishing it as humanity's home.

Figure 7.2 Apollo 17 View of Earth

Source: NASA

II Paths of return: ways of re-membering home

In what follows I will give a few examples of how our technological culture has already begun to travel a path of return, has already been engaged in ways of remembering home. I take these examples as indications of the breakdown of the cultural psychology of distance and the breakthrough of a new cultural–psychological style, as moments when the shadows of technology have found a place. As their presence will also illustrate, these shadows embody that attitude of re-entry marked with a sense of eros, and each of these cultural moments has been in its fashion a moment of homecoming. But by no means do these examples claim to be exhaustive or even the most significant. Rather, I choose them because they are the ones I know best, the shadows that have caught my eye in the light of technology. Moreover, in presenting them, in becoming, as it were, a witness for them at the end of the tale, I make no claims regarding their efficacy in having brought about a change. I make no pretense about such judgements here, and this is especially the case with respect to psychoanalysis. If some would say that psychoanalysis has miserably failed to realize its potential for cultural change (and there are many today who would say so), I would reply that it is we who engage psychoanalysis and its potential, we who foster it or refuse it. In any case, regardless of this issue, I make room for these shadows, including and perhaps especially psychoanalysis, mindful of their original moments. At those moments some new cultural seeds were being sown. Those seeds are still there. They need only to be continually nourished. They need to be remembered by us.

A   Psychoanalysis and the symptomatic body

Of all that can be said of psychoanalysis, perhaps the most pertinent item with respect to our story is that it is, in its theory and its praxis, a full shadow of technology. To the distant spectator self behind the window of his or her consciousness, a consciousness detached from the world and the body, psychoanalysis opposes its notion of the unconscious, of a self that is already borne by its embodied desires into the world, a self in intimate proximity with things. Whatever else may or may not be said of this unconscious, it must be said that it is the 'self incarnate', a self restored to the thickness of flesh and to the depth of the world, a self with a history and in a situation.

To the spectacle of things, reduced in the space of explanation to mere physical objects of calculable measure, psychoanalysis opposes the symbolic character of things. It not only restores the self to the world, but it does so in a concrete way through the intermediary of things, through the way in which the things of the world are already tied to the body through the bonds of libidinal desire. Caught up in the circuit of the instincts and their vicissitudes, things are not mere objects on 'that' side of the world, separate from a subject on 'this side'. Rather, they are the terminus of the instinctual body's intentions, the fulfillment of its desires. As such and most importantly, things are gifted with a certain flexibility, allowing them a range of meaning, placing them within a symbolic and figurative field where they can, for example, combine with one another to condense multiple meanings or displace meaning from one to another. Psychoanalysis recovers how we live every day of our lives with things, how through things and over things we speak to each other of who we are. It restores to us our emotional commerce with things, revealing, for example, how in losing the gift which you gave to me I speak of what our relationship has become.

Finally, with respect to the specimen body, to that body which arises from and belongs to the anatomical context, psychoanalysis opposes the libidinal body, the body of desire. To the corpse, it opposes the hysteric body. In short, to the body of technical functioning, a body without either situation or history, it opposes the symptomatic body which suffers, which bears its history.

With respect to self, things, and the body, then, we can say that psychoanalysis is the other side of technology. Within the field of its vision the self is not a spectator, the world is not a spectacle, and the body is not a specimen.[8] At its origins, in the late nineteenth and early twentieth centuries, psychoanalysis is the breakthrough of another cultural dream, and in our discussion we shall focus on the symptomatic body as an indicator of this breakthrough.

Anyone who would discuss the body in psychoanalysis is faced at the very start with several options. One could, for example, show how the body in psychoanalysis is a return home to the living body of everyday life by focusing on the symptomatic body of the hysteric, or the libidinal body of the developmental stages, or the instinctual body in Freud's theories. But whichever option one chooses, one soon discovers a concordance of these views around several themes. Because, however, we have already met the hysteric in the shadows of the abandoned body, I shall focus my discussion on the symptomatic body.

In one of his earliest publications on hysteria, Freud noted the challenge which the hysterical symptom presented to the physicians of the abandoned body. He wrote:

> In its paralysis and other manifestations, hysteria behaves as though anatomy did not exist or as though it had no knowledge of it. . . . It takes the organs in the ordinary, popular sense of the names they bear: the leg is the leg as far up as it insertion into the hip, the arm is the upper limb as it is visible under the clothing.[9]

At the outset of his investigations, therefore, Freud saw and acknowledged that the neurotic symptom was not a fact to be explained by the
structures and functions of the anatomical body. On the contrary, he saw
and again acknowledged that the neurotic symptom was betraying another
body, a different body, a body which belonged to the structures of everyday
life. The symptom was not so much a mechanism as a meaning, and yet
Freud's genius was to recognize that even as meaning the symptom was not
the creation of a pure consciousness divorced from the body. Its meaning
was a dense and fleshy matter, a matter of the body's life in the world and
not a matter of mind, not a meaning dreamed up by the spectator self and
imposed upon the dumb mechanisms of the body. In short the symptom,
for example, a hysterical paralysis, was as far from being a fiction of a
diseased mind to be reasoned away by the superior logic of the physician as
it was from being a fact of the diseased body whose cause could be discovered in the anatomical structures of the corpse. The symptomatic body
of the hysteric presented a new reality. It confronted the physicians of the
abandoned body with a body which was, so to speak, midway between the
corpse and the spectator self in its splendid isolation from the body. The
symptom, like Freud's definition of the instinct as '. . . a concept on the
frontier between the mental and the somatic . . .',[10] presented a body
mindful of the world, a self incarnate.

In his work with the neurotic body Freud discovered that the symptom is
a memory which both preserves and disguises a traumatic past. 'Hysterics,'
he wrote, 'suffer mainly from reminiscences.'[11] Such a discovery gave a
place to the body as a historical, socially situated reality, to the body as a
matter of time, to the body whose flesh suffered its history. Moreover,
insofar as the symptom was always in one sense or another rooted in a
conflict between desire and prohibition, Freud's work indicated that the
body was essentially and primarily an erotic history. In this way, he
extended the sexuality of the flesh, freeing it from the tyranny of the
genitals, suffusing the entire body with desire, discovering in the body's
activities reference not to its anatomical structures or biological functions,
but to its history of passion and hunger for connection with the world and
with others. Whether it was the mouth, or anus, or phallus, or eye, or skin,
or heart or stomach, the organs of the body revealed themselves as con-
figurations of desire and its woundings. In such ordinary activities as eating
or sleeping or playing, or nursing and weaning an infant, or toilet training a
child, Freud discovered a body entangled in a network of familial relations,
embedded in a culture, shaped and formed in its desires through these
relations.

Here, then, in the context of psychoanalysis was a resurrection of the
flesh, a resurrection not of a corpse reanimated by electricity but of a living
body animated by desire, a body of history and passion, a body seeking its
place in the world, a body that could weep and suffer, a body that could

appeal to us for understanding. Perhaps it is all the more surprising that the living, human body should have been reborn in the context of psycho-analysis through the work of Freud, who was a medical doctor. But then again perhaps it is not so surprising, and perhaps it was even necessary. Freud, trained in the tradition of the abandoned body, knew very well the body of anatomy. He knew very well indeed the corpse that is always in the background of the medical body, that body which belongs nowhere and to no one, that anonymous body with neither a history nor a situation, that body as far from life as it is from death, that body which, lacking the events of death or of birth, could neither live amongst us nor be buried. And perhaps only by someone who knew that body so well could the difference between the medical body, the dissected corpse, the body cut in anatomy, and the hysteric body, the symptomatic body, the body cut by time, be heard. Perhaps only someone who knew so very well the body discovered – invented through the gaze of distant vision could allow it to approach and to speak of its denied passions and desires in the more intimate and proxi-mate space of human conversation. Perhaps only then, in that space, could the body as specimen, as a matter for the eye alone, become a body to be heard and understood.

Today there is much criticism of Freud's work. More often than not the charge is made that in his theoretical formulations, as well as in his practice with hysteric patients, he was guilty of imposing the patriarchal structure of Victorian society. Hélène Cixous' play, *A Portrait of Dora*, is an excellent example of this criticism. There is, without any doubt, much merit in this criticism, but any treatment of it would take us far beyond our present concerns. I mention it, however, because in one very important way it accords perfectly with a recurring theme in our story. Most of Freud's hysteric patients were women, and in this respect we would have to say that the resurrection of the body in psychoanalysis is the return not only of a historical, socially situated, erotic body of desire, but also a return of this body in the guise of the feminine. It was the woman, again, as our shadow history of the abandoned body has indicated, who was forced to carry the body from exile, the woman who was asked to be culture's reminder of what it would deny and forget, and the woman who was punished for becoming that memory. In giving a place for this shadow body to emerge from exile and to speak, Freud does deserve our praise. But, again, in silencing the speaking of this body, either by his imposition of the patriarchal values of industrial – technological Victorian society upon his theoretical formulations, or by failing to hear in the hysteric's suffering an indictment of a cultural dream which had imposed upon her the burden of carrying all that that dream would repress, Freud may deserve, if not our blame, then at least our disappointment.[12]

As I have indicated, however, the intention of this part of our story is neither to blame nor to praise. Rather, it is only to indicate those cultural moments, however brief or unfulfilled they may have been, when something of a return from exile appeared. The psychoanalysis of the body is one such moment. Its birth lies in its confrontation with the hysteric body, with the abandoned body reawakened as passion and desire. Its origins are inseparable from the body's desire to return from exile and banishment.

B   Pornography and the feminine as shadow

Feminist criticism of psychoanalysis is part of a larger whole. Indeed, the rise of a feminist consciousness in our time is perhaps the most intense appearance of the shadow of technology, a situation which is not surprising given the fact that the feminine side of humanity's cultural–psychological life has more or less carried the shadow throughout the history of linear perspective vision. This has been especially the case, moreover, at the most concrete level of our dreams of distance, at the level of the body. The feminine, almost more or less exclusively, has been the shadow of the abandoned body, from its initial appearance as witch to its latest as anorexic. The woman's body, again almost exclusively, has been charged with the burden of remembering what the cultural–psychological dream of refashioning the body would forget. From the discovery–invention of the corpse, through its resurrection as machine and reanimation via reflex, to its appearance as industrial worker, robot, and astronaut, the abandonment of the body has been in the service of re-creating a body as distant from life as from death, a body purified of passion and history, an efficient body of technical functioning. The matter of the body has been washed clean of all the impurities of life, of all those qualities which would make the body difficult to quantify, control, and dominate, and part of that process of purification has been the inscription of all those undesired elements onto the flesh of the feminine body. Not surprisingly, then, this body became identified as marked by excess, by an excess of emotional life, making it wild, brutish, unpredictable and uncontrollable; and especially by an excess of passion, making it threateningly erotic, and even sinful, and hence requiring its burning or imprisonment or even death, requiring at any cost its obedience and its silence. Consigned to a shadowy existence, to a realm on the margins of the official consciousness of culture, this body of passion, of life, of death, of history, of desire, could appear only in broken, twisted form, only in guises easily assigned a negative index, only as witch or madwoman, only dazed in the safe and controllable sleep of hypnosis, only as monster, only as neurotic to be diagnosed and cured. A fine and convenient separation, therefore, was dreamed. A split was established between the feminine shadows of the abandoned body, displaced over there on that side of the window, and the essentially masculine dreams of a spectator self on this side of the window. Safely placed over there on that side of the window, the feminine shadows of the abandoned body, wild and disordered pieces of nature, could be coupled with the disorders of nature itself. More-over, as Carolyn Merchant[13] so clearly demonstrates, this coupling allowed the scientific subjugation of nature and the cultural subordination of women to proceed hand in hand. The dark, shadowy presence of a body and a nature essentially feminine was observed, watched, manipulated, and shaped to fit the space of a geometrized world, a space purified of all but mechanism and number, envisioned by a spectator self, by an essentially masculine consciousness safely isolated from any contact with and contami-nation by the feminine.

Surely there is much about this description of the abandoned body and its shadow history that evokes and imitates the situation of pornography, and that similarity, I would add, is not completely accidental. I am not saying here that linear perspective vision and the scientific vision of the world which it generates are pornographic. Rather, I am saying only that this vision, which establishes the conditions for transforming the world into a spectacle, also allows the appearance of another kind of vision which would objectify, dominate, purify, and ultimately deaden matter. Linear per-spective space nourishes a scientific vision of the world, but also allows a pornographic vision of it.

Susan Griffin, in her excellent book *Pornography and Silence*, gives a vivid account of these issues, and especially of the place which rites of puri-fication have in the pornographic imagination. Such rites ultimately deaden the flesh, and indeed the pornographic body, which in our culture is over-whelmingly the woman's body, bears an unmistakable resemblance to the corpse. Griffin's description of the pornographic display of the woman's body vividly portrays how very much this body is an abandoned body. She writes:

> Like a piece of furniture, she must be pictured from the side, and particular parts of her body, those intended for use — her breasts, her vulva, her ass — must be carefully examined. And yet at each turn of her body, at each face or curvature exposed, we see nothing. *For there is no person there.*[14]

The woman's body on pornographic display is very much like the corpse on the dissecting table. Both are anonymous. Moreover, they share a similar space. The space of linear perspective vision within which this anonymous, impersonal body as corpse is discovered–invented is very much like the space of the voyeur. The space of linear perspective vision, a space which essentially presents a spectacle, a matter for observation, a matter for the gaze of the fixed eye and for the eye alone, is a space which one can enter without either being moved or touched or otherwise changed by what one sees. It is a space of separation and a space within which depth as a matter of vertical levels has been replaced by depth as a matter of distance.

Griffin's description of voyeuristic space shows many of these same qualities:

> The man who *stares* at a photograph of a nude woman is a voyeur. He can look freely and turn away when he wishes. He can run his hands over the two-dimensional surface, but he will *not be touched*. He can know the body of a woman, and yet encounter a knowledge which will *not change him*. We read that the sight of a woman contains 'the image of everything which *rises up from the depths*'. But the voyeur, when he sees a photograph of a woman's body, keeps these *depths at a distance*. An invisible line *separates* him from the image he perceives.[15]

There is the same fixity of vision, the same denial of depths in favor of distance, the same separation, the same one-sided spectator non-involvement in both spaces, strengthening the suggestion of a connection between pornographic vision and the history of the abandoned body. Moreover, the same dynamic patterns are present in each instance. There is a *splitting* of the self into masculine and feminine aspects, a subsequent *denial* of the feminine, and finally its *projection* onto the woman, now regarded as alien and other. As a consequence of these dynamics there is a literalization of the feminine in the woman and a reduction of the woman to the sexual, the latter being an issue which is thematic in pornography and a very strong current in the history of the abandoned body and its shadows, as we indicated in the discussions of the witch, the mesmerized body, and the hysteric.

The value, I believe, of indicating a connection between pornographic vision and the abandoned body with its shadow history is that this connection allows us to understand more deeply how very much our cultural–psychological dreams of distance, of departure and escape, of domination, mastery, and control of nature, are an incomplete and unbalanced masculine dream which has lost touch with the feminine. Moreover, this connection graphically and frighteningly illustrates how deeply opposed to life these cultural dreams of distance and mastery are. The split-off feminine fragment of the cultural–psychological life of humanity is not only murdered, it is also pushed beyond death. The discarded feminine is reduced to mere matter, which is the other side of the masculine spirit's flight from matter, a reduction achieved primarily through a *humiliation* of the woman's body, a term which literally indicates a coming back down to earth which in this context has nothing to do with return but rather with its opposite, escape. In humiliating the woman's flesh, the pornographic vision even deadens death, enacting an 'objectification of a whole being into a thing', which, Susan Griffin reminds us, 'is the central metaphor of the form.'[16] Through the lens of the pornographic eye, we are invited to see that a cultural psychology which emphasizes only its masculine side is in pursuit of violence and death. Moreover, insofar as violence always signals a failure of the imagination, we can add that pornography forces us to acknowledge that a society enmeshed in a one-sided masculine dream of distance, departure, and escape from matter is a society hostile and alien to the powers of the imagination, to those powers which generate the stories, myths, metaphors, and symbols which hold a society together. Adrienne Rich sums up these points in a direct, powerful way. She writes:

> One of the devastating effects of technological capitalism has been its numbing of the powers of the imagination — specifically, the power to envision new human and communal relationships. I am a feminist because I feel endangered, psychically and physically, by this society, and because I believe that the women's movement is saying that we have come to an edge of history when men — insofar as they are embodiments of the patriarchal idea — have become dangerous to children and other living things, themselves included; and that we can no longer afford to keep the female principle enclosed within the confines of the tight little post-industrial family, or within any male-induced notion of where the female principle is valid and where it is not.[17]

Nothing that has been said about pornography is meant to imply that its presence can be tolerated because of the function it can serve of reminding us of the dangers of a one-sided masculine dream of distance. I mean to say only that pornography is a symptom, a particularly disturbing one to be sure, and that as such we need to hear its message and not simply legislate its abolition. To do the latter would only continue the cultural repression which denies the feminine and objectifies it. A change can come about, with respect to pornography *and* the destructive dreams of which it is a symptom, only if we remember that what it indicates has been forgotten, only if we *remember the split* of humanity's cultural–psychological life into an official, conscious, masculine side and a rejected, shadow, feminine side. Indeed, the issue here is no different than that with respect to the bomb. It too is a symptom, and if we content ourselves with simply being against it we continue that very split of which it is a symptom.

Moreover, I am making this point with respect to both of these examples, pornography and the bomb, because today we are witnessing a dangerous inflation of each of these issues, amplified by their conjunction. In the increasing drift toward a simplistic fundamentalism, in both religion and politics, we see a self-righteous, moralizing condemnation of pornography coupled with a rhetoric which would make the bomb an instrument of our purification and our salvation. The primary danger here, of course, is that such reasoning (if it can be called that) perpetuates those dynamics of splitting, denial, and projection which divide and separate everything into one side which is just, right, holy, and pure, and another side which is evil, wrong, wicked, and impure, and therefore justifiably in need of punishment and perhaps even extinction. As a consequence nothing of either pornography or the bomb as a symptom of *who we are* is heard. On the contrary, it all has to do with the *other one*. We learn nothing, therefore, and we do not change. Furthermore, a real secondary danger is that the bomb we would grasp as our sword of salvation is as deadly for all humanity as the bomb we would eschew as evil. The bomb embraced is no different from the bomb negated. Either one would ravage the entire earth.

In the cultural–psychological condition in which we find ourselves, the creation of saviors is as strong as the creation of shadows. Indeed, each is a consequence of that splitting, and the savior is only the other face of the shadow, the shadow's twin, as it were. This dynamic, moreover, is quite visible with respect to the feminist movement, particularly with respect to the two ways in which it is regarded. Like the bomb it is either negated as the shadow, or embraced as the savior. Women, then, become newly deified, charged with no less a task than saving the planet. Much to their credit, most feminist writers, like Adrienne Rich, Susan Griffin, Mary Daly, Shulamith Firestone, and Kate Millett, resist this dubious honor and see it for the lie that it is.[18] For indeed, the identification of woman as savior is a lie insofar as it repeats the identification of the feminine with the woman, which led to the creation of the woman as shadow in the first place. The woman deified is no better off than the woman enslaved. The virgin is still the sister of the whore, her elevation the opposite pole of the other's debasement. If we are to benefit culturally and psychologically from the presence of the symptom of pornography, then we have to recognize that the feminine is no more exclusively the woman than the masculine is exclusively the man. If we are to learn anything about 'return' from this symptom, then we have to begin by acknowledging that it calls for a radical cultural–psychological change in women and in men.

In saying as much, however, I would have to add that in this task men, for the most part, will have to learn silence, and that much of the task will entail dismantling many of the old, familiar structures of our society which institutionalize the assumptions and values of patriarchy. In our educational systems, in our economic systems, in our child-rearing patterns, and even in our psychiatric and psychological therapies, as Mary Daly[19] so powerfully demonstrates, we reincarnate the one-sided masculine dreams of distance, departure, and escape which define our cultural–psychological lives, and it is for the most part men who practice, enforce, and control these structures. Change, therefore, will have to be generated outside these structures, these strongholds of masculine dominance *and* male presence. To illustrate what I mean here very briefly, consider what a feminist, woman therapist might have done with Dora, one of Freud's most celebrated hysteric patients. Or consider, as again Mary Daly forcefully urges, abandoning the gynecological medical structures which, she argues, do not serve women's health but continue 'to repress and depress female be-ing.'[20]

Her chapter 'American gynecology: gynocide by the holy ghosts of medicine and therapy' is something which must be acknowledged by every masculine dreamer, whether man or woman, who is seriously interested in hearing the shadow side of our technological culture, and who wishes to be seriously attentive to the rise of feminist consciousness as a vehicle of return. It is important because it indicates so forcefully that the task of return, the work of change, cannot be accomplished without much anxiety and pain. Re-entry is a critical and dangerous moment.

Adrienne Rich notes: 'The mid-twentieth-century wave of feminism has gone further and asked more than its predecessors.'[21] That is, of course, true, but our history of the abandoned body and its shadows has indicated that feminism has been present throughout this history. The feminine has more or less been the figure, the guise, of the shadow, and although it has gathered strength in our day, it has never been completely absent from the scene. To conclude my remarks on feminism as a cultural–psychological moment in the breakdown of our primarily masculine dreams of departure and escape, I will cite two curious and ironic historical instances of feminism. Each betrays the connections among the abandoned body, its shadow, and the feminine; the second instance also illustrates the violence practiced against this shadow, and in a way recalls the connection with pornography.

The first instance returns us to the creature of Frankenstein, the monstrous shadow of the abandoned body. He was conceived in the fertile imagination of Mary Shelley but in such a fashion that within her story the monster is exclusively 'manmade'. He is the offspring of Victor Frankenstein alone, of the doctor's unbridled knowledge and unchecked desire to create a race of beings which would never know the pain of death. The monster is truly the son of man, a creature not of woman born, and in this respect he is the incarnation of those masculine dreams to dominate, control, and master nature. As such he is a monstrosity, a haunted, hunted, isolated being whose end is not death, but exile in the barren, frozen wastelands of the cold and dark Arctic night. Mary Shelley imagined this being whose birth bears no trace of the feminine. She imagined this creature with a life devoid of the feminine.

Mary Shelley was the daughter of William Goodwin and Mary Wollstonecraft, one of the earliest feminists. Her life and her book, *A Vindication of the Rights of Women*,[22] published in 1791, have earned her a well deserved place in the history of the feminist movement. Daughter and mother have been voices of the denied feminine, each in their own ways. May we not suggest, moreover, that there is something of a lesson to be learned in this historical fact? A world in which the rights of women remain unsupported is an alien world, a world of isolation, a solitary world of broken and absent connections. From *A Vindication of the Rights of Woman* to *Frankenstein* lies the path of an appeal, its refusal, and the consequences. A world in which the voice of the feminine remains unheard, in which the feminine plays no part and has no place, can produce only monsters of destruction.

My second historical example returns us to the hysteric, and specifically to those with whom Charcot worked. In a remarkable and informative book entitled *The Birth of Neurosis: Myth, Malady and the Victorians*, G. F. Drinka notes that several of Charcot's hysteric patients at the Salpetrière gained a certain public notoriety because of their grand hysterical symptoms and their often exaggerated, powerfully evocative behavior under hypnosis. One such woman was Blanche Wittman, who had even earned the title 'Queen of the Hysterics'. Her notoriety, as well as that of the others, was, however, somewhat short-lived. Beginning their 'careers' in the 1870s and lasting well into the 1890s, these grand ladies of the Salpetrière were all but forgotten by the turn of the century. Although her hysterical crises had disappeared, Blanche Wittman never left Charcot's clinic. Rather, she found another place for herself as a radiology technician in the new field of X-rays just discovered by the Curies. As her luck would have it, however, she became 'a victim of the new profession', contracting the ' "abominable cancer of the radiologist." ' And as Drinka points out, 'As the cancer had spread, her limbs, one by one, had been amputated.'[23]

Nothing in this story, of course, would be remarkable except for the fact that Blanche Wittman as a grand hysteric belongs to that shadow history of the abandoned body we have presented. Within that context, she was the visible memory of an erotic body of desire which the cultural–psychological dream of abandoning the body would forget. She, along with her sister hysterics, carried this body of denied passion. 'Blanche and the other hysterical women truly suffered from a psychocultural disturbance', Drinka notes. But, 'Told by domineering men to be quiet and bear their pain, women had no option but to faint and throw their fits.'[24]

Yes, that is so, and indeed that was their hysteria: a compromise, as it were, between bearing the memory of what would otherwise be forgotten and keeping silent. But the image of Blanche, with her body not only progressively eaten away by an X-ray induced cancer but also surgically dismembered, suggests more. It suggests, I believe, that silencing this body is not enough. It suggests that the memory of the vital body, which the woman's body bears as a shadow within a cultural psychology that would deny and escape the flesh, is so painful and disturbing that we need to convince ourselves once more and in the most dramatic way that the body is in reality a corpse. Blanche's amputated body is within the context of the surgery theater the anatomical body dismembered. There on the surgery table the body which would vindicate its rights to life, to passion, to history, and to place, this body which carries these shadows primarily in the guise of the feminine, is once again made into a corpse. The rise of a feminist consciousness is a much-needed avenue of return. But Blanche Wittman's fate reminds us that it is a painful and even dangerous work.

C The eye of the painter, once again

In our story of technology as a cultural–psychological dream of distance, departure, and escape from matter, we began with the eye of the painter. The discovery–invention of the technique of linear perspective in the fifteenth century originated with the artist, but, as we have seen, this artistic technique finally became a new cultural–psychological metaphor of humanity's place in space, and its relationship to self, body, and world. Now near the end of our tale, when we are considering cultural moments of breakdown of this vision, moments of transformation in this dream, we encounter the eye of the artist again. With the rise of Impressionist painting in the mid- to late-nineteenth century we find the birth of a new eye and a new sense of light. Impressionism, like psychoanalysis in the same period and the rise of feminist consciousness, is a path of return.[25]

Of the many ways in which Impressionism indicates the breakdown of a cultural–psychological dream of infinite distance and the breakthrough of another dream, I will cite four. The canvases of these painters betray an end to the eye of distant vision, reconstruct the geometric landscape of linear perspective vision as a space of time, of dream, and of imagery, reintroduce a sense of vertical depth or levels into the horizontal space of depth as spatial distance, and finally register the breakdown of the body as anatomical object and the breakthrough of another bodily reality.

The eye of distant vision is, as we said earlier, an eye of fragmentation. In organizing the world as a geometric spectacle, it looks at the world through a window which is in fact a grid, a grid which serves the purpose of decomposing the whole into parts. The illustration depicted in Figure 3.2 demonstrates the fragmenting function of this spectating eye, and the reader might wish to look at it again and to recall that portion of the tale.[26]

Quite different from the vision of that eye is the vision of a painter like J. M. W. Turner (1775–1851). In the painting *Valley of Aosta — Snowstorm, Avalanche and Thunderstorm*, depicted in Figure 7.3, we are presented with a scene in which the disparate components of the visible world are all but drowned in the impalpable. Turner's eye does not select, divide, or otherwise fragment the visible world. On the contrary, his eye seems more to recompose it. His painting offers some evidence that the fragmentation of the world in relation to the eye of distant vision has been transformed, as well as the eye itself. His painting suggests that our anatomization or dismemberment of the world is being re-membered in a swirl of activity and movement.

With the Impressionist painter a new world space is opened up, as we move from the well ordered geometric space of linear perspective vision to a kind of space which is, in the descriptive sense of the word, surreal. The Impressionist artist rejects the illusory depth of linear perspective vision and tends toward flattened spaces where the minimizing of perspective opens up

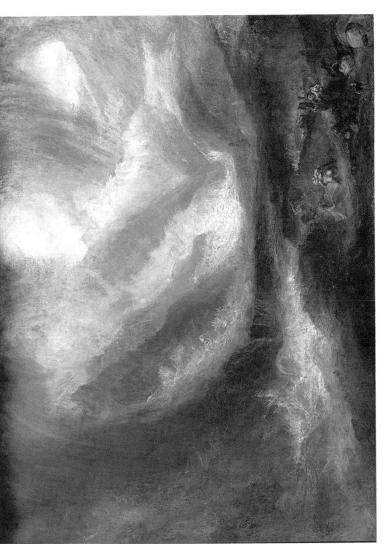

Figure 7.3 J. M. W. Turner, *Valley of Aosta — Snowstorm, Avalanche and Thunderstorm*, 1836—7

Figure 7.4 Caspar David Friedrich, *The Polar Sea*, 1824, Kunsthalle, Hamburg

a dreamlike atmosphere. The fixed, observing eye of linear perspective vision is set free, and our vision appears to float in this other, more fluid, space, in a space not ruled by geometric lines. It is as if the Impressionist artist displays on canvas the psychoanalytic discovery of the unconscious. Dreams, memories, fantasies, and images invade this space, much as they invade the space of spectator consciousness. Something of the surreal, dreamlike quality of this space can be seen in Caspar David Friedrich's *The Polar Sea*, shown in Figure 7.4. A dreamy, liquid quality haunts this icy landscape.

The Impressionist artist does not, however, feel restricted to contrasting the linear, geometric space of waking life with the dream space of the night. It is not merely an opposition of light and dark, day and night, objective and subjective, the mathematical and the dream, which Impressionism offers. On the contrary, its vision of reality is much more radical than any mere contrast or opposition would convey. Within nature itself, within the world itself which we perceive, there is a kind of life, a movement, an animation. Time enters the previous static space of linear perspective vision, and the frozen landscape fixed by rules of geometric composition becomes a temporal, transient landscape, a world flooded with time. In other words, the space of the world is no longer one in which temporal change is reduced to changes in position in space, in which time is reduced to space, but one in which there is, we would have to say, a space–time. Moreover, in this respect we would have to add that again the painter anticipates the physicist, that the artist first imagines the world space for the science of his time. As the artistic eye of linear perspective vision prepared the space for Galileo, Vesalius, Harvey, Descartes, Newton, and others, the artistic eye of impressionistic vision prepared the space of space–time for Einstein. In Manet (1832–1883) and especially, I think, in Cézanne (1839–1906), one begins to see the interpenetration of things, an erotic bond between and among things which has them reaching, turning, twisting toward each other, almost as if they are in a frenzy of newly released passion. One looks at some of their landscapes and one recognizes that indeed, as the Spanish philosopher Ortega y Gasset will later say, '[things] desire each other as male and female; . . . they love each other and aspire to unite, to collect in communities, in organisms, in structures, in worlds.'[27]

No discussion of Impressionism can proceed too far without Cézanne. He is, we might suggest, to Impressionism what Freud is to psychoanalysis. Each is the one name indissolubly linked with the respective terms. But each, of course, deserves it, and with Cézanne we are invited without any doubt to witness a new world. His vibrating brushstrokes not only capture that erotic character of nature which we have just described, but also its multiple depths. The flat, lavish strokes destroy perspective, explode linear, horizontal space where depth is measured as spatial distance, and liberate the vertical depths of the world, that space within which depth becomes once again a matter of levels.

But, of course, Cézanne was no more alone than was Freud, and his destruction of perspective and the liberation of the vertical depths of the world can be found in others both before and after him. What matters here is not so much who did it, but that it happened. Beginning in the mid-nineteenth century the *unitary* concept of space, the level space of one plane retreating toward a vanishing point, that space of explanation and horizon line isocephaly, is broken down as the artist rediscovers and reinvents a kind of medieval narrative space, placing different spaces side by side, compressing, or even abolishing, the distance between background and foreground, diminishing the distance and separation between the one who sees and the world that is seen. There is, as it were, a return from our journey toward infinite distance. The window is broken. The see-er is no longer just a spectator of, but rather a participant in, the world.[28]

The Impressionist artist not only registers the birth of a new world, he also displays the birth of a new form and style of embodiment. Movement becomes a particular concern, with an emphasis on the restlessness of everyday gestures. It is not the body of anatomical motion in space which is presented, but the moving body whose gestures generate and outline the space of a living situation. The artist with an Impressionist eye places the body back in the world and in such a way that there is often an intertwining between the body's flesh and that of the world. Cézanne often said, for example, that he wanted 'to marry the curves of women's bodies to the shoulders of the hills.'[29] One needs only to look at a painting like *Luncheon on the Grass* to see that Cézanne accomplished that marriage. In his work one sees a chiasm or crossing between body and world.

With Impressionism, then, we are witnessing a moment of return insofar as there is a new emphasis on the relations between things, compared with their isolation and fragmentation in the eye of distant vision; insofar as there is a new emphasis on the situated body as the genesis of space, compared with the abandoned body in the neutral space projected by linear perspective vision; and finally insofar as there is a rejection of perspective itself in favor of a new space which opens up the depths and levels of the world. In all of this, however, Impressionism does not reject the notion that the world matters as light, nor could we expect it, since painting's vocation is the light. Its canvases, however, are enough to persuade us that with the Impressionist's eye the light of the world has changed as well as the eye which sees it. We are not presented here with the light of geometric vision, of straight lines and level planes, the light through which the distant eye of the spectator behind the window views the world. Rather, we are offered a light which is bent and shaped by its commerce with things; a light which bedazzles the eye and bathes the world, suffusing it with color; a light which takes up the eye and carries it swimmingly into a riot of colors. It is an eye, then, situated in the world, and if it is not yet fully embodied, if it is still something of a spectator's eye on the verge of tumbling into the mix of the world, it is nevertheless an eye in touch with the world, a vision that has been impressed and moved by the world.

D Energy revisited

In an earlier part of our story we spoke of energy as the new light of the world, and specifically of $E = mc^2$ as the symbol of an enlightened and energetic age which reveals to us that matter is energy and that within its heart lies the power of the stars. At the same time, moreover, we indicated the danger involved in the energizing of matter, and we suggested that in our efforts to energize matter we recall the figure of the monster Frankenstein. Frankenstein, we said, stands in relation to our efforts to energize the body as the bomb stands in relation to our efforts to energize matter. Each indicates the shadow side of our effort to reanimate deadened matter. We also suggested that as shadows the monster and the bomb were inviting us to acknowledge that we cannot energize dead matter and that if we start here we will end in destruction. In other words, we suggested that the shadow sides of our efforts to energize matter were inviting us toward a revisioning of matter itself, and at that time we promised to describe that new vision. It is time now to make good that promise and to show that there is another code in the symbol of our age, another message about matter in the equation $E = mc^2$ which places at the core of physics itself a moment of return. If physics can be called a planetary neurosis, then like all neuroses it contains a deeper wisdom which remembers something we would otherwise forget. $E = mc^2$ is not just a symbol of our age, it is also a symptom, inviting us to recover something that has been lost or displaced.

The realization of $E = mc^2$, the realization of the conversion of matter as mass into energy, itself requires very high energies. For matter to become energized it has to be exponentially enlightened, as it were, and it is only when physics enters the very energetic realms of atomic and sub-atomic particles that the law of the conservation of matter falls away, leaving in place only the law of the conservation of energy. At those very high energy levels matter is not conserved; it becomes energy. At those levels there is a dematerialization, a vaporization of matter. Matter becomes energy at the cost of its annihilation and disappearance. The shadow of the bomb haunts us here, for that is precisely what will happen to all material things at ground zero. They will disappear. They will be destroyed, or, as the photographs from Hiroshima make chillingly clear, matter at some distance from ground zero will become a shadow.

I would propose, however, that this is the fate of matter, and our own fate, when we energize matter that is already dead. Starting with deadened matter, with the matter of the world from which we have already withdrawn, its energizing can result only in its explosion and disappearance. The bomb is a reality in our time because we need it. It is here because it is the most explosive way in which matter can protest our withdrawal, our deadening objectification of it. In creating the bomb we did not simply discover the energy of the sun within the heart of matter, we also affirmed a prescription we had already written about matter itself. Creating the bomb we said in effect that matter once deadened could be energized. Indeed, given the historical sequence of events from a Newton to an Einstein in that order, the bomb was our way of saying that only deadened matter could be energized. The bomb, however, has its own voice. It is not a reality which works because there is the energy of the sun in the nucleus of deadened matter. Rather, it is a reality and it works because it is the way in which matter first deadened and then energized explodes, protests, and signals its resistance to our deadening objectification. When deadened matter is energized by discovering–inventing a nuclear sun at its core, it explodes. It explodes because there is a real difference between a *nucleus at the core* and *eros at the heart* of matter. We can perhaps recognize this difference more concretely when we recall that today our nuclear family is falling apart; that in 1986, for example, half of our marriages ended in divorce. With both spouses in so many families working today; with the entertainments so diverse and so multiple; with the busy schedules of parents, children, and adolescents; with the hectic pace and pressures, there is much energy expended. But energy at the core of the family cannot replace eros at its heart. Like matter itself the family cannot withstand increasing energization when what lies at the heart is dead.

Perhaps you can already guess the direction of my story from the above distinction between the nuclear core and the erotic heart of things. Language makes a difference. It matters, because what we say bespeaks how we see what the world shows of itself. At the high energy levels where matter is energized, we see the nuclear core of things, but it is also possible to see something else, and to see in a different way. Indeed physics itself invites this way of seeing. It is there in the work of David Bohm,[30] for example, whose notion of the 'implicate order' reveals a wholeness of the universe. And it is there most radically at the level of events, at those very same high energy levels where matter is vaporized, for what happens at these levels is that our vision *and* matter change. At these very high energy levels, we are invited, so to speak, by matter itself, to witness its web of relations, its dance of interactions, its net of interconnections. We are invited at these levels to witness not only the dematerialization of matter but also its transformation. Hans Stapp makes the point this way. At high energy levels 'an elementary particle is not an independently existing, unanalyzable entity [but] a set of relationships that reach outward to other things.'[31]

If we are so inclined, then at these high energy levels we can bear witness to the fact that matter as mass exponentially enlightened, that matter energized, is a reaching out of matter toward other things, a yearning or a desire, we might say, which matter has for itself. Indeed, we are invited to witness and to acknowledge something even more radical and astonishing, that particles do not desire one other but in essence *are* desire, that they are connections and not entities connected. In his most provocative work, *Beyond the Pleasure Principle*,[32] Freud suggested that every cell of the body has a libidinal quotient. The physicist, however, is indicating something even more radical. He is not only theorizing that every bit of matter, including the cellular matter of the body, has, so to speak, a libidinal charge, he is also demonstrating that matter in its essence is libidinal, erotic, a matter of desire. We are being invited, therefore, to discover the libido at the heart of matter, asked to remember that matter is not dead but alive, called to acknowledge that at its heart and not its core matter is erotic. At these very high levels of energy we are being offered the opportunity to witness that the energizing of matter need not mean simply the dematerialization of matter, its destruction, but also, in a more radical and profound way, its rebirth as something passionate and alive. We are offered this opportunity as the other side of the danger involved in energizing dead matter to the point of explosion.

That moment where danger lurks and opportunity beckons is a crisis. What the physicist offers us, at these high levels of energy, therefore, is matter in crisis. What he or she offers is the terrible culmination of our cultural–psychological dream of distance in destruction *and* the breakthrough of another dream which returns us to the mythic Eros as the first and originating source of all creation. $E = mc^2$ means energy is mass exponentially enlightened. But it also means that when mass is exponentially enlightened Eros appears.

If we emphasize the moment of opportunity more than the moment of danger, then we begin our energizing of matter with more eros and less death, with more love and less violence, drawing nearer in intimacy and withdrawing less into distance. What difference such a beginning might make is difficult to say, but it is not difficult to say that how we begin does make a difference. At the very least, if we were to begin in this way, it might mean that we had heard the symptom in our energizing of dead matter, that we had heard the bomb as symptom. It might mean that we had heard the bomb as matter's way of saying that if we energize it as deadened matter it will destroy us, *and* that we had heard the bomb as matter's way of saying that it will be energized without such destruction only when we acknowledge that it is alive. This acknowledgement might be a first step away from the bomb as weapon of destruction. Then, perhaps, in place of incarnating our vision of energized matter in a bomb designed to radiate the nuclear fires of destruction, we might begin to incarnate our vision of eroticized matter in ways which would radiate new relations and connections among us, and between us and things, and ourselves and the earth. Emphasizing the moment of opportunity more than the moment of danger, speaking more of eros at the heart of matter and less of a nucleus at its core, how we see and what we see of the world might be transformed. We might, I think, begin to feel ourselves drawn into the spreading web of relations cast by eroticized matter, and we might respond, I believe, by adding our own erotic life to that of the world. We might be warmed, then, by the fires of matter, by its erotic fires of desire, making it, perhaps, less likely that we will be burned by its nuclear fires of destruction.

That we emphasize, however, the danger, that we emphasize the de-materialization of matter, says more about us, about our cultural–psycho-logical dreams of distance, departure, and destruction, than it does about matter. We cannot, of course, choose only the opportunity and erase the danger. The shadow is always with us, as our history of the abandoned body has indicated. Matter, therefore, will always be in crisis, because it registers for us, it reflects to us, the crisis we always are as psychological beings. It will always burn with the fires of destruction as well as with those of desire. There will always be that tension, because again matter mirrors us, because it mirrors the tensions which are psychological life, the tensions, for example, of birth and death, of living and dying, of wanting and not having, of rest and activity, of sleep and wakefulness, of illness and health, of masculine and feminine, of conscious and unconscious. Physics, then, invites us to embrace that tension, to live it as the rhythm of life. The fact that we emphasize the danger says of us, therefore, that we reject that tension, that we attempt to dissolve it. It says, perhaps, that we even prefer the certainty of an 'either/or' over the ambiguity of 'both/and', even when that preference might mean choosing the fires of death over living the tensions, rhythms, dangers, and opportunities of life.[33]

The physics of high energy is a path of return. It is the breakthrough of another cultural–psychological dream. Because, however, we are still enmeshed in our dreams of departure and escape, much of what the physicist tells us seems surreal, and indeed is surreal insofar as this new dream is simply imposed upon our older one. Physics offers us a new vision, a new knowledge, for which we are culturally–psychologically unprepared. It is as if the physicists, at least those like David Bohm, for example, who are able to see the new world which this knowledge opens up, have awakened to a new dream while the rest of us continue to sleep and to dream in old ways. We cannot, however, dis-invent what we have invented. We cannot un-discover the knowledge we have discovered. Therefore, *we* must change. We must awaken from one dream if we are to be gripped by another. Our cultural–psychological dreams must change. We desperately need physics as a path of return, as a stimulus toward awakening. We need to be informed of its visions insistently and continuously. We need, as we have perhaps never needed before, the spark and vitality of its imagination. I take it as a good sign, therefore, that so many physicists today publish books with a popular appeal, that there are people like Carl Sagan, Fritjof

Capra, and Gary Zukav[34] to name only a few to inspire the public imagination. There are, of course, dangers here, the primary one being our predisposition to present science within the context of old dreams; to become merely apologists for science; and for us, the public, to hear it in this fashion. But again where there is danger there is opportunity, and so I judge the risk to be one worth taking. Perhaps more than anything else, however, we need good physicists as teachers: they should be men and women not only of character, which goes without saying, but of wisdom, imagination, inspiration, and intuition. We need them as guides to open the paths of a new world for those just beginning. To this end, therefore, we must seriously reconsider our teaching of science and our teaching of teachers of science. We must begin to teach science as a way of envisioning reality and not just the reality it envisions, because we must come to understand our own participation in the world. Moreover, we must begin teaching our teachers of science with full recognition of the fact that today the physicist is our new magician and our new philosopher. In teaching the teaching and the teachers of science, therefore, we must find ways of allowing them to emphasize above all else, above content or method or technique, the necessity to marry the power of the magus with the wisdom of the philosopher.[35]

E Depression and the mood of return

The cultural–psychological dream of infinite distance has realized itself historically as our technological world. In considering several cultural moments of return from this distance — psychoanalysis, the rise of feminist consciousness, Impressionist painting, and contemporary physics — we have indicated the breakdown of this dream of distance, departure, and escape, and we have suggested the possible breakthrough of another cultural–psychological dream. Whether or not this dream will be realized, I do not know. Nor do I know how to name the world which may be realized out of this dream. Such baptisms belong to the artist, to the poet and the painter, whose imaginative gifts assist the birth of dreams into reality. They give voice and figure to the myths and epics of a new age, and we still await, I think, those myths and epics which can join together these discrete moments of breakthrough into a world. Or perhaps I should say *worlds*, since the breakdown of the cultural–psychological dream of distance is the breakdown of a linear, fixed perspective, and the breakdown of all that goes with it, including literal, univocal, singular modes of perceiving and thinking. As the work of James Hillman[36] so eloquently indicates, the shadow of our age is characterized by plurality, by a polytheistic rather than a monotheistic presence. Or as the great scholar of western mythology, Joseph Campbell, has put it, 'There is no general mythology today, nor can there ever be again.' In indicating why this is so, he adds that 'Our lives are too greatly various in their backgrounds, aims, and possibilities for any single order of symbols to work effectively on us all.'[37]

There are, however, signs and portents of a new age, as the writings of Marilyn Ferguson, for example, indicate, as do those of David Bohm and James Hillman, mentioned above, and E. F. Schumacher, Robert Sardello, and William Irwin Thompson.[38] All of these people, among many others, need to be read, because in each of them there are hints and whispers of another dawn and of its face.

To describe their work here would be, however, a task well beyond the scope of this tale, so I must content myself with citing them and with offering the briefest of comments on what the four cultural moments of return intimate about the features of a new world. Taken together, they suggest that the breakthrough of a new cultural dream will realize a world whose *form* is figurative and imaginative as well as literal and factual, whose *structure* is relational and plural more than individual and singular, whose *atmosphere* is dream-like and mythical in addition to logical and rational, whose *style* is told and storied more than seen and explained, whose *landscape* is multi-perspectival and vertically leveled more than fixed and infinitely distant, and whose *energy*, finally, is more erotic and, one hopes, less destructive.[39]

These are, I admit, guesses, perhaps even wild speculations or vain hopes. Nevertheless, within the same vein of guesswork, I would like to add one other feature. I would like to suggest that the breakthrough of a new cultural–psychological dream will realize a new world whose mood is low. With this guess, however, I enter into another domain: into a brief defense of depression.

We avoid depression and its lows as we avoid perhaps nothing else, and it is for us in our society, as it is in any highly medicalized society, a symptom to be treated, an illness to be cured. In a society that values progress and equates progress with upward mobility — the rise up the corporate ladder, as it were — depression is profoundly anti-progress, not to say anti-efficient and even anti-technological. Indeed, in one respect it may even be said that depression is anti-American, insofar as we declared at our founding that one of our inalienable rights along with life and liberty is the pursuit of happiness. This pursuit is our right and perhaps even our duty, and depression is one of those elements, perhaps even *the* most primary element, which indicates the failure of our pursuit. I am not saying here that our founding fathers were misguided in naming the pursuit of happiness as one of humanity's sacred rights. Within the context of the Enlightenment dream of reason in which they wrote and of which they were a part, this definition made more than common sense. It was an inspired, noble dream, one of the best fruits of the infinite vision of the Enlightenment. Rather, I am saying only that within the context of the increasing industrialization of society since the mid-eighteenth century, and especially within the context of the technological revolution of the last thirty years or so, the pursuit of happiness has become a frenzied hunt married to a success measured more often than not in material possessions, in dead things. Perhaps no better symbol of this inflationary spiral of the pursuit of happiness and success exists than that of the credit card, the plastic money which is the key to unlock almost any dream. Robert Sardello[40] has indicated how its presence actually devalues our sense of money and the things which we buy with it. To this symbol, however, I will add the figure and the story of Willie Loman, Arthur Miller's salesman, whose pursuit of the American dream, whose quest for happiness measured as success, has become almost archetypal. Willie Loman — without, of course, credit card in hand — is 'the quintessential American dreamer',[41] whose tragedy has become almost worldwide weekly television fare in the life of J. R. Ewing, the quintessential American schemer. It may seem odd, and perhaps to some even profane, to speak of Willie and J.R. in the same breath, but the difference between them is an important barometer of depression in our culture. Depression is 'the other face of the American dream',[42] and Willie Loman's life and his death in pursuit of that dream are a tragedy, because in pursuit of a happiness made visible as success for himself and especially for his son Biff, Willie loses his way home. J. R. Ewing's life and near death, however interesting, are not tragic, largely because, despite his house, J. R. Ewing has no home. Willie Loman's life and pursuit of happiness are a journey in search of home, not unlike the other great epic journeys of our western literary tradition, beginning with *The Odyssey*. J. R. Ewing's life and his pursuit of success are — and here our contemporary jargon fits well — a trip.

Depression, then, is a matter of home, of coming home or trying to, of being called home. It is not an illness to be cured. It is the cure.

The psychiatrist Walker Percy appreciates depression in this way, and like all good depressives, of which I suspect he is one, his appreciation is laced with irony and wit. Calling into question the usual therapeutic rationale that depression is a symptom of an illness which implies that there is something wrong with you, he reverses it and says that *not* to be depressed today can only be a sign of your derangement. Indeed, 'you are entitled to your depression.' Addressing us personally he says:

No member of the other two million species which inhabit the earth — and who are luckily exempt from depression — would fail to be depressed if it lived the life you lead. You live in a deranged age — more deranged than usual, because despite great scientific and technological advances, man has not the faintest idea of who he is or what he is doing.[43]

And lest we miss his point Percy goes on to advise us to 'consider the only adults who are never depressed: Chuckleheads, Californian surfers, and fundamentalist Christians who believe they have had a personal encounter with Jesus and are saved for once and all.' It may very well be good advice. In any case, 'Would you trade,' he asks, 'your depression to become any of these?'[44]

I cite Percy because his irony and wit lighten the leaden heaviness of depression which, although it rightfully belongs to depression, is too often used to mask one's resistance to depression. Depression is a call home and in our lives we would resist that call, because having already resisted the knowledge it would give us, it is forced to appear as alien to our lives, in the guise perhaps of something like that ugly, strange alien E.T., who says 'phone home'. We would resist such alien things, and so depression itself becomes a resistance to depression and we become depressed about being depressed, and so on.

Nevertheless, for a spectator too distant from a world that has become only a spectacle and too distant even from his or her body, which has become only a specimen, depression is a cure. It is the cure for a life on the run, for a life 'on the road', as Dean Moriarty lives it in Jack Kerouac's now classical novel of the same name.[45] Depression is the cure for men and women who have become fugitives. Of course, to say it in this way, to say that depression is the cure does not mean that this is an easy thing to do. It is not simply a matter of accepting one's depression, of passively resigning oneself to it. On the contrary, depression as cure entails a willingness to allow oneself to be guided and to be taught by one's depression, to work with it and to let it work over one's life. For a life on the run and on the way up, it means specifically a willingness to allow the depression to slow you down and bring you down, and to turn you around and to demand that you remember home even as you leave it.

In the opening of his 'Ninth Elegy' the poet Rilke asks why we long for destiny, and in first reply he answers himself in the negative. He says,

> Not because happiness really
> exists, that premature profit of imminent loss.[46]

It is, I think, a line of poetry which has to make one pause. Happiness as a profit made too early and from things that will too easily pass away. It may be too dark a vision, and yet the depressive, I believe, knows something of what Rilke speaks. He or she knows that it is not happiness in itself, and certainly not its pursuit under the guise of success and as an inalienable right, which is the stuff of life. He or she knows that happiness is not a goal to be achieved at the end of a journey but is rather a way of going along the path. 'Depression,' the Jungian analyst John Layard says, 'is withheld knowledge.'[47] I believe that is essentially correct, and I would add only that it is withheld by the deeper levels of who we are, because who we are refuses to listen. But if we did listen, if we heard, then the knowledge which depression is would teach us that happiness is not life shaped as a line of progress, but that happiness is life shaped in the round. Depression as the mood of return is the call of ourselves to ourselves, saying that all departure must also and always be in the light of a return.

III Conclusion: a final word and a final gathering

Our tale has now come to its end. Only a final gathering and a few parting words remain. Those figures who have played a part in our story appear and in the weakened light of either dawn or dusk we can catch a last glimpse of them.

Enter the Little Cosmonaut and the two kissing figures, images of the artist who stirred our story into life; make room also for Galileo, Newton, and Harvey too, and for Descartes, Vesalius and others of their kind, as the procession of founding fathers of modern science takes its place; Brunelleschi is there, as is Alberti, with their sketches and projects of infinite vision, and coming to greet them explorers of the camera eye and its limits: Hockney with his moving eye and Uelsmann with an eye that can see into dreams — and of course amongst them all the painters impressed with the rhythms and depths of the world; enter too Mesmer and Freud and the patients they attended, to whom we owe so much for not letting us forget; there is Mary Shelley, too, whom we should not forget, and nor should we forget those later sisters of her mother who have awakened the feminist shadows of our cultural dreams. We recognize ourselves there, too, in the guises of those who have preceded us, as figures of our dreams: the spectator self behind a window now made in infinite variations; and the self of infinite vision, with a body and its shadows, corpse, machine, and robot, reflex man and woman, industrial worker and, of course, the astronaut, the last and now the first in this pantheon of images. Witch and madwoman shadow the background, together with the hypnotist and the hypnotized and mesmerized patients in their twilight state between waking to a new dream and sleeping; there too, of course, are the hysteric and the anorexic, forgotten daughters of the astronaut.

They, we, are all there. Originators and continuing players who belong to this, our world. Gathered together within a dream, drawn together by a vision. It is over there in front of us again, as we envisioned it before, the earth as seen from space, the image we saw in Figure 7.2. We should all look at the earth again in this way, while we continue to dream our cultural dreams of distance, departure, and escape. We should look and in this, the final moment of our tale, hear the words of the poet:

> We shall not cease from exploration
> And the end of all our exploring
> Will be to arrive where we started
> And know the place for the first time.[48]

Notes

PROLOGUE: ADDRESS TO THE READER

1 Marshall McLuhan, *The Gutenberg Galaxy*, New American Library, New York, 1969, p. 43.
2 See, for example, Figure 2.5 in this text. McLuhan notes with respect to Bosch that he '. . . injected the spaces of the medieval dream world into the new Renaissance spaces': *Through the Vanishing Point*, Harper & Row, New York, 1968, p. 77. The unfolding of our tale will tell us what has happened to those dreams injected into the space of rational vision.
3 Rainer Maria Rilke, *Duino Elegies*, trans. J. Leishman and S. Spender, W. W. Norton & Co., New York, 1939, p. 77.
4 For an excellent presentation of the many overlaps between science and art in the twentieth century, see C. H. Waddington, *Behind Appearances*, Edinburgh University Press, Edinburgh, 1969. The book is especially inviting for its many illustrations.
5 Frederick Turner, 'Design for a new academy,' *Harpers* 273, No. 1636, September 1986, p. 50.
6 Paul Bob, 'Openings inside and out,' *Esquire* 103, No. 3, March 1985, p. 284.
7 Patricia Brady, 'A conversation with Alex Grey,' *Boston Visual Arts News* 12, January 1984.
8 Ibid.
9 Norman Cohn, *Europe's Inner Demons*, New American Library, New York, 1977, p. 258.
10 Ibid., p. 263.
11 See, for example, J. H. van den Berg, *The Changing Nature of Man* (W. W. Norton & Co., New York, 1983) and *Divided Existence and Complex Society* (Duquesne University Press, Pittsburg, 1974). Unfortunately the two major works of van den Berg dealing with his notion of *metabletics*, a theory of changes, are not available in English translation. A very fine overview of van den Berg's work can be found, however, in *Humanitas* 7, no. 3 (Winter 1971). In addition, there is the recent *Festschrift* volume honoring van den Berg's work edited by Dreyer Kruger and entitled *The Changing Reality of Modern Man: Essays in Honor of J. H. van den Berg*, Juta & Co., Capetown, 1984.
12 See, for example, note 1. In addition the reader is advised to consult *Through the Vanishing Point*, Marshall McLuhan and Harley Parker, op. cit.
13 The work of Harold Innis has been largely neglected. He was, however, a strong influence on McLuhan. See, for example, *The Bias of Communication* (University of Toronto Press, Toronto, 1964) and *Empire and Communication*

(University of Toronto Press, Toronto, 1972). With respect to Ong, his studies are indispensable for this type of research, in which culture, history, and psychology intersect. The reader is especially advised to consult *Rhetoric, Romance, and Technology* (Cornell University Press, Ithaca, 1971), *Interfaces of the Word* (Cornell University Press, Ithaca, 1971) and *Orality and Literacy* (Routledge & Kegan Paul, London, 1982). Finally, the work by Donald M. Lowe, *History of Bourgeois Perception* (University of Chicago Press, Chicago, 1983), is especially readable. His discussion of the temporal, spatial, and bodily style of bourgeois life is a rich and valuable source of reflection.

14 Dianne Connelly, *All Sickness is Homesickness*, Centre for Traditional Acupuncture, Columbia, Maryland, 1986. In addition to its presentation of the symptom as a guide to healing, this book offers an excellent introduction to traditional acupuncture as an alternative mode of therapeutic work. Connelly's stories of her work with patients are especially instructive.

15 William Barrett, *The Illusion of Technique*, Doubleday & Co., Garden City, 1978. See also *Time of Need*, Harper & Row, New York, 1972.

16 I wish to acknowledge here a colleague, David Gentry, who, as a practicing psychotherapist like myself, has taught me to know and to appreciate how very much music is a matter of psychotherapy and psychotherapy a matter of music. Since this work is something of a psychotherapy of technological culture, I would very much wish that in place of giving you a book to read I could sing the song of technology's dreams and symptoms. Really, I would very much rather give you a song and a dance than feed you a line.

CHAPTER 1 LIFT-OFF: WE ARE ALL ASTRONAUTS

1 Charles Wentinck, *The Human Figure*, Livingston Publishing Company, Wynnewood, 1971, p. 157.

2 *The Dallas Morning News*, November 24, 1984.

3 Walker Percy, *Lost in the Cosmos*, Washington Square Press, New York, 1983. A witty, irreverent and serious book highly recommended for those readers already displaced and far from a sense of home.

4 Loren Eiseley, *The Invisible Pyramid*, Charles Scribner's Sons, New York, 1970, p. 80.

5 Timothy Leary, *Neuropolitics*, Starseed/Peace Press, Los Angeles, 1977, p. 49.

6 Ibid., p. 49.

7 One should read this book by Crick for its *psychological* significance. Whether the scientific data he offers in support of his theories are true or not, there is a fantasy of origins at work here which says a great deal about our culture's relation with and attitudes toward the earth. For an illustration of how to read a scientific work as a cultural–psychological document, see my discussion of William Harvey in *Psychological Life: From Science to Metaphor*, University of Texas Press, Austin, 1982.

8 Joseph Weizenbaum, *Computer Power and Human Reason: From Judgement to Calculation*, W. H. Freeman, New York, 1976, p. 276.

9 Ibid., p. 259.

10 Jonathan Schell, *The Fate of the Earth*, Avon Books, New York, 1982. We should read this book in order to weep. It is a sane and sober analysis of the plight of our nuclearized world. In its impact and importance it is the literary counterpart of the film *Testament*. Hans Jonas, a philosopher of science, has written in a recent work, *The Imperative of Responsibility* (University of Chicago Press, Chicago, 1985), of the necessity to develop an ethics of fear. We

need to imagine the horrible destructiveness of nuclear war if we are to take a moral stand against it. Jonas' argument is a cogent one and one which the Harvard psychologist James Blight has just recently demonstrated in his as yet unpublished manuscript, *Fear and Learning in a Nuclear Crisis*. Fear of the consequences of nuclear inadvertence in the Cuban missile crisis was largely responsible for its peaceful outcome. I am very much persuaded by Blight's evidence and presentation. But I would add that we also need an ethics of sorrow in our nuclear age. It is not enough only to fear the horrible destructiveness of an imagined holocaust. We also need to mourn now, in the present, the loss of *all* that faces us, that is near to us, that matters to us. We need to develop the capacity to feel the sorrow of the trees, the lament of the oceans, the sadness of the stars, if we are to survive. We need to sense how things are making their appeal to us.

11 Walter M. Miller, *A Canticle for Leibowitz*, Bantam Books, New York, 1959, p. 312.
12 Ibid., p. 313.
13 Paul Boyer, *By the Bomb's Early Light*, Pantheon, New York, 1986, p. 362.
14 William Barrett, *Time of Need*, Harper & Row, New York, 1972, p. 386.
15 Leary, op. cit., p. 138.
16 Ibid., pp. 70−1.
17 Isaac Asimov, in Gerard O'Neill, *The High Frontier*, Anchor Press/Doubleday, Garden City, 1976, p. 35.
18 O'Neill, op. cit.
19 Barrett, op. cit., p. 385.
20 Jeremy Rifkin, *Algeny*, Penguin Books, New York, 1984, p. 42.
21 Barrett, op. cit., p. 385.
22 David Michael Levin, *Pathologies of the Modern Self*, New York University Press, New York, 1987.
23 Eiseley, op. cit., p. 65.
24 James Hillman, *The Dream and the Underworld*, Harper & Row, New York, 1979.
25 Eiseley, op. cit., p. 71.
26 Rilke, op. cit., p. 77.
27 The allusion, of course, is to T. S. Eliot's *Four Quartets*. We shall meet the poet and hear his words again later in the story.

CHAPTER 2: THE WINDOW AND THE CAMERA

1 For the references to the work of van den Berg see p. 230.
2 Samuel Y. Edgerton, *The Renaissance Rediscovery of Linear Perspective*, Harper & Row, New York, 1976, p. 4.
3 Horst de la Croix and Richard G. Tansey, *Gardner's Art Through The Ages*, Harcourt Brace Jovanovich, New York, 1975, p. 434.
4 William Ivins, *On the Rationalization of Sight*, Da Capo Press, New York, 1975, p. 12.
5 Edgerton, op. cit., p. 165.
6 Ibid., p. 9, my italics.
7 Ibid., pp. 9−10.
8 It should be apparent that this chapter is very much indebted to the work of Edgerton cited above. In what follows I shall be dealing with Alberti's procedures only insofar as they relate to the theme of this work. For a more comprehensive treatment, and one which supplies a good historical context for Alberti's

work, see Edgerton. His book is a masterpiece of clarity and insight.

9 Leon Battista Alberti as quoted in Edgerton, op. cit., pp. 42–3, my italics.

10 Ibid., p. 196.

11 Ibid., p. 43.

12 Ibid., p. 200.

13 Hannah Arendt, *The Human Condition*, University of Chicago Press, Chicago, 1958, p. 6.

14 Alberti as quoted in Edgerton, op. cit., p. 43.

15 For a discussion of this theme of nuclear winter, see Paul R. Ehrlich, Carl Sagan, Donald Kennedy, and Walter Orr Roberts, *The Cold and the Dark*, W. W. Norton & Co., New York, 1984.

16 Arendt, op. cit., p. 265.

17 For the actual line and its context see *The Poetry and Prose of William Blake*, ed. David V. Erdman, University of California Press, Berkeley, 1981, p. 693.

18 Title of first chapter of C. S. Lewis's *The Abolition of Man*, Macmillan, New York, 1974.

19 Alberti as quoted in Edgerton, op. cit., p. 44.

20 For a thorough discussion of this notion of the mathematical and its relation to the experimental character of *modern* science, see Martin Heidegger, *What is a Thing?*, trans. W. Barton, Henry Regnery Co., Chicago, 1967. In addition, the reader who is interested in the phenomenological approach to modern science is well advised to consult Edmund Husserl's, *The Crisis of European Science and Transcendental Phenomenology*, trans. D. Carr, Northwestern University Press, Evanston, 1970. Finally, for a less philosophically technical application of phenomenology to the study of the science of psychology, see Robert Romanyshyn, *Psychological Life: From Science to Metaphor*, University of Texas Press, Austin, 1982.

21 Marshall McLuhan, *Understanding Media*, New American Library, New York, 1964, p. 145.

22 Alexander Koyre, *From the Closed World to the Infinite Universe*, John Hopkins University Press, Baltimore, 1968. This text is a readable and interesting companion piece to the references cited in note 20 above.

23 For a full discussion of this point about the birth of psychology as a science, see Romanyshyn, op. cit. In that work the genesis of modern psychological humanity is shown to be inextricably tied to the emergence of the modern sciences of nature and the body. The present work is a complement to, and a deepening of, this earlier one insofar as it attempts to describe the genesis of the technological world in that dream of distance and departure inaugurated in linear perspective vision. It is this new vision which makes possible those new sciences of nature and the body, which in turn require and call into being the new science of psychology. Our technological world, then, is one in which psychological humanity functions within a world whose reality is defined by physics and with a body whose reality is defined by anatomy and physiology; and all of this begins with the imaginal eye of the artist. It is there and then that a new cultural–historical dream emerges.

24 David Hockney, *Cameraworks*, Alfred A. Knopf, New York, 1984, p. 9, my italics.

25 Ibid., p. 23.

26 Lawrence Weschler, in Hockney, ibid., p. 26. Weschler is referring here to a specific piece entitled *The Brooklyn Bridge*.

27 Hockney, *New York Times*, October 7, 1984.

28 Hockney, *Cameraworks*, p. 17, his italics.

29 Hockney, *Dallas Morning News*, January 6, 1985.

30 Hockney, *Cameraworks*, p. 20.
31 Hockney, *New York Times*, October 7, 1984.

CHAPTER 3: SELF AS SPECTATOR

1 William Shakespeare, *King Lear*, Act IV, Scene 6.
2 Marshall McLuhan and Harley Parker, *Through the Vanishing Point*, Harper & Row, New York, 1968, p. 75.
3 Horst de la Croix and Richard G. Tansey, *Gardner's Art through the Ages*, Harcourt Brace Jovanovich, New York, 1975, p. 433.
4 Walker Percy, *Lost in the Cosmos*, Washington Square Press, New York, 1983, p. 17.
5 William Ivins, *Art and Geometry*, Dover, New York, 1964, p. 69.
6 J. H. van den Berg as quoted in Robert Romanyshyn, *Psychological Life: From Science to Metaphor*, University of Texas Press, Austin, 1982, pp. 24, 25.
7 Ibid., p. 24.
8 See Marshall McLuhan and Harley Parker, op. cit., pp. 99, 105, for the fittingness of these quotations within the context of a predominantly visual culture.
9 Christopher Lasch, *The Culture of Narcissism*, W. W. Norton & Co., New York, 1979, p. 135.
10 Nicolo Machiavelli, *The Prince*, trans. L. P. de Alvarez, University of Dallas Press, Irving, 1984, p. 108.
11 This point is discussed in a rich and delightful work by Joseph Lyons, *Ecology of the Body: Styles of Behavior in Human Life*, Duke University Press, Durham, 1987, p. 294.
12 A. C. Harwood, *Shakespeare's Prophetic Mind*, Rudolf Steiner Press, London, 1977, p. 35.
13 William Shakespeare, *Hamlet*, Act II, Scene 2.
14 Alberti as quoted in Samuel Y. Edgerton, *The Renaissance Rediscovery of Linear Perspective*, Harper & Row, New York, 1976, p. 115.
15 For a discussion of this point the reader is well advised to consult Maurice Merleau-Ponty, *Phenomenology of Perception*, Routledge & Kegan Paul, London, 1962, especially chapter 6. In addition, his essay entitled 'Eye and mind' in *The Primacy of Perception*, Northwestern University Press, Evanston, 1964, is an excellent presentation of how we are borne into the world by our perceptions and of the relations between perceiving, thinking, and speaking. Finally, for the reader who is interested in pursuing this topic in more detail see Maurice Merleau-Ponty, *The Prose of the World*, Northwestern University Press, Evanston, 1973.
16 Edgerton, op. cit., p. 119.
17 Alberti as quoted in Edgerton, ibid.
18 Rudolf de Lippe, *La Géometrisation de l'homme en Europe à l'époque moderne*, Bibliotheks- und Informationssystem der Universität Oldenburg, Oldenburg, 1985. Rudolf de Lippe's work is an indispensable companion to much of what is presented in this text. This particular piece is noteworthy for its fine illustrations.
19 Martin Heidegger, *What is a Thing?*, trans. W. Barton, Henry Regnery Co., Chicago, 1967. For a discussion of the mathematical project of modern science see especially pp. 65–108.
20 Galileo as quoted in E. A. Burtt, *The Metaphysical Foundations of Modern Science*, Doubleday & Co., Garden City, 1954, p. 75.
21 All the quotations in this section are taken from Hannah Arendt, *The Human Condition*, University of Chicago Press, Chicago, 1958, pp. 265–7.

22 Ibid., p. 266.

23 Ibid., p. 265.

24 Ibid., pp. 265, 262.

25 Jonathan Schell, *The Fate of the Earth*, Avon Books, New York, 1982, p. 11.

26 Arendt, op. cit., p. 269.

27 Joseph Weizenbaum's *Computer Power and Human Reason*, W. H. Freeman, New York, 1976, is an excellent discussion of the implications of and dangers inherent within an unexamined use of our technological powers and skills. Written by one of the pioneers of computer technology, it is a sensitive plea for reason in an age much given to madness born of an unreflective and unresponsive use of its powers.

28 Paul Ricoeur, *Freud and Philosophy: An Essay on Interpretation*, Yale University Press, New Haven, 1970, p. 31.

29 Quoted in Marshall Berman, *All that is Solid Melts into Air*, Simon & Schuster, New York, 1983, p. 69. Berman's text is an instructive and exciting essay on the spirit of modernity as illustrated through the establishment of the modern city landscape.

30 De la Croix and Tansey, op. cit., p. 434.

31 As quoted in McLuhan and Parker, op. cit., p. xxiv.

32 Robert Romanyshyn, *Psychological Life: From Science to Metaphor*, University of Texas Press, Austin, 1982, p. 28.

33 Newton as quoted in Romanyshyn, ibid., p. 26.

34 Arendt, op. cit., p. 250.

35 Robert Romanyshyn, 'The despotic eye,' in *The Changing Reality of Modern Man*, ed. Dreyer Krueger, Juta & Co., Capetown, 1984, p. 98.

36 McLuhan and Parker, op. cit., p. 77.

37 Jean-Paul Sartre, *Nausea*, New Directions, Norfolk, 1964, p. 158.

38 David V. Erdman (ed.), *The Poetry and Prose of William Blake*, University of California Press, Berkeley, 1981, p. 27.

39 Ibid., p. 693.

40 Jack Stillinger (ed.), *The Poems of John Keats*, The Belknap Press, Cambridge, 1978, pp. 472–3.

41 Percy, op. cit., p. 77.

42 Ivan Illich, *Medical Nemesis*, Bantam Books, New York, 1977, pp. 40, 41.

43 Percy, op. cit., p. 17.

44 McLuhan and Parker, op. cit., pp. 10, 131.

45 Hannah Arendt, *Eichmann in Jerusalem*, Viking Press, New York, 1965. Arendt's study of Eichmann is a chilling portrait of that image of efficiency wedded to indifference which we described earlier in the text.

46 Arendt, op. cit., pp. 263, 264.

47 Romanyshyn, *Psychological Life: From Science to Metaphor*. For a discussion of the relation between Copernicus and Vesalius, between the moving earth and the corpse, see especially chapter 1.

48 Arendt, *The Human Condition*, p. 259.

49 Edgerton, op. cit., p. 165.

50 Percy, op. cit. For his amusing and perceptive discussion of modern modes of re-entry, see especially chapter 14.

51 Ivins, op. cit., p. 71.

52 For a discussion of this connection between vision and landscape in Shakespeare, see McLuhan and Parker, op. cit.

53 Maurice Merleau-Ponty, *The Primacy of Perception*, p. 25.

54 Thomas Sprat as quoted in Romanyshyn, *Psychological Life: From Science to Metaphor*, p. 175.

55 Joseph and Frances Gies, *Life in a Medieval City*, Harper & Row, new York, 1981, p. 46.
56 Bernard Grun, *The Timetables of History*, Simon & Schuster, New York, 1975, p. 259.
57 After finishing this book a newspaper story about attempts to revive the Cornish language was brought to my attention. Of interest to our tale is the fact that this effort has had to include the coining of new words. The word for 'television' in the resurrected Cornish tongue is 'Pellwrlok,' which means 'seeing at a distance.' When we look upon the modern world with fresh eyes, which in this case means through the eyes of an ancient language in need of a word to describe a new experience, we see how very much this world is a matter of distant vision. For the article in question, see *Dallas Times Herald*, April 16, 1987.

CHAPTER 4: BODY AS SPECIMEN

1 Charles Wentinck, *The Human Figure*, Livingston Publishing Company, Wynnewood, 1971, p. 157.
2 For a discussion of this relation between belief and the human heart see Robert Romanyshyn, *Psychological Life: From Science to Metaphor*, University of Texas Press, Austin, 1982, chapter 4. The point of this connection is that we conduct our lives not primarily in terms of what we know but rather in terms of what we can bear to believe. As psychological beings, truth is always a matter of what the human heart, our organ of belief, can stand. If this tarnishes our image of truth, so much the better, since the image of a pure truth seeded and nourished in a rational mind divorced from our living situation is an unbearable fiction.

   Along these same lines let me mention a manuscript being prepared for publication by Professor James Blight of the John F. Kennedy School of Government at Harvard University. Entitled *Fear and Learning in a Nuclear Crisis*, this work offers a persuasive psychological account of the Cuban missile crisis, and by extension the crisis of any nuclear confrontation, by treating the participants in that crisis as human beings who acted as they did because of what they believed about the impending nuclear catastrophe. Kennedy and Khruschev, among others, were not rational actors playing a game of nuclear poker. They foresaw with fear and trembling the outcome of a nuclear war started by inadvertence, and, believing that matters were reaching a point beyond their ability to control them, they acted on those beliefs. Blight's manuscript is a working example that the living of life is a *matter of belief* and that in that living *belief matters*.
3 I speak somewhat loosely here when I say the body is 'in' a situation — hence the quotation marks. Later in the text the reader will appreciate that it is much more appropriate to speak of how the human body *is* a situation. For the moment, however, let me illustrate the difference between a body being *in* and *being* a situation. A smile which I see on the face of the woman I love is inseparable from my face which I present to her. Her smile has nothing to do with her insides. It has to do with my face, with our relationship. Moreover, her smile gathers a space around us in a specific felt bodily way. Her smile does not exist in a space which contains us. Rather, her smile forms and shapes a space for us. It creates and radiates its space.
4 Horst de la Croix and Richard G. Tansey, *Gardner's Art through the Ages*, Harcourt Brace Jovanovich, New York, 1975, p. 323.
5 Ibid.
6 That most minimal sense of the human body which allows us to divorce the body

from culture so that it can be fully consigned to the realm of nature is the sense which is operative today. It is the sense of the body as mechanism, as object, as anatomical structure and physiological function; it is the medical body. That this body is a physical matter, a piece of nature, is not in question. What is in question, however, is that it *matters* only as physical matter. The point of these pages on the medieval body is to indicate that the human body as a part of nature is a *cultural matter*. The body of earlier ages is not just a different perception. It is a different body. *It is a different matter.* Some work in progress by Ivan Illich and Barbara Duden on the historicity of the body is quite relevant here. See, for example, Duden, *Geschichte unter der Haut*, Klett-Cotta, Stuttgart, 1987. For an illustration of the body as cultural matter see my discussion of the heart in *Psychological Life: From Science to Metaphor*, chapter 4.

7 See for example, J. H. van den Berg, *Het Menselijk Lichaam: Het Goepende Lichaam*, G. F. Callenbach, Nijkerk, 1959; *Het Menselijk Lichaam: Het Verlaten Lichaam*, G. F. Callenbach, Nijkerk, 1961; *Metabletica van den Materie*, G. F. Callenbach, Nijkerk, 1969; *Gedane Zaken*, G. F. Callenbach, Nijkerk, 1977.

8 Jeremy Rifkin, *Algeny*, Penguin Books, New York, 1984, p. 59.

9 David Abrahamson, 'Tamarins in the Amazon,' *Science 85* vol. 6, no. 7, p. 63.

10 This allusion to cartoon figures is not without seriousness. The cartoon figure, like the pantomimic body, is a body whose exaggerated gestures incarnate a situation. In other words, in cartoons we read the situation in relation to the body and vice versa. The cartoon body is the e-motional outline, the form, the definition of the situation. It is the situation made visible. Moreover, the cartoon body shares another feature with the pantomimic body of medieval art. Both are bodies without interiors. That is, the body in each of these instances matters as a situation. It does not matter as an interior space stuffed with organs. Cartoons, then, as medieval artistry! Medieval art as cartoon!

11 De la Croix and Tansey, op. cit., p. 323.

12 As we shall see in this chapter the body as an interior space stuffed with organs begins with the corpse. It may be, then, that our health spas actually resurrect and condition the corpse-like body. Our manic pursuit of health may actually be taking place in the shadows of death. It may, ironically, be a loss of life.

13 The body of anatomical structure is a cultural–psychological *invention* which has become a *convention*. I see the value of this study to be precisely that it allows us to become *unconventional* and thereby recover ('re-member') what has become uncritically assumed. For a detailed example of how the body is a cultural–psychological matter see the discussion of the heart as a pump in my earlier work, *Psychological Life: From Science to Metaphor*, especially chapter 4.

14 The reader is reminded here of our earlier discussion in chapter 2 of the window as grid in linear perspective vision. Here is a vivid illustration of those remarks.

15 Alberti as quoted in Edgerton, *The Renaissance Rediscovery of Linear Perspective*, Harper & Row, New York, 1976, p. 119.

16 John Berger, *Ways of Seeing*, Penguin Books, New York, 1977, p. 62. For another discussion of Dürer, one which is excellent and most comprehensive in treating Dürer's conception of beauty as contained in his treatise on human proportions, see *The Life and Art of Albrecht Dürer*, ed. Erwin Panofsky, Princeton University Press, Princeton, 1955, pp. 242–84. Panofsky does note a certain violence to nature in Dürer's scheme. 'It denied', he says, 'individual differences and hardened into geometrical curves what should be an organic undulation . . .', p. 264.

17 William S. Heckscher, *Rembrandt's Anatomy of Dr Nicolaas Tulp*, New York University Press, Washington Square, 1958, pp. 28, 32.

18 J. H. van den Berg, *Medical Power and Medical Ethics*, W. W. Norton & Co., New York, 1978, pp. 67–85.

19 Robert Romanyshyn, op. cit., pp. 20–2.

20 Van den Berg, *Medical Power and Medical Ethics*, p. 70.

21 Ibid., pp. 71, 70.

22 Ibid., p. 83.

23 P. Aries, *The Hour of Our Death*, Alfred A. Knopf, New York, 1981, p. 318.

24 Ivan Illich, 'H₂O and the waters of forgetfulness,' *Resurgence*, No. 112, September/October 1985, p. 11.

25 E. M. Cioran, *The Fall into Time*, trans. R. Howard, Quadrangle Books, Chicago, 1970, p. 61.

26 Van den Berg, *Medical Power and Medical Ethics*, p. 83.

27 Ibid., p. 83.

28 Illich, op. cit., p. 10.

29 Ibid., p. 10.

30 It would be foolish to assume that in this text we are decrying technology. Certainly it is a positive boon to man- and womankind to wash the city. Linear perspective vision has positive features and advantages. Nevertheless, it is necessary to recognize how the advantages of technological vision are also dangers. This is precisely the case when, for example, our scrubbing of the city becomes a sterilization of it, producing cities which are easily forgetful of the fact of our incarnation. An ideal of purity which denies the flesh distances us not only from our bodies but also from the history and myth of water, which irrigates the soul. The value of Illich's article cited in note 28 is that it reawakens the historical and mythical depths of water so clearly threatened in our imagined purification of it.

31 I cannot help but recall here as an example the exercised, well muscled body which is a product of our health spa industry and visible in our television advertisements. This body of interior muscle, which fits everywhere and any-where and hence belongs nowhere, has become a commercialized product, a saleable item, a purchasable thing.

32 Van den Berg, *Medical Power and Medical Ethics*, pp. 79–80.

33 Barbara Duden, 'Historical concepts of the body', *Resurgence* No. 112, September/October 1985, pp. 24–6. This article is an exceptionally important piece which has recently been elaborated in book form under the title *Geschichte unter der Haut*.

CHAPTER 5: THE ABANDONED BODY AND ITS SHADOWS

1 Robert Romanyshyn, *Psychological Life: From Science to Metaphor*, University of Texas Press, Austin, 1982.

2 Romanyshyn, 'The despotic eye', *The Changing Reality of Modern Man*, ed. Dreyer Krueger, Juta & Co., Capetown, 1984, pp. 87–109.

3 Randolf Severson, 'Money and Nature', *Money and the Soul of the World*, eds R. Sardello and R. Severson, The Dallas Institute for Humanities and Culture, Dallas, 1983, p. 52.

4 Romanyshyn, *Psychological Life: From Science to Metaphor*, pp. 107–34. Each of these terms is like a switch word in the text describing the heart not only from a physiological point of view, but also from a cultural–psychological per-spective. The heart is empty, for example, insofar as it is the systolic moment, that moment when the heart discharges blood, which defines for Harvey the true character of the heart as a pump. But at that moment in history, the heart is not

only empty of blood, but also emptied of its beliefs, as the rise of the cult of the Sacred Heart illustrates. In short, I indicated in that work how a text in physiology can be read as a cultural-psychological document. While the terms 'empty', 'divided' and 'equal' have a basis in Harvey's text, they are also psychological realities, mirrored or reflected in the events of the age.

5 J. H. van den Berg, *Reflex and Revolution*, pp. 56, 63. I am citing here an English translation of van den Berg's *De Reflex*, G. F. Callenbach, Nijkerk, 1973. The translation, which has never been published, was done by Marius Jacobs, a long-time friend and associate of van den Berg.

6 David Michael Levin, *The Body's Recollection of Being: Phenomenological Psychology and the Deconstruction of Nihilism*, Routledge & Kegan Paul, London, 1985. This work is a scholarly and comprehensive treatment of the denial of the body in the tradition of western thought. It is also a highly original presentation of the necessary place of the body in understanding the way in which we bear our thoughts, incorporate a living tradition, achieve a felt sense of moral value, become a body politic, and take in our stride the measure of the earth. It is one of those rare texts whose philosophical depths of understanding are matched by poetic heights of expression.

7 Romanyshyn, 'Das Auge der Distanz und der Lieb des Begehrens: eine Metabletik des Wohnens', *Poesis 3/1987*, pp. 3–21.

8 Van den Berg, *Reflex and Revolution*, p. 89. See note 5.

9 Karl Marx and Friedrich Engels, *The Communist Manifesto*, trans. S. Moore, Foreign Languages Press, Peking, 1965.

10 John Cohen, *Human Robots in Myth and Science*, Allen & Unwin, London, 1966.

11 Karel Capek, *R.U.R.*, ed. H. Shefter, Pocket Books, New York, 1973. A somewhat neglected play, it has the virtue of dramatizing the birth of the robot within the context of forced, repetitive, mechanical, and meaningless labor. In dramatic fashion it allows us to appreciate how *we* have invented the robot, how the robot belongs exclusively to the landscapes of the industrial and technological world.

12 Norman Cohn, *Europe's Inner Demons*, New American Library, New York, 1977.

13 My discussion of these shadows of the abandoned body owes much to my conversations with Angelyn Spignesi. In her own work she has investigated the psychological connections among the figures of the witch, the hysteric, and the anorexic. For an excellent treatment of the anorexic see her book *Starving Women*, Spring Publications, Dallas, 1983.

14 Carolyn Merchant, *The Death of Nature*, Harper & Row, New York, 1983.

15 Michel Foucault, *Madness and Civilization: A History of Insanity in the Age of Reason*, Random House, New York, 1973.

16 Ibid., pp. 24, 25.

17 Ibid., p. 48.

18 Ibid., p. 59.

19 Ibid., p. 66.

20 J. H. van den Berg, *Divided Existence and Complex Society*, Duquesne University Press, Pittsburg, 1974, chapter 5. I am very much indebted in this discussion of the mesmerized and hypnotized bodies to van den Berg's excellent account of the historical and cultural conditioning which gave rise to the unconscious.

21 Ibid., p. 81.

22 Ibid., p. 82.

23 Mary Shelley, *Frankenstein*, Bantam Books, New York, 1981, p. 33.

24 Joyce Carol Oates, 'Frankenstein's fallen angel', in *Frankenstein: or the Modern*

Prometheus, by M. W. Shelley, University of California Press, Berkeley, 1984, pp. 241–52.

25 Ibid., p. 252.

26 Ibid., p. 249.

27 J. H. van den Berg, op. cit., pp. 68–91.

28 George Frederick Drinka, *The Birth of Neurosis*, Simon & Schuster, New York, 1984, pp. 74–151.

29 J. H. van den Berg, *The Changing Nature of Man*, W.W. Norton & Co., New York, 1983, p. 118. See also Josef Breuer and Sigmund Freud, *Complete Psychological Works of Sigmund Freud Vol. II: Studies on Hysteria*, ed. J. Strachey, The Hogarth Press, London, 1955.

30 Breuer and Freud, ibid. That the hysteric body is not reducible to the anatomical body is evident in the case histories and theoretical discussions presented in their work. That the body of psychoanalytic investigation will become increasingly the symbolic body of everyday lived life is also evident in the development of Freud's work. That Freud will never quite fully abandon the concept of the medical body, the body of anatomical structure and physiological function, is, however, also evident. What initially appears as contradiction, is, however, upon closer inspection, a source of the fruitful ambiguity of Freud's vision. Trained in medicine *and* faced with the symptoms of the hysteric, Freud sought a way of understanding the symptom as between the mechanism of matter and the ideality of mind. For a rigorous philosophical defense of this fruitful ambiguity in psychoanalysis see Paul Ricoeur, *Freud and Philosophy: An Essay on Interpretation*, Yale University Press, New Haven, 1970.

31 Sigmund Freud, *Complete Psychological Works of Sigmund Freud Vol. VII: Fragment of an Analysis of a Case of Hysteria*, ed. J. Strachey, The Hogarth Press, London, 1953.

32 Ibid., p. 40.

33 The reason for the quotation marks around 'discovers' should by now be obvious. The hysteric body, as much as the corpse, is discovered *and* invented. The history and shadow history of the body are a creation of culture and a discovery in nature. Or to put all this another way, the figures of the abandoned body (corpse, machine, reflex, robot, etc.) and its shadows (witch, hypnotized and mesmerized bodies, hysteric, etc.) are metaphorical bodies. They are neither things of nature nor thoughts of mind, but realities brought into being between nature and culture. They are all as much ways of perceiving the human body as they are bodily incarnations to be perceived. For a full discussion of this use of metaphor in dealing with the 'discoveries' of science, see my earlier work *Psychological Life: From Science to Metaphor*, University of Texas Press, Austin, 1982.

34 Josef Breuer and Sigmund Freud, *Studies on Hysteria*, p. 7.

35 Maurice Merleau-Ponty, *The Visible and the Invisible*, Northwestern University Press, Evanston, 1969.

36 Angelyn Spignesi, op. cit. In mentioning her work in passing I do not want to miss the opportunity to recommend highly this remarkable book. Its psychological insights into the suffering soul of the anorexic are matched by the style of presentation, which successfully draws the reader into the emotional depths of this figure.

37 Hilda Bruch, *The Golden Cage*, Harvard University Press, Cambridge, 1978.

38 Mary Daly, *Gyn/Ecology: The Metaethics of Radical Feminism*, Beacon Press, Boston, 1978. Not a book for the faint-hearted: Mary Daly manages to upset and to explode many cherished and unexamined assumptions of a masculine-oriented culture. What I value in the work, apart from its power to disrupt fossilized

modes of thinking, is the way in which it demonstrates the alliance between technological modes of culture and masculine modes of damnation.

39 Susan Griffin, *Pornography and Silence*, Harper & Row, New York, 1981, p. 139.

40 Susan Griffin, *Made from this Earth*, Harper & Row, New York, 1982, p. 165.

41 Bruch, op. cit., p. 5.

42 Barbara Duden, 'Historical concepts of the body', *Resurgence* No. 112, September/October 1985, p. 25.

43 Griffin, *Pornography and Silence*, pp. 36–80. In these pages especially Griffin offers a powerful description of the emptying of the body through the pornographic gaze. The body is de-souled in pornographic vision and such a body becomes what it can only become: dead, inanimate matter quickened by the projected impulses of the invisible voyeur, the spectator at a distance hidden in shadows.

44 Ivan Illich, *Medical Nemesis*, Bantam Books, New York, 1977. While this book is already more than ten years old, little, if anything, in the way of health care has been changed. Indeed, the spiral of increasing costs unmatched by more effective control of diseases only reinforces Illich's point regarding the dangers involved in the medicalization of life. Perhaps today even more than ten years ago at its publication this book needs to be appreciated.

CHAPTER 6: WORLD AS SPECTACLE

1 Each of these transformations is already prescribed by the procedures for the construction of a linear perspective space described in chapter 2. In this chapter, we shall only allude to that earlier discussion. The reader who wishes to refresh himself or herself about these matters should, therefore, consult the relevant portions of chapter 2. For the matter of explanation, see pp. 43–4; for the matter of light, see pp. 42–3; and for the discussion of things, see pp. 52–7.

2 See chapter 2, p. 41.

3 Bert Hansen, 'The complementarity of science and magic before the Scientific Revolution', *American Scientist* 74, March/April 1986, p. 130. For the Chaucer text from which Hansen quotes see, Geoffrey Chaucer, *The Canterbury Tales*, trans. R. M. Lumiansky, Washington Square Press, New York, 1971, pp. 270–3.

4 Ibid., p. 130–1.

5 Ibid., p. 130.

6 The appellation is bestowed upon Bacon by Loren Eiseley, *The Man who saw through Time*, Charles Scribner's Sons, New York, 1973.

7 James L. Enyeart, *Jerry Uelsmann, Twenty-Five Years: A Retrospective*, Little, Brown, Boston, 1982, p. 37. This text contains many fine illustrations of Uelsmann's work.

8 Marshall McLuhan and Harley Parker, *Through the Vanishing Point*, Harper & Row, New York, 1968, p. 77.

9 For a discussion of the etymology of the word 'story' and its psychological implications, see my earlier text *Psychological Life: From Science to Metaphor*, University of Texas Press, Austin, 1982, pp. 86–9.

10 For a discussion of the need for myth and its place in our lives see James Hillman, *Re-Visioning Psychology*, Harper & Row, New York, 1975, and a more recent and quite interesting text *Inter-Views*, Harper & Row, New York, 1983.

11 I say 'probably' because insofar as increasing accountability pervades our society — for teachers, lawyers, doctors, etc. — we get into a fantasy of purity. Within

the fantasy we begin to believe that if we try hard enough we can enlighten everyone about everything every time, that we can scrub the world clean of all shadows. Accountability is a positive value, but we should acknowledge that there are limits to how far we should and can go.

12 See, for example, Marshall McLuhan, *Understanding Media*, New American Library, New York, 1964.
13 Donald M. Lowe, *History of Bourgeois Perception*, University of Chicago Press, Chicago, 1983, p. 9.
14 Loren Eiseley, *The Invisible Pyramid*, Charles Scribner's Sons, New York, 1970, p. 65.
15 Martin Heidegger, *Discourse on Thinking*, trans. J. Anderson and E. Freund, Harper & Row, New York, 1966, p. 50.
16 Jeremy Rifkin, *Algeny*, Penguin Books, New York, 1984, pp. 3–4.
17 Ibid. Rifkin's work, while quite controversial, raises important questions about the unreflective style and unchecked pace of technology. The easy style of his writing and the popularity of his work does not and should not detract from the seriousness of the issues which he raises.
18 For a discussion of this theme of nuclear winter see Paul R. Ehrlich, Carl Sagan, Donald Kennedy, and Walter Orr Roberts, *The Cold and the Dark*, W.W. Norton & Co., New York, 1984.
19 Fritjof Capra, *The Tao of Physics*, Bantam Books, New York, 1977, p. 186.
20 Harold Fritzsch, *The Creation of Matter: The Universe from Beginning to End*, trans. J. Steinberg, Basic Books, New York, 1984.
21 Capra, op. cit., p. 51.
22 The phrase is Martin Heidegger's, applied to the eclipse of Being in the history of western metaphysics. In using it here with respect to things I do not intend to equate beings and Being. Rather, my use of this pregnant phrase is meant only to call to mind for the reader the connection in Heidegger's thought between this eclipse of Being and technology. For a fine series of essays on this whole topic see *Heidegger and the Path of Thinking*, ed. John Sallis, Duquesne University Press, Pittsburg, 1970.
23 Capra, op. cit., p. 190.
24 J. H. van den Berg, *Divided Existence and Complex Society*, Duquesne University Press, Pittsburg, 1974, p. 132.
25 See chapter 2, pp. 52–7.
26 Rainer Maria Rilke, *Duino Elegies*, trans. J. Leishman and S. Spencer, W.W. Norton & Co., New York, 1939, p. 77.
27 Randolph Severson, 'Money and nature', in R. Sardello and R. Severson, *Money and the Soul of the World*, Dallas Institute for Humanities and Culture, Dallas, 1983, p. 52.
28 Lewis Hyde, *The Gift: Imagination and the Erotic Life of Property*, Vintage Books, New York, 1979, p. 239.
29 Robert Sardello, 'Money and the city', p. 21.
30 These words, of course, are from the song written by Neil Diamond.
31 Rilke, 'The task of transfiguration', in *Duino Elegies*, p. 129.
32 J. H. van den Berg, *The Phenomenological Approach to Psychiatry*, Charles C. Thomas, Springfield, 1955, p. 32.

CHAPTER 7: RE-ENTRY: PATHS OF RETURN

1 *Dallas Times Herald*, June 13, 1983.
2 Ibid.

3 Walker Percy, *Lost in the Cosmos*, Washington Square Press, New York, 1983, p. 142.

4 Ibid., p. 47.

5 For a discussion of this theme, see Dorella H. Meadows *et al.*, *The Limits to Growth*, New American Library, New York, 1972.

6 For a discussion of how small is beautiful, see E. F. Schumacher's *Small is Beautiful*, Perennial Library, New York, 1975.

7 Timothy Leary, *Neuropolitics*, Starseed/Peace Press, Los Angeles, 1977, p. 138.

8 Certainly there would be those who would deny psychoanalysis the status of a critique, at least an implicit one, of technological consciousness. But if, as the thesis of this book has maintained, technological consciousness arises out of the eye of distant vision, a vision which in separating itself from the body re-creates the body 'over there', as object, then certainly the situation of analysis, in which physician and patient are drawn into the space of intimate conversation, challenges that vision. In any case, I make the effort here to redeem the radical and critical nature of psychoanalysis *vis-à-vis* the culture of technology.

9 Sigmund Freud, 'Some points for a comparative study of organic and hysterical motor paralyses', *Complete Psychological Works of Sigmund Freud Vol. I*, ed. J. Strachey, The Hogarth Press, London, 1966, p. 169.

10 Freud, 'Instincts and their vicissitudes', ibid., Vol. XIV, pp. 121–2.

11 Freud, op. cit.

12 A consideration of Freud and feminism deserves a book of its own, and such a book requires a most delicate approach to, and appreciation of, the genius of Freud and the genuine merits of psychoanalysis as well as the legitimate and much needed criticisms of feminist thinkers. To cite only one example of the difficulty of this task, consider the criticism that Freud *reduces* female sexuality to its anatomy, and specifically to an anatomy that suffers an absence. 'Anatomy is destiny', is the way it goes. But even the least sympathetic reader of Freud would have to acknowledge that the body of Freud's work works against such simplistic reductionism. After all, psychoanalysis regards the body and its organs as forms of desire already enmeshed in the cultural world and in a landscape of social relations. If feminine sexuality, and masculine sexuality too, are founded in the body, then it is this cultural body which Freud means — even, I would say, in spite of some of his words. Passages in a text belong to a body of work, and to isolate this or that passage or this or that text is to deny the body, a move which repeats in kind that dismemberment of the body in patriarchal consciousness, that discovery–invention of the corpse to which the hysteric body calls attention. I think one could quite legitimately fault Freud for not saying explicitly that human sexual identity is a matter of the *cultural* body and not of the body of anatomy. But to emphasize only this complaint would be to fail to appreciate how deeply embedded we always are in culture and history. Even Freud's genius, which was responsible at least for opening a space for the hysteric to speak, could not detach itself from its cultural matrix to penetrate the assumptions of a cultural dream of which he was a part. But who can? One can no more jump outside one's culture and history than one can jump outside one's skin. One can only speak from within it, forgetfully or with some small measure of reflection. Freud, I believe, has that measure.

13 Carolyn Merchant, *The Death of Nature*, Harper & Row, New York, 1983.

14 Susan Griffin, *Pornography and Silence*, Harper & Row, New York, 1981, p. 36. My italics.

15 Ibid., p. 34. My italics.

16 Ibid., p. 36.

17 Adrienne Rich, *On Lies, Secrets, and Silence*, W.W. Norton & Co., New York, 1979, pp. 83–4.

18 For references to Adrienne Rich see note 17 and also *Of Woman Born*, W.W. Norton & Co., New York, 1986. In addition to note 14 for Susan Griffin, see also *Made from this Earth*, Harper & Row, New York, 1982. Regarding the other authors cited in the text see: Mary Daly, *Gyn/Ecology: The Metaethics of Radical Feminism*, Beacon Press, Boston, 1978; Shulamith Firestone, *The Dialectic of Sex*, Bantam Books, New York, 1971; and Kate Millett, *Sexual Politics*, Doubleday & Co., Garden City, 1970.

19 Daly, ibid. See especially chapter 7 for a discussion of this point.

20 Ibid., p. 229.

21 Rich, *Of Woman Born*, p. 79.

22 Mary Wollstonecraft, *A Vindication of the Rights of Women*, in *The Feminist Papers*, ed. Alice S. Rossi, Columbia University Press, New York, 1973. Rossi's text is not only a valuable resource which gathers together in one volume many significant writings, but also a valuable commentary on the writings. Her introductory essays provide a useful context.

23 G. F. Drinka, *The Birth of Neurosis: Myth, Malady, and the Victorians*, Simon & Schuster, New York, 1984, p. 150.

24 Ibid.

25 Much the same, and perhaps even more, could be said about post-Impressionism, specifically Surrealism. But that would take us beyond the scope of this narrative — and at a point where we want only to indicate another moment of return, another road of remembrance.

26 See chapter 3, p. 75.

27 Jose Ortega y Gasset, *Meditations on Quixote*, W.W. Norton & Co., New York, 1961, p. 88.

28 Although it is not possible in this text to illustrate all the points just discussed, I can nevertheless cite some examples. For an illustration of how background and foreground space interpenetrate each other, see Delacroix's *St George destroying the Dragon*. Edgar Degas' *Reclining Nude* is a good example of how the painter diminishes the distance between viewer and the model, inviting the viewer, as it were, into her space. On the other hand, his *Ballet Dancers Climbing a Flight of Stairs* offers a beautiful illustration of the multi-leveled depths of the world. Similarly Gaugin's *La Belle Angèle* and Picasso's *The Burial of Casagenias* illustrate depth as a matter of levels. With regard to how Cézanne works this theme, see *Le Chateau Noir* and his 1905 painting, *Mont Ste-Victoire*.

29 Paul Cézanne as quoted in *Impressionism*, Editors of Réalitiés, Chartwell Books, Secaucus, 1973, p. 112.

30 David Bohm, *Wholeness and the Implicate Order*, Ark Paperbacks, London, 1983. The radicality of Bohm's vision is all the more impressive because of his standing as a theoretical physicist. Within the context of the present work, readers are especially advised to consider his first chapter, in which the issues of fragmentation and wholeness are discussed.

31 Hans Stapp as quoted in Gary Zukav, *The Dancing Wu-Li Masters*, William Morrow, New York, 1979, p. 94.

32 Sigmund Freud, *Complete Psychological Works of Sigmund Freud Vol. III: Beyond the Pleasure Principle*, ed. J. Strachey, The Hogarth Press, London, 1955. It is astonishing to me that of all Freud's major writings, this one is the least attended. Although the notion of a death instinct is a difficult and unpleasant thought, its power to tie together such diverse phenomena as repetitive behaviour, transference, and daily acts of aggression make it a powerful idea. The work also provides a wonderful opportunity to appreciate the workings of a gifted, imaginative mind. For a discussion of the specific point mentioned in the text, see pp. 50–61.

33 When in 1986 all the nations of the world spent on average 1.7 million dollars per minute on weapons, with the US in first place, there can be little doubt about preferences. See the *Virginian Pilot* (Norfolk), November 24, 1986.

34 See for example, Carl Sagan, *Cosmos*, Random House, New York, 1980; *The Dragons of Eden*, Ballantine Books, New York, 1977; and *Broca's Brain*, Ballantine Books, New York, 1974. For Capra, see *The Tao of Physics*, Bantam Books, New York 1977, and *The Turning Point*, Simon & Schuster, New York, 1982. Regarding Zukav see *The Dancing Wu-Li Masters*, op. cit. Although I include Sagan in this list, I do so with some reservation, since much of his work seems to be an unreflective apology for science. See, for example, Walker Percy's satirical comment on Sagan in *Lost in the Cosmos*, pp. 171–3. Nevertheless, I admire Sagan's work on the issue of nuclear winter.

35 For an excellent and extended treatment of this issue, see John Davy's *On Hope, Evolution, and Change*, Hawthorn Press, Stroud, 1985.

36 See, for example, James Hillman, *Re-Visioning Psychology*, Harper & Row, New York, 1975, and *Inter-Views*, Harper & Row, New York, 1983.

37 Joseph Campbell, 'The need for new myths', *Time*, January 17, 1972, p. 51.

38 See, for example, Marilyn Ferguson, *The Aquarian Conspiracy*, J. P. Tarcher, Los Angeles, 1980; E. L. Schumacher, *Small is Beautiful*; Robert Sardello, 'Money and the city' in R. Sardello and R. Severson, *Money and the Soul of the World*, Dallas Institute for Humanities and Culture, Dallas, 1983; William Irwin Thompson, *The Time Falling Bodies take to Light*, St Martins Press, New York, 1981. For works by Bohm and Hillman see notes 30 and 36 respectively.

39 We should add to this characterization the recognition that the new world will and must be a recovery of the feminine. Such a recognition is very much in accordance with our narrative, especially with respect to the discussion of the shadow history of the body in chapter 5.

40 Robert Sardello, op. cit.

41 Michiko Kakutani, 'Arthur Miller: view from maturity of a life tempered by skepticism', *The New York Times*, May 9, 1984.

42 For a discussion of this issue, see Robert Romanyshyn and Brian Whalen, 'Depression: the other face of the American Dream', in *Pathologies of the Modern Self*, ed. D. M. Levin, New York University Press, New York, 1987.

43 Percy, *Lost in the Cosmos*, p. 79.

44 Ibid.

45 At one point in the novel Moriarty expresses his fugitive style of living when he says, 'we gotta go and never stop going till we get there.' When asked, however, by Sal, the character who narrates the story, where it is that they are going, Moriarty says, 'I don't know but we gotta go.' See Jack Kerouac, *On the Road*, New American Library, New York, 1968, p. 196.

46 Rainer Maria Rilke, *Duino Elegies*, trans. J. Leishman and S. Spender, W.W. Norton & Co., New York, 1939, p. 73.

47 This quote is taken from the page preceding the Contents page in a remarkable work by Penelope Shuttle and Peter Redgrove, *The Wise Wound*, Penguin Books, Harmondsworth, 1980. For some interesting papers by Layard see, 'The virgin archetype: two papers', and 'A Celtic quest: sexuality and soul in individuation', *Spring Publications*.

48 T. S. Eliot, 'Little Gidding', *Four Quartets*, Harcourt, Brace & World, Inc., New York, 1971, p. 59.

Bibliography

Abrahamson, D. (1985) 'Tamarins in the Amazon,' *Science 85* 6, 7: 58–63.
Arendt, H. (1958) *The Human Condition*, Chicago: University of Chicago Press.
Arendt, H. (1965) *Eichmann in Jerusalem*, New York: Viking Press.
Aries, P. (1981) *The Hour of Our Death*, New York: Alfred A. Knopf.
Barrett, W. (1972) *Time of Need*, New York: Harper & Row.
Barrett, W. (1978) *The Illusion of Technique*, Garden City: Doubleday & Co.
Berger, J. (1977) *Ways of Seeing*, New York: Penguin Books.
Berman, M. (1983) *All That is Solid Melts into Air*, New York: Simon & Schuster.
Blight, J., *Fear and Learning in a Nuclear Crisis*, unpublished manuscript.
Bob, P. (1985) 'Openings inside and out,' *Esquire* 103, 3, March: 284.
Bohm, D. (1983) *Wholeness and the Implicate Order*, London: Ark Paperbacks.
Boyer, P. (1986) *By the Bomb's Early Light*, New York: Pantheon.
Brady, P. (1984) 'A conversation with Alex Grey, performance artist,' *Boston Visual Artists Union News* 12, January.
Breuer, J., and Freud, S. (1895) *Complete Psychological Works of Sigmund Freud Vol. II: Studies on Hysteria*, ed. J. Strachey, London: The Hogarth Press.
Bruch, H. (1978) *The Golden Cage: The Enigma of Anorexia Nervosa*, Cambridge: Harvard University Press.
Burtt, E. A. (1954) *The Metaphysical Foundations of Modern Science*, Garden City: Doubleday & Co.
Campbell, J. (1972) 'The need for new myths,' *Time* January 17.
Capek, K. (1973) *R.U.R.*, ed. Shefter, H. New York: Pocket Books.
Capra, F. (1977) *The Tao of Physics*, New York: Bantam Books.
Capra, F. (1982) *The Turning Point*, New York: Simon & Schuster.
Chaucer, G. (1971) *The Canterbury Tales*, trans. R. M. Lumiansky, New York: Washington Square Press.
Cioran, E. M. (1970) *The Fall Into Time*, trans. R. Howard, Chicago: Quadrangle Books.
Cohen, J. (1966) *Human Robots in Myth and Science*, London: Allen & Unwin.
Cohn, N. (1977) *Europe's Inner Demons*, New York: New American Library.
Connelly, D. (1986) *All Sickness is Homesickness*, Columbia, Maryland: Center for Traditional Acupuncture.
Crick, F. (1981) *Life Itself: Its Origins and Nature*, New York: Simon & Schuster.
Daly, M. (1978) *Gyn/Ecology: The Metaethics of Radical Feminism*, Boston: Beacon Press.
Davy, J. (1985) *On Hope, Evolution and Change*, Stroud: Hawthorn Press.
De la Croix, H. and Tansey, R. (1975) *Gardner's Art Through The Ages*, New York: Harcourt Brace Jovanovich.

Drinka, G. F. (1984) *The Birth of Neurosis: Myth, Malady, and the Victorians*, New York: Simon & Schuster.

Duden, B. (1985) 'Historical concepts of the body,' *Resurgence* September/October, 112: 24–6.

Duden, B. (1987) *Geschichte unter der Haut*, Stuttgart: Klett-Cotta.

Edgerton, S. Y. Jr. (1976) *The Renaissance Rediscovery of Linear Perspective*, New York: Harper & Row.

Ehrlich, P., Sagan, C., Kennedy, D. and Roberts, W. O. (1984) *The Cold and the Dark*, New York: W. W. Norton & Co.

Eiseley, L. (1970) *The Invisible Pyramid*, New York: Charles Scribner's Sons.

Eiseley, L. (1973) *The Man Who Saw Through Time*, New York: Charles Scribner's Sons.

Eliot, T. S. (1971) *The Four Quartets*, New York: Harcourt, Brace, & World, Inc.

Enyeart, J. L. (1982) *Jerry Uelsmann, Twenty-Five Years: A Retrospective*, Boston: Little, Brown.

Erdman, D. (ed.) (1981) *The Poetry and Prose of William Blake*, Berkeley: University of California Press.

Ferguson, M. (1980) *The Aquarian Conspiracy*, Los Angeles: J. P. Tarcher.

Firestone, S. (1971) *The Dialectic of Sex*, New York: Bantam Books.

Foucault, M. (1973) *Madness and Civilization: A History of Insanity in the Age of Reason*, New York: Random House.

Freud, S. (1953) *Complete Psychological Works of Sigmund Freud Vol. VII: Fragment of an Analysis of A Case of Hysteria*, ed. J. Strachey, London: The Hogarth Press.

Freud, S. (1955) *Complete Psychological Works of Sigmund Freud Vol. VIII: Beyond The Pleasure Principle*, ed. J. Strachey, London: The Hogarth Press.

Freud, S. (1957) *Complete Psychological Works of Sigmund Freud Vol. XIV: Instincts and their Vicissitudes*, ed. J. Strachey, London: The Hogarth Press.

Freud, S. (1966) *Complete Psychological Works of Sigmund Freud Vol. I: Some points for a comparative study of organic and hysterical motor paralyses*, ed. J. Strachey, London: The Hogarth Press.

Fritzsch, H. (1984) *The Creation of Matter: The Universe from Beginning to End*, trans. J. Steinberg, New York: Basic Books.

Gies, J. and Gies, F. (1981) *Life In A Medieval City*, New York: Harper & Row.

Griffin, S. (1981) *Pornography and Silence*, New York: Harper & Row.

Griffin, S. (1982) *Made From This Earth*, New York: Harper & Row.

Grun, B. (1975) *The Timetables of History*, New York: Simon & Schuster.

Hansen, B. (1986) 'The complementarity of science and magic before the Scientific Revolution,' *American Scientist* 74, March/April: 128–36.

Harwood, A. C. (1977) *Shakespeare's Prophetic Mind*, London: Rudolf Steiner Press.

Heckscher, W. (1958) *Rembrandt's Anatomy of Dr Nicolaas Tulp*, New York: Washington Square Press.

Heidegger, M. (1966) *Discourse on Thinking*, trans. J. Anderson and E. Freund, New York: Harper & Row.

Heidegger, M. (1967) *What Is A Thing?*, trans. W. Barton, Chicago: Henry Regnery Co.

Hillman, J. (1975) *Re-Visioning Psychology*, New York: Harper & Row.

Hillman, J. (1979) *The Dream and The Underworld*, New York: Harper & Row.

Hillman, J. (1983) *Inter-Views*, New York: Harper & Row.

Hockney, D. (1984) *Cameraworks*, New York: Alfred A. Knopf.

Husserl, E. (1970) *The Crisis of European Science and Transcendental Phenomenology*, trans. D. Carr, Evanston: Northwestern University Press.

Hyde, L. (1979) *The Gift: Imagination and the Erotic Life of Property*, New York: Vintage Books.

Illich, I. (1977) *Medical Nemesis*, New York: Bantam Books.

Illich, I. (1985) 'H₂O and the waters of forgetfulness,' *Resurgence* 112, September/October: 9–13.

Impressionism (1973) Editors of Réalités, Secausus: Chartwell Books.

Innis, H. (1964) *The Bias of Communication*, Toronto: University of Toronto Press.

Innis, H. (1972) *Empire and Communication*, Toronto: University of Toronto Press.

Ivins, W. (1964) *Art & Geometry*, New York: Dover.

Ivins, W. (1975) *On the Rationalization of Sight*, New York: Da Capo Press.

Jonas, H. (1985) *The Imperative of Responsibility*, Chicago: University of Chicago Press.

Kakutani, M. (1984) 'Arthur Miller: view from maturity of a life tempered by skepticism,' *The New York Times*, May 9.

Kerouac, J. (1968) *On the Road*, New York: New American Library.

Koyre, A. (1968) *From the Closed World to the Infinite Universe*, Baltimore: Johns Hopkins University Press.

Krueger, D. (ed.) (1984) *The Changing Reality of Modern Man: Essays in Honor of J. H. van den Berg*, Capetown: Juta & Co.

Lasch, C. (1979) *The Culture of Narcissism*, New York: W. W. Norton & Co.

Layard, J. (1972) 'The Virgin Archetype: Two Papers,' New York: Spring Publications.

Layard, J. (1975) 'A Celtic Quest: Sexuality and Soul in Individuation,' Zürich: Spring Publications.

Leary, T. (1977) *Neuropolitics*, Los Angeles: Starseed/Peace Press.

Levin, D. M. (1985) *The Body's Recollection of Being: Phenomenological Psychology and the Deconstruction of Nihilism*, London: Routledge & Kegan Paul.

Levin, D. M. (1987) *Pathologies of the Modern Self*, New York: New York University Press.

Lewis, C. S. (1974) *The Abolition of Man*, New York: Macmillan.

de Lippe, R. (1985) *La Géometrisation de l'Homme en Europe à L'Époque Moderne*, Oldenburg: Bibliotheks — und Informationssystem der Universität Oldenburg.

Lowe, D. M. (1983) *History of Bourgeois Perception*, Chicago: University of Chicago Press.

Lyons, J. (1987) *Ecology of the Body: Styles of Behavior in Human Life*, Durham: Duke University Press.

Machiavelli, N. (1984) *The Prince*, trans. L. P. de Alvarez, Irving: University of Dallas Press.

Marx, K. and Engels, F. (1965) *The Communist Manifesto*, trans. S. Moore, Peking: Foreign Languages Press.

McLuhan, M. (1964) *Understanding Media*, New York: New American Library.

McLuhan, M. (1969) *The Gutenberg Galaxy*, New York: New American Library.

McLuhan, M. and Parker, H. (1968) *Through the Vanishing Point*, New York: Harper & Row.

Meadows, D. H., Meadows, D. R., Randers, J. and Behrens, W. W. (1972) *The Limits to Growth*, New York: New American Library.

Merchant, C. (1983) *The Death of Nature*, New York: Harper & Row.

Merleau-Ponty, M. (1962) *Phenomenology of Perception*, London: Routledge & Kegan Paul.

Merleau-Ponty, M. (1964) *The Primacy of Perception*, Evanston: Northwestern University Press.

Merleau-Ponty, M. (1969) *The Visible and the Invisible*, Evanston: Northwestern University Press.

Merleau-Ponty, M. (1973) *The Prose of the World*, Evanston: Northwestern University Press.

Miller, W. (1959) *A Canticle for Leibowitz*, New York: Bantam Books.

Millett, K. (1970) *Sexual Politics*, Garden City: Doubleday & Co.

Oates, J. C. (1984) 'Frankenstein's fallen angel', in *Frankenstein: or the Modern Prometheus*, by Mary Wollstonecraft Shelley, Berkeley, University of California Press.

O'Neill, G. (1976) *The High Frontier*, Garden City: Anchor Press/Doubleday.

Ong, W. (1971) *Rhetoric, Romance, and Technology*, Ithaca: Cornell University Press.

Ong, W. (1977) *Interfaces of the Word*, Ithaca: Cornell University Press.

Ong, W. (1982) *Orality and Literacy*, London: Routledge & Kegan Paul.

Ortega y Gasset, J. (1961) *Meditations on Quixote*, New York: W. W. Norton & Co.

Panofsky, E. (1955) *The Life and Art of Albrecht Dürer*, Princeton: Princeton University Press.

Percy, W. (1983) *Lost in the Cosmos*, New York: Washington Square Press.

Rich, A. (1979) *On Lies, Secrets, and Silence*, New York: W. W. Norton & Co.

Rich, A. (1986) *Of Woman Born*, New York: W. W. Norton & Co.

Ricoeur, P. (1970) *Freud and Philosophy: An Essay on Interpretation*, New Haven: Yale University Press.

Rifkin, J. (1984) *Algeny*, New York: Penguin Books.

Rilke, R. M. (1939) *Duino Elegies*, trans. J. Leishman and S. Spender, New York: W. W. Norton & Co.

Romanyshyn, R. (1982) *Psychological Life: From Science to Metaphor*, Austin: University of Texas Press.

Romanyshyn, R. (1984) 'The despotic eye,' *The Changing Reality of Modern Man*, in D. Krueger (ed.) *The Changing Reality of Modern Man*, Capetown: Juta & Co.

Romanyshyn, R. (1987) 'Das Auge der Distanz und der Lieb des Begehrens: Eine Metabletik des Wohnens,' *Poesis 3/1987*, ed. Rudolf de Lippe, Oldenburg: Universität Oldenburg, 5–21.

Romanyshyn, R. and Whalen, B. (1987) 'Depression: the other face of the American Dream,' *Pathologies of the Modern Self*, ed. D. M. Levin, New York: New York University Press.

Sagan, C. (1974) *Broca's Brain*, New York: Ballantine Books.

Sagan, C. (1977) *The Dragons of Eden*, New York: Ballantine Books.

Sagan, C. (1980) *Cosmos*, New York: Random House.

Sallis, J. (1970) 'Towards the moment of reversal: science, technology, and the language of homecoming,' in J. Sallis (ed.) *Heidegger and the Path of Thinking*, Pittsburgh: Duquesne University Press.

Sardello, R. (1983) 'Money and the city,' in R. Sardello and R. Severson, *Money and the Soul of the World*, Dallas: The Dallas Institute for Humanities and Culture.

Sartre, J. P. (1964) *Nausea*, Norfolk: New Directions.

Schell, J. (1982) *The Fate of the Earth*, New York: Avon Books.

Schumacher, E. F. (1975) *Small is Beautiful*, New York: Perennial Library.

Severson, R. (1983) 'Money and nature,' in R. Sardello and R. Severson, *Money and the Soul of the World*, Dallas: The Dallas Institute for Humanities and Culture.

Shakespeare, W. (1977) *King Lear, The Complete Pelican Shakespeare*, New York: Viking Press.

Shakespeare, W. (1977) *Hamlet, The Complete Pelican Shakespeare*, New York: Viking Press.

Shelley, M. (1981) *Frankenstein*, New York: Bantam Books.

Shuttle, P. and Redgrove, P. (1980) *The Wise Wound*, Harmondsworth: Penguin Books.

Spignesi, A. (1983) *Starving Women*, Dallas: Spring Publications.

Stillinger, J. (ed.) (1978) *The Poems of John Keats*, Cambridge: The Belknap Press.

Thompson, W. I. (1981) *The Time Falling Bodies take to Light*, New York: St Martins Press.

Turner, F. (1986) 'Design for a new academy,' *Harpers* 273, no. 1636. September: 47–53.

Van den Berg, J. H. (1955) *The Phenomenological Approach to Psychiatry*, Springfield: Charles C. Thomas.

Van den Berg, J. H. (1959) *Het Menselijk Lichaam*, I. *Het Goepende Lichaam*, Nijkerk: G. F. Callenbach.

Van den Berg, J. H. (1961) *Het Menselijk Lichaam*, II. *Het Verlaten Lichaam*, Nijkerk: G. F. Callenbach.

Van den Berg, J. H. (1969) *Metabletica van den Materie*, Nijkerk: G. F. Callenbach.

Van den Berg, J. H. (1973) *De Reflex*, Nijkerk: G. F. Callenbach.

Van den Berg, J. H. (1974) *Divided Existence and Complex Society*, Pittsburgh: Duquesne University Press.

Van den Berg, J. H. (1977) *Gedane Zaken*, Nijkerk: G. F. Callenbach.

Van den Berg, J. H. (1978) *Medical Power and Medical Ethics*, New York: W. W. Norton & Co.

Van den Berg, J. H. (1983) *The Changing Nature of Man*, New York: W. W. Norton & Co.

Waddington, C. H. (1969) *Behind Appearances*, Edinburgh: Edinburgh University Press.

Weizenbaum, J. (1976) *Computer Power and Human Reason: From Judgement to Calculation*, New York: W. H. Freeman.

Wentinck, C. (1971) *The Human Figure*, Wynnewood: Livingston Publishing Company.

Wollstonecraft, M. (1973) *A Vindication of the Rights of Women*, in *The Feminist Papers: From Adams to de Beauvoir*, ed. Alice S. Rossi, New York: Columbia University Press.

Zukav, G. (1979) *The Dancing Wu-Li Masters*, New York: William Morrow.

Index